THE MANAGEMENT OF PEOPLE

SPIRO BUSINESS GUIDES
HUMAN RESOURCES AND TRAINING

Spiro Business Guides are designed to provide managers with practical, down-to-earth information, and they are written by leading authors in their respective fields. If you would like to receive a full listing of current and forthcoming titles, please visit www.spiropress.com or email spiropress@capita-ld.co.uk or call us on +44 (0)870 400 1000.

The Management of People

HRM in Context

Dr Chris Rowley

First published in 2003 by
Spiro Press
17–19 Rochester Row
London
SW1P 1LA
Telephone: +44 (0)870 400 1000

© Chris Rowley 2003

ISBN 1 904298 88 5
Reprinted 2004

British Library Cataloguing-in-Publication Data.
A catalogue record for this book is available from the British Library.

Disclaimer: This publication is intended to assist you in identifying issues which
you should know about and about which you may need to seek specific advice. It
is not intended to be an exhaustive statement of the law or a substitute for seeking
specific advice.

Spiro Press USA
3 Front Street, Suite 331
PO Box 338
Rollinsford NH 03869
USA

Typeset by: Monolith – www.monolith.uk.com
Printed and bound in Great Britain by Cromwell Press, Trowbridge, Wiltshire
Cover design by: REAL451

This book is dedicated to my parents, Clive and Jean Rowley,
with love and thanks for all their patience and continual support.

Contents

· ·

List of figures

List of tables

List of case studies

List of tasks

List of questions to think about

4.4	158	5.5	237
4.5	161	5.6	240
4.6	174	5.7	241
4.7	176	5.8	245
4.8	185	5.9	247
4.9	187	6.1	261
4.10	189	6.2	263
5.1	209	6.3	275
5.2	211	6.4	275
5.3	212	6.5	275
5.4	216	6.6	283

About the author

Chris Rowley (BA, MA, DPhil) is Reader in Human Resource Management and editor of the journal *Asia Pacific Business Review*. He has taught at Cardiff Business School and the University of London. His previous employment experience includes a variety of work in the public and private sectors. He has given a range of talks and lectures to universities and companies internationally. Chris has had consultancy experience with unions, business enterprises and government departments.

Chris researches in a range of areas, including international and comparative human resource (HR) management, employee relations, flexibility and Asia Pacific management and business. He has recently won a research grant from the British Academy to examine employment practices in Korean multinational corporations in Malaysia. Chris has published widely, writing over 60 articles, over 60 book chapters and other contributions, and 16 edited and sole authored books. He has recently co-edited *Globalization and Labour in the Asia Pacific Region* (Frank Cass, London, 2001), *Managing Korean Business* (Frank Cass, London, 2002), *Human Resource Management in the Asia Pacific Region* (Frank Cass, London, 2003) and this book *The Management of People: HRM in Context*. He also regularly contributes to *Mastering Management Online* from *The Financial Times*.

The author may be contacted at:

E-mail: c.rowley@city.ac.uk

CHAPTER 1

Introduction: context, development and scope

Introduction

Human resource management (HRM) remains crucial to all organisations and the achievement of business strategies and is at the heart of many important debates, including political, economic and social. It also has impacts from, and on, these areas. Simultaneously, HRM also remains an area of management that retains elements of both continuity and flux. This introductory chapter presents both the concept of HRM and the philosophy of this book. This overview includes some of the different perspectives and views of HRM, its history and evolution as an area of management, and some of the main factors that have critically influenced its development, variations and practices. It will be apparent that HRM not only retains its ongoing importance and relevance, but also evolves and remains complex and varied.

It can be argued that some changes in HRM's operating environment and context have actually made HRM more important, diffuse and widespread. This makes this book relevant, especially for managerial and student non-specialists, one of its markets. One consequence is that the spreading waves of people management wash over ever-broader aspects of business and work. Changes driving this tide include the increase in ideas such as knowledge management, with its assumptions of human resources (HRs) as critical. Then there are notions concerning the competitive advantage that stems from HRs in a globalised world of fast take-up of other means of competing, such as location, technology and so on. In some countries, such as the UK, HRM's influence has also spread due to the encroachment of laws into what was traditionally a less regulated arena.

It terms of this book's stance, content and coverage, several points need to be made. If some specific areas are of particular interest, other books in this series (and elsewhere – see Further reading and background information) can be consulted for further details. These include the spheres of recruitment, rewards and employee appraisals, among many others. Similarly, this book is not a prescriptive, 'how to' guide for 'best' HRM practice per se. Rather, where these practices are noted, it often goes on to provide a more general overview and feel for the area and the main practices and issues involved. As in many aspects of life, the specific HR area, issue and problem may result in going in turn to a specialist, in some cases within HRM itself. Furthermore, the legal aspects to

HRM increasingly require consultation with specialists in an era of increasing juridification and aggressive legality of the work sphere.

Questions to think about, Overviews and Further readings

During the course of the following chapters in this book, several issues and questions are regularly raised for readers to think about, reflect on and even note down some responses to before moving on. This exercise enhances the learning process by, for instance, challenging the reader to address some of the issues and bring their own viewpoints, perspectives, experiences and understandings to bear, and in turn become exposed to other options. In this way the complex, contested and dynamic nature of HRM will become apparent. Also, each of the main chapters is provided with its own 'Overview' at the start. The reading of these, and the completion of any tasks within them, will allow readers a quick grasp of the whole chapter, as these are 'stand-alone' sections. Also, these Overviews are interactive since they allow readers to undertake some activities themselves. Lists of Further reading are provided at the ends of chapters, with a more comprehensive list of titles in the Further reading and background information section at the end of the book. This will provide readers with a resource to allow them to take their learning and interests further under their own steam.

Wider relevance

The enduring relevance of the management of people in popular culture and artifacts is apparent. One of the most explicit examples of this was in the former Soviet Union's 'socialist realism' movement in which art depicted certain values, the dignity and importance of work, and so on. The Further reading and background information section indicates other cultural dimensions. This provides a range of 'lighter' ways in which people management is portrayed or can be witnessed, ranging from books and novels to television programmes, dramas and films. These include Bafta award-winning television series. One example is *Back to the Floor* with its variety of real-life job-swaps undertaken by senior management from various business sectors, providing fascinating and unforgettable moments in a range of related areas, including rewards. Another example is *The Office* and its insights into office life in a paper materials company. For instance, the role of management, recruitment, training and employee performance appraisals all appear. Films range from *Modern Times* and its classic view of Tayloristic working life, to *The Man in the White Suit* concerning management–trade union connivance to halt technology, and *I'm All Right Jack* with its satire on postwar UK employee relations. More recent films include *Gung-Ho*, with its backdrop of faltering US economic performance and cross-cultural views on management and workers in a car factory taken over by the Japanese. More recently, there has been *Bread and Roses* with its portrayal of non-union immigrant Mexican cleaners in California.

The rest of this chapter takes the following format. There are sections on what HRM is and its development, some of the rhetoric, reality and tensions in the area, strategy and context. The scope of the book is also outlined.

What is HRM?

Question to think about 1.1

What practical areas of business and work is HRM concerned with?

In the most general sense, HRM refers to the management of people in relation to work. Such 'people management' is largely concerned with the more practical aspects of the employment relationship. Nevertheless, HRM is also underpinned by some theory, with motivation as one of the more obvious examples. HRM involves: people 'processing', such as staffing requirements and planning, recruitment and selection of employees; 'developing', such as organising training and setting up appraisal systems; 'rewarding', such as establishing pay systems and non-monetary rewards; and 'relations', such as dealing with rules and grievances.

For some commentators, HRM goes further than this. For instance, in somewhat simplistic terms, the central claims of HRM are as follows:

- By matching productive requirements and the workforce and raising its quality, organisations can significantly improve performance.

- HRs are the key organisational assets, and organisational performance depends on the quality of workforce efforts, and hence on their ability and motivation.

The lead in people management within organisations is often taken by the HR department, which is charged with the key areas. A variety of methods are used within these areas, with the exact mix varying and influenced by history, organisational size, sector, location and so on. Consequently, HR work is diverse and multifaceted, requiring a considerable amount of not only specialist knowledge and expertise, but also understanding and tact on the part of practitioners.

Contemporary issues

Furthermore, while HRM's core activities are relatively easy to identify, new HR issues continually appear or reappear. Many of these issues may arouse attention for a while and become the subject of debate, then pass and fade quickly. Yet other issues may have more profound and longer-term effects.

Question to think about 1.2

What issues do you think have become more important in HRM recently?

Fresh issues come to the fore through changes in the economy and society or in the state of knowledge. These range from changes in labour markets (such as more diverse workforces) to technological changes (such as different processes, skills, means of control, injuries). Some of these environmental and contextual shifts can be monitored, and even to some extent predicted, in a variety of ways. In short, the context of HRM is vitally important.

Development of HRM

There is, obviously, a long history of the practice of people management. Indeed, writing on the area dates back to at least the first century AD and Columella, a Roman farmer whose *De Rustica* featured one of the earliest tracts on people management.

Question to think about 1.3

What earlier forms of people management can you note? Do they have any relevance to businesses today?

The most recent incarnation of people management as HRM has earlier guises such as personnel management (PM), 'welfarism' and 'paternalism'. While somewhat historical, these forms are not totally exclusive and modern versions and examples of these can be seen, to greater or lesser extents. The history and development of HRM needs to be noted and covered, not least as it, and the goals and values of a company's culture, may influence more contemporary HRM roles. A variety of different terms and schema have been used in this area by various authors. Some of the more common categories are as follows.

Welfare tradition

This area developed during the late nineteenth century. This was associated with the paternalism of larger companies, sometimes extending to creating whole communities and towns forged on the beliefs (often religious) and ideas of their founders. Practical and welfare-type employee provisions were often provided.

Examples in the UK included Owen's New Lanark experiment early in the Industrial Revolution, Lever at Port Sunlight and Clarks at Street. Titus Salt, a Yorkshire wool baron and pioneer of 'caring capitalism', built his new mill just outside the polluted town of Bradford in 1848 and over 20 years created Saltaire, a model community for his staff, with every home having running water. Then there were the Quakers, such as George Cadbury, at Bourneville, and Joseph Rowntree, who in 1904 built Rowntree village in York. Here houses stood around a community hall; in 1906 he set up a pension fund, in 1916 a profit-sharing scheme and in 1918 staff shareholding (see Chapter 3), a revolutionary concept at the time. An example from the USA, also in the confectionery sector, is Milton Hershey, a Mennonite, whose factory town is of the same name. A Dutch example is the chemicals group DSM, with its mining past and employees' well-being high on its agenda. It built houses for workers and funded generous social policies, including medical help and alternative factory work for disabled miners.

Developments such as these can be seen reflected in the founding of the Institute of Welfare Officers in 1913. The concerns of welfare officers ranged from areas such as housing and education to canteens and other amenities at work. Modern versions of paternalism include companies such as Marks & Spencer, while there is also the John Lewis Partnership, with their particular forms of HRM. In the 1980s other examples included the Body Shop and Ben & Jerry's Ice Cream, with links under the rubric of ethical practices. Large enterprises in countries such as the former Soviet

Union, Eastern bloc countries, South Korea, Japan and China are also examples. The level of such provision in these enterprises was very high, including company accommodation, and the idea of 'cradle to grave' employment with the same company.

Administrative tradition

This form of people management was concerned with much of the long-standing work of personnel departments. This included administration in areas such as recruiting, preparing job descriptions, arranging promotion panels, and so on. This personnel tradition dates from the early twentieth century. It is linked to the ideas of the scientific management (such as Taylor) and administration (such as Fayol) movements.

Negotiating tradition

A strong tradition of negotiating can also be identified in people management. This was personnel's involvement in negotiations with workers on both a daily and periodic basis, and individually and collectively. In the UK this aspect of personnel work became especially important from the Second World War onwards. A satirical view of this can be seen in part of the film *I'm All Right Jack* (see Further reading and background information at the end of the book). This spread from traditional areas of production and manufacturing to other spheres such as the public sector. Personnel management existed to 'defend' organisations. This sort of tradition was popular in the 1970s in the UK. Nevertheless, examples still remain, as witnessed by contemporary events in sectors ranging from the train operating companies, the Post Office and the fire service to the healthcare sector and teaching. Other countries such as Germany, Sweden and Finland also retain this form of people management tradition across a range of sectors.

HR development tradition

This tradition of people management is more recent, from the 1960s, 1970s and 1980s. This perspective argues that employees need to be seen as a strategic resource of the business. Profitability and success are closely related to the way an organisation manages its HRs. It propounded that in the past management have been too concerned with investments in technology, marketing and so on, neglecting the 'human' contribution to a company's strategy. It was argued that personnel were not there as reactive 'glorified social workers' or 'rubbing rags' (mediators) between management and employees. Rather, HR managers were now 'key players' in the business.

The crucial point is that there are varied traditions in HRM, and the contexts in which it operates. This influence persists to a greater or lesser extent. These traditions also partly help to shape the way in which HRM is integrated, or not, into the organisation.

Rhetoric and reality in HRM

When one asks managers 'what is your organisation's greatest asset?' they can usually be relied upon to answer in unison: 'our people'. Yet this platitude is often simply not borne out in reality by anecdotal evidence or research. It is sometimes asserted that HRM has little (or even no) role in organisations, or, even worse, HRM 'interferes' with strategy and prevents managers from doing what they want, how they want and when they want. After all, this line often continues, HRM does not 'add value' to the business (especially not in easily quantifiable and 'hard' terms) in the manner of some other managerial functions. This sort of view is indicated by the decidedly non-politically correct term previously used to describe personnel's role – as a 'handmaiden' to serve and service other functions from which it was 'downstream'. HRM implemented business decisions, it did not help to make them, let alone get involved with strategy. The implication was that HRM was subsequently less important than other functional areas.

One view stemming from this sort of perspective is: 'why should we bother to study HRM?' Sometimes such a view is reinforced by the area being perceived as 'soft' or 'woolly', not 'hard' or 'clear', with 'real' numbers and single, simple, universal truths, verities and answers that only need to be learnt by rote. This would allow HR issues to be dealt with successfully from then on, almost on automatic pilot, irrespective of business, time or place. This search for such a corpus of 'one best way' practices to manage people is not new. For instance, we only need to think back to the ideas and practices of Frederick Taylor and Henry Ford and the whole scientific management movement, whose very label clearly indicates its views on managing, including people management. Similar ideas became popular in academia, particularly from the 1950s. This came to be known as convergence theory, and this area has recently become revitalised in the guise of powerful potential role models, such as

Japanese management practices and corporations (with ideas of the 'Japanisation' of businesses) in the 1980s, and now more recently the area of globalisation. However, this universalistic 'best practice' drive remains unfulfilled, with many caveats to cloud the issue. We will return to this area in Chapter 6.

Question to think about 1.4

Why should we bother to study HRM?

The position concerning the 'vagueness' of HRM, and thus its 'less useful' role, can be countered at several levels. First, numbers do occur in HRM, at both macro and external as well as micro and internal levels. These include unemployment, inflation, productivity, labour turnover, labour costs, pay rates and so on. People cost money and valuable people cost a lot of money. While these figures can be questioned in terms of their construction and collection, this is the case with all 'numbers'. Indeed, some aspects of the above views about the 'robustness' of some areas of management are more difficult to sustain in the aftermath of debacles such as Enron, WorldCom and others, where it turns out that 'numbers' actually mean very little. We only need to recall Disraeli's famous dictum that there are 'lies, damn lies and statistics' to see this problem.

Second, we only have to look at areas such as the UK public healthcare system or German or Japanese business to see many critical HRM forces in action. Likewise, UK private services, especially in the South-East of England, are impacted on by core HRM issues. These include recruitment and selection, retention and rewards in 'tight' labour markets with poor training provision.

In short, organisational changes here are tightly bounded and constrained by HRM issues.

Third, it is propounded that the style of much management in the area has been changing. Indeed, the hierarchical 'command and control' approaches to managing are seen by many as less appropriate with a greater emphasis on discretion, self-direction and teamwork. This is linked to areas such as 'responsible autonomy' and empowerment. We will return to such areas in Chapter 5. Of course, some types of employment have always required this sort of managing.

Fourth, it is 'the people' that are the organisation; it would not exist without them. People make money, technology and physical assets work; they generate innovation, give a distinctive edge in the marketplace, and provide service. How people are resourced, rewarded and developed ensures organisations have these skills and use them effectively. In particular, one only needs to recall all the debate about 'knowledge management' and the 'knowledge-based economy' to see the relevance of HRs. Companies are coming to depend less on the ownership of physical assets and resources than on their ability to select, pay, train and manage HRs. Therefore, the decline in the uniqueness of physical assets may actually give quality HRs more outside employment opportunities. Furthermore, people, unlike other resources, can walk out at any time they choose, taking their talent, skills and knowledge with them. A contemporary example of this concerns the UK academic system, with one grading format (the Research Assessment Exercise) based on 'quality' publications, which have a life span and are predominantly portable. This has created a 'market' for academics with these assets, who have become sought after to boost departmental ratings and hence have become very mobile HRs. What this does for the motivation of other staff and developing talent internally is problematic to say the least.

Fifth, managing people is not easy. HRM is not a science; rather, it involves choices and judgement. Making the right choice is important to how organisations perform.

Sixth, institutions, society and culture differ between countries. HRM and business have to be sensitive to this (see examples in other chapters, especially Chapter 6). As a result, HRM is challenging and difficult.

Tensions in HRM

From the start, it is important to outline the current tensions in the field of HRM. These are the following, which run through all the subsequent chapters in this book.

Universal versus contingent perspectives

The universal view in management believes we can search out and focus on a single approach to dealing with each of the major policies and issues that can be shown (often via a range of proxy variables) to have the 'best' record for practice. For instance, the notion of 'benchmarking' fits in here. This claims that it is possible both to identify the most effective way to manage, as in HRM, and that these practices are also readily transferable. While not a new area, ideas such as globalisation have given such universal views renewed vigour (Bae and Rowley, 2001).

An alternative view to this is the contingent perspective. This argues that methods and general approaches in management, and especially HRM, vary and are dependent on a range of factors. They are influenced by the specific circumstances and environments of the organisation. This includes not only size and sector, but also location, with its particular frameworks of institutions and culture. This latter school makes the production of a 'one size fits all' HRM prescriptive prognosis (and book) very difficult, even within one country (Rowley and Benson, 2002).

The lack of a simple, universal 'best way' to manage HRs may be somewhat difficult and unpalatable to some of the more naive management gurus (and managers) who want to receive 'the answer'. This can then simply be regurgitated. Yet HRM deals not with inanimate objects but with people who are complex social beings, making their management messy and not conducive to standard 'answers' but rather a contingent range of perspectives. What may be 'best' at one time may not be 'best' on the next occasion, even in exactly the same context. When the context changes as well, we see the chasm of contingency, a kaleidoscope of different possibilities, opening up before us. It is this uncertainty that often infuriates people and leads, in part, to HRM's 'bad press'.

Integration versus independence views

A second tension concerns the area of HRM policies and practices in terms of their integration versus stand-alone nature. For some commentators, it is not just that HRM practices are present, but there is a need for HRM congruence. This 'joined up', integrated HRM can be in two dimensions: horizontal (with internal fit across the areas of HRM) and vertical (with external fit between HRM, management of the organisation and broader business strategies and environment). This sort of view is in stark contrast to the almost 'pick and mix' approach to HRM policies and practices found in many organisations.

Simplicity versus complexity approaches

A further common thread is the tension between the opposing camps in HRM practice. On the one hand, there is a common desire for simple, cheap practices that are usable and complied with. However, on the other hand, the drive and search to overcome possible limitations and biases in some HRM practices leads to increasingly complex, costly methods, which may be less likely to be carried out. One problem is that they may come to be seen as chores, imposing extra paperwork, bureaucracy and costs on busy managers and employees.

These tensions can be seen in Figure 1.1. These tensions indicate that there may often be no 'right' answer to HRM questions.

A strategic role?

In the 1980s came the rise of the term 'HRM' and its replacement of the leitmotif of PM in lexicons and jobs. PM and HRM are often used to refer to the same set of issues and activities, and used interchangeably. However, it is worth recognising some differences between them, and how the area of people management is seen to have become more central to management. For some, HRM was simply 'old wine in new bottles'. For others, it was what 'good' PM should have been all along.

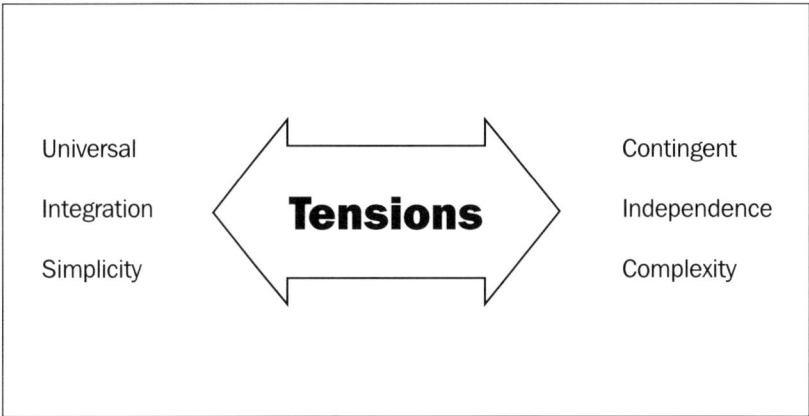

Figure 1.1 Tensions within HRM.

Question to think about 1.5

What, if anything, do you think distinguishes HRM from PM?

For some commentators, such distinctions could, and should, however roughly, be made. This can be seen in Table 1.1. Also, many models of HRM have been developed. The most famous are shown in the Figures 1.2 and 1.3.

Thus, a key PM/HRM distinction revolves around the concepts of strategy, integration and implementation. This raises a set of related questions. How strategically do organisations use the HRM function? How integrated are HR policies and decisions with both

---

key business decisions at the strategic level and with each other? Do line managers, rather than HR managers, play a role in developing and implementing HRM?

Table 1.1 PM and HRM compared

Dimension	PM	HRM
Implementation	Specialists	Line
Stance	Reactive	Proactive
Practices	Ad hoc	Integrated
Timescale	Short-term	Long-term
Importance to business	Marginal	Key
Level	Operational	Strategic

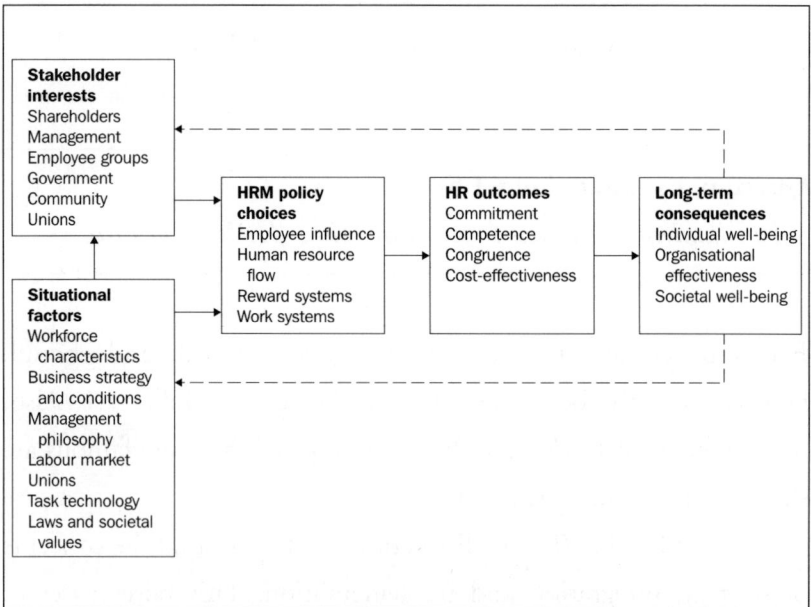

Figure 1.2 The Harvard framework for human resource management. (*Source*: Beer et al., 1984.)

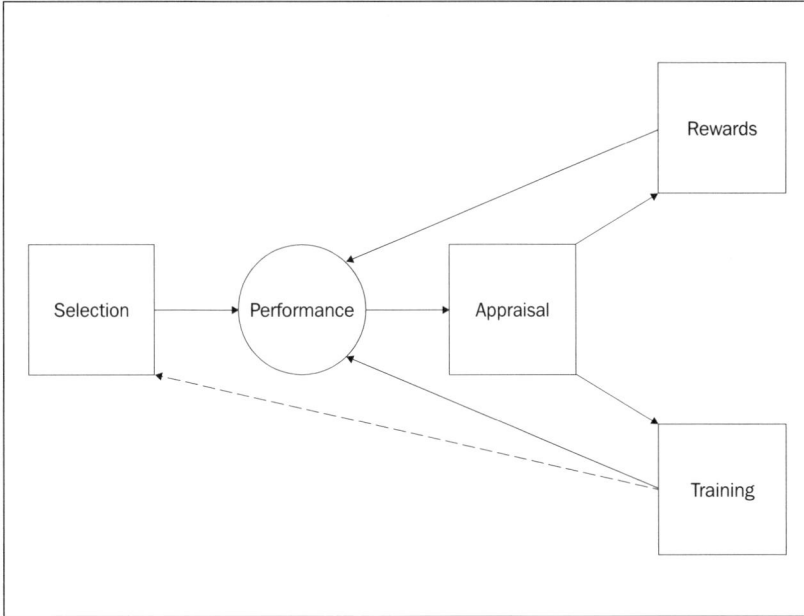

Figure 1.3 The human resource management cycle. (*Source*: Fombrun et al., 1984: 41.)

Some research has gone beyond the proselytising of management gurus, and examined real attempts to develop HRM in practice. This has found that, yes, there has often been some take-up of HRM-type practices, but such findings are also tempered by the following. First, many HRM experiments were often less than successful, such as quality circles and performance-related pay (we will return to these in Chapters 3 and 5). Second, practices hailed as 'new' had actually often been in use for some time, their newness simply reflected relabelling. Third, attempts to introduce change rarely occurred in a strategic and planned way, but rather in an incremental or ad hoc fashion. Fourth, there was resistance to change, and this was from not only employees, but also often from managers who preferred previous working practices.

In sum, while there is concern to make HRM a key component of senior management decision-making, in practice only a few companies have been successful in integrating HRM with the competitive strategy of their organisation. Why might this be? Furthermore, why is there such a huge variation in what HRM does and how it does it?

The context of HRM

Clearly HRM does not exist in a vacuum, but rather operates within changing contexts. Within this, trends and changes in contingent factors exert a varying influence over aspects of people management and HR departments and managers. This varies in many ways, including historical influences, business strategy and competitive position taken, environment, size of department, type of manager and organistion.

Business strategy

One key variable in the practice of HRM is business strategy. Organisations have varied business strategies. We can see these at work in so-called life cycle models (such as Kochan and Barocci, 1985), with 'start-up', 'growth', 'maturity' and 'decline' phases. Porter (1985) has 'cost reduction', 'quality enhancement' and 'innovation' as strategies. The earlier 'defender' and 'prospector' (Miles and Snow, 1978) strategies have been developed into 'internal' and 'market type' employment systems (Delery and Doty, 1996). Another version is by Grubman (1998) and his attempt to align HRM practices to strategic styles labelled 'products', 'operations' and 'customers'. Needless to say, each of these classifications has radically different HRM implications.

Environments

Furthermore, the internal and external environments of organisations are critically important to HRM and its role and operation. These can be analysed within a PEST (Political, Economic, Social, Technological) framework. Within this, the labour market (LM) is one of the most important contextual and contingent factors. The type and structure of the LM radically influences HRM. Therefore, it is worth spending some time exploring this factor in further detail.

Labour markets

An LM may be viewed as 'the way work is distributed within a society' (Salamon, 2000: 24). Labour markets can be formed on the basis of geography and skill. Generally, the higher the skill level, the greater the geographic scope of the LM. Unskilled HRs are often recruited locally, while more highly skilled professional, technical and managerial posts may be resourced nationally and even internationally.

According to a traditional model, an LM is a place where individuals freely exchange their labour in return for a wage so as to achieve the goods they want and need. Such a model assumes that individuals are rational animals who calculate their optimum utility in terms of the hours and rates of pay they receive. Such views of the LM tend to see employees in a fairly neutral way. For example, wages are determined in relation to the supply of, and demand for, labour. So, in 'tight' LMs (i.e. economic booms), when there is a shortage of skills or labour, employers have to offer higher wages. In times of 'slack' LMs (i.e. economic downturns), when there is a surplus of skills and labour, employers can offer lower wages. According to the human capital school of thought, employees can improve their earnings by investing in education and qualifications (i.e. they can increase their human capital), with training that is general and transferable or organisational-specific skills. This view assumes that there is a trade-off between skills and wages. Yet, to what extent is this always the case?

Question to think about 1.6

How do such LM views explain wages not declining in recessions, or pay inequalities based on factors such as gender or ethnicity?

Such perspectives are criticised for not taking into account the way institutions shape and structure LMs according to the relative power and influence they can exert. Thus they ignore the structural organisation of LMs. Some commentators argue that social and political factors structure LMs. Therefore, some employees find themselves in protected spheres and internal LMs (ILMs) while others are located in peripheral jobs and sectors and external LMs (ELMs). There are some key differences between ELMs and ILMs. Various characteristics of strong ILMs can be seen in Table 1.2.

Table 1.2 Characteristics of internal labour markets

HRM area	Characteristics
External recruitment	Confined to junior positions: limited 'ports of entry'
Other vacancies	Filled internally: promotions and transfers
Jobs	Designed and arranged for career progression, by experience in lower levels
Tenure	High
Training	Firm-specific (reinforces above)
Rewards	Structure rigid and unresponsive to ELM pressures

It has been argued that organisations distinguish between those employed in primary ILMs and those from secondary ELMs in the HRM used. Therefore, LMs affect HRM and how firms manage HRs. For instance, those who belong to ELMs were more likely to be on precarious work contracts, have inferior conditions and lower pay. In ILMs HRs were shielded from ELMs, such as competition from workers. Traditionally, some large corporations, such as in the USA, Japan and Korea, developed strong ILMs. These led to the creation of HRM practices such as lifetime employment and seniority-based rewards in such businesses.

Question to think about 1.7

What are the advantages and disadvantages of ILMs?

Companies developed ILMs for a range of reasons. Some of these can be seen in Table 1.3.

Table 1.3 Advantages and disadvantages of internal labour markets

Advantages	Disadvantages
Motivation boosted	Lack of responsiveness
Willingness to innovate (without fear of job loss)	Workers become increasingly expensive
Costly training kept	Recruitment needed at various times
Cheap new workers	Lack of new ideas

The flexible firm

Such notions of LMs as 'divided' or 'segmented' have been adapted in ideas of flexibility and the famous so-called 'flexible firm' model (Atkinson, 1984). This argued that changes in product markets, technology and so on impacted on organisations which then searched for ways to increase their flexibility. In terms of HRs, this meant reducing so-called rigidities and enhancing flexibilities in the resourcing, use and rewarding of HRs in a new, strategic fashion. This can be seen in Figure 1.4 in which the main segments of employment are clear.

There are various forms of flexibility resulting from structuring firms in such a manner. These are as follows:

- *functional* – moving between tasks, blurring of demarcations and multiskilling;

- *numerical* – changing workforce size;

- *financial* – rewards, such as performance-related pay;

- *temporal* – adjusting employment over time, both within and between days.

Some, more macro, supportive evidence on the growth of such flexibility is available. However, the flexible firm model has been criticised for several reasons.

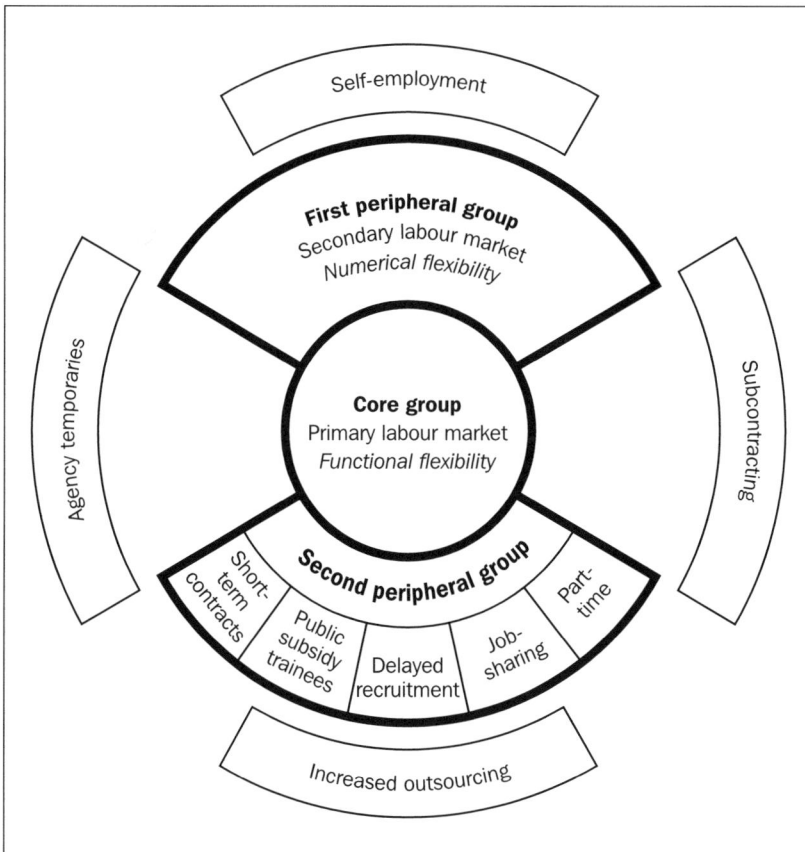

Figure 1.4 The flexible firm model. (*Source*: Atkinson, 1985.)

Question to think about 1.8

What might be some of the problems encountered with the flexible firm model?

The concept of the flexible firm has been attacked for many reasons. Table 1.4 shows some of these reasons.

Table 1.4 Criticisms of the flexible firm model

Area	Reasons
Empirical base	Manufacturing, yet many changes are in services
Newness	Long history of use, such as part-timers in services, subcontractors in textiles
Strategy	Changes often rather reactive and ad hoc
Contradictions	Practices/outcomes mutually exclusive, e.g. motivation, careers, training
Dichotomy	Some peripheral jobs are critical to organisations while some in the core are not
Contrast	Not all rigidities are 'bad' nor all flexibilities 'good'

Some of these points can be seen in the example of IT and computing services workers. Their conditions and importance do not support their commonly located periphery status. Likewise, some service sectors rely on peripheral workers for delivery and customer interface, in contrast to those in the core. Other examples may include UK outdoor entertainment and holiday centres which are often reliant on part-timers at times of peak demand but who also come into close customer contact. Some of the other problems in terms of training provision are discussed in Chapter 4. Flexibility in terms of numerical 'hire and fire' can weaken not only training (as people may well leave after it), but also motivation as well as innovation, particularly if this is risky or may lead to job losses. In contrast, the benefits of inflexibility, or job security, are obvious.

HR departments

A further variation is that HR departments themselves vary greatly in size, structure and role depending on the size, complexity and structure of the organisation, as well as its history. In larger organisations HR activity may be supervised by a member of the board of directors or senior management group. The HR director may have the support of several senior executives, each responsible for specialist functions, for example training managers. Under this there may be a hierarchy of middle-management personnel professionals, with clerical/administrative staff at lower levels.

In contrast, in smaller organisations there is much less scope for HRM specialisms and managers become generalists, taking responsibility for a wider range of functions. HR may not have direct representation at board or senior management level. In the smallest organisations there may be no HR specialists at all. Here HR functions may be taken over by general managers or owner-managers.

HR managers

Another variation is in terms of the nature of HR managers themselves. Here the framework developed by Tyson and Fell (1986) of types of 'people manager' retains its usefulness. This is reproduced in Table 1.5. This table clearly indicates that even those managers sharing a title, be it PM or HRM, may be radically different in what they do and what is expected of them.

Table 1.5 Types of HR manager

Aspects	Type of HR manager		
	'Clerk of the works'	**'Contracts manager'**	**'Architect'**
Discretion	Little	Some, within limits	High
Planning horizons	Short-term	Medium-term	Long-term
Roles	• Services junior line managers • Administrative support • Follows routines • Looks for leadership from others	• Services and advises middle managers • Provides knowledge of systems/practice • Follows systems, modifies to some extent • Gives leadership within existing structures	• Consultant to senior managers • Conceptualiser, inventive, problem solver • Changes routines/systems as necessary • Copes rapidly with change • Leads/participates with top management

Source: Adapted from Tyson and Fell (1986).

Flexible management for flexible firms

A further factor is that organisational positioning can lead to variations in HRM. First, in terms of organisational variation by competitive position and success, we can develop two models with radically different HRM:

• *short-term, cost-cutting survival approach* – here HRM may be downgraded. A 'clerk of works' (administrative support) mode prevails;

- *stronger position enabling a focus on long-term change* – here HR's position is more robust. HRM may be more likely to adopt an 'architect' of change mode.

Within this is the impact of the organisation's employment choices on HRM. Again, we can tease out two broad models:

- *'macho management' type* – this may be applied to peripheral (secondary) LM jobs;

- *more sophisticated, consultative role* – this may be applied to core (primary) LM jobs.

So, there is much variability in HRM. There are wide differences between businesses in the way HR activity is organised and delivered. Some of this may be due to organisational and employment variations.

Scope

In terms of coverage, the scope of this book extends to employee resourcing, rewards, development and relations, and some of the questions these areas raise. (Redundancy and dismissal are not a primary focus as these are increasingly quick-changing and litigious areas requiring specialist treatment.) Along with the final conclusion, these form the sequential structure of the rest of the book. These, and their links, can be seen in Figure 1.5. This figure will also allow you to quickly see what each chapter is about and make a decision to 'dip in' where you want.

Employee resourcing

The initial phase of HRM starts with HR planning. This is an obvious place to begin, as it is concerned with the HR requirements of organisations and how their business strategies can be resourced. This involves forecasting the numbers and types of HRs required from various sources and taking into account the impacts and developments on these. Then there is recruitment and selection. Given the HR plan, the necessary HRs need to be attracted and chosen by reliable, valid and cost-efficient methods – this is critical to organisational success.

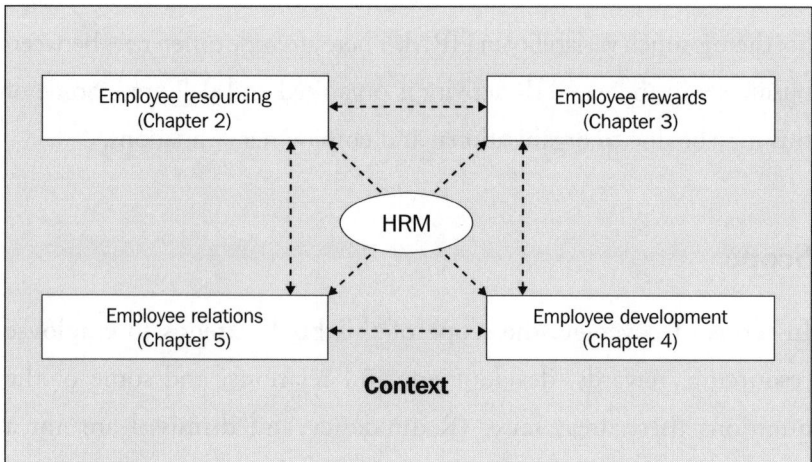

Figure 1.5 Overview and integration of HRM.

Employee rewards

This includes the mix and types of rewards required to try to ensure attraction, retention and commitment of HRs and what reward levels might be based on. There are numerous types of rewards and systems. The issue of 'fairness' remains key. The area of 'performance' in rewards has become increasingly important with the greater belief in its wider relevance across all employment sectors and countries. This view has taken root, despite thorny issues such as criteria and measurement in such reward systems.

Employee development

There is the perennially important area of training and development. The requirement and evaluation of the level and type of training, on-the-job or off-the-job, in-house or brought-in, remain key aspects of this area. A comparative examination of training shows its provision and underpinning to be very varied, with implications for methods of competition, and so on. Once in place, management needs to try to discover how well HRs are working, to provide feedback on performance, and indicate future directions and business objectives. This includes employee performance appraisal. This is another tricky area, with well-known problems for management and organisations to be very cautious of even within countries, while cross-cultural systems are even more problematic.

Employee relations

This contentious and contested area forms the final substantive part of the book. The ideas of a 'system' and 'actors' (groups, parties) operating within a context and the frameworks and perspectives of unitarism and pluralism, individualism and collectivism, remain relevant. This also varies internationally. Indeed, the post-1997 political envionment has contributed to this in the UK and can be seen in the European Union (EU) and many of its Directives. This area includes employee involvement, its numerous practices, and the raft of benefits it is believed to bring to businesses. Yet this is an elastic concept, allowing most people to support it, although its various forms have radically different implications.

Conclusion

The area of people management in its various guises is not new. The topic retains its crucial importance to management, either from a positive (to bring benefits) or negative (to avoid losses) stance. There may be increasing recognition of the importance of HRM for the competitive success of many organisations. We can still note criticisms. It is argued that HRM should be closely tied to the competitive strategy of the business and internally integrated between its policies. Yet this coordinated strategic stance is often missing, especially in the UK where HRM tends to operate in a more pragmatic and short-term orientation with ad hoc policies. It is argued that HR specialists should 'give up' HRM and devolve it to line management. Trends and developments in environmental contexts impact on HRM. An important factor is the labour market and its flexibility. Yet how does this impact on any 'strategic' role, especially in a context of organisational decentralisation, for HRM? We will return to such areas in the conclusion to this book.

All of the above have crucial impacts on ideas of universalism ('best practice') versus contingency in HRM. This is one of the common themes and tensions that run through the rest of the chapters in this book. In sum, HRM remains vitally important for all organisations yet diverse in its applicability and operation.

References

Atkinson, J. (1984) 'Manpower strategies for the flexible organisation', *Personnel Management*, August: 28–31.

Bae, J. and Rowley, C. (2001) 'The impact of globalization on HRM: the case of South Korea', *Journal of World Business*, 36, 4: 402–28.

Beer, M., Spector, B., Lawrence, P., Quinn Mils, D. and Walton, R. (1984) *Managing Human Assets*. New York: Free Press.

Delery, J. and Doty, H. (1996) 'Modes of theorizing in strategic HRM: tests of universalistic, contingency and configurational performance predictions', *Academy of Management Journal*, 39, 4: 802–35.

Fombrun, C., Tichy, N. and Devanna, M. (1984) *Strategic Human Resource Management*. New York: John Wiley.

Grubman, E.L. (1998) *The Talent Solution*, New York: McGraw-Hill.

Kochan, T. and Barocci, T. (1985) *Human Resource Management and Industrial Relations*. Boston: Little Brown.

Miles, R. and Snow, C. (1978) *Organizational Strategy, Structure and Process*. New York: McGraw-Hill.

Porter, M. (1985) *Competitive Advantage: Creating and Sustaining Superior Performance*. New York: Free Press.

Rowley, C. and Benson, J. (2002) 'Convergence and divergence in Asian HRM', *California Management Review*, 44, 2: 90–109.

Salamon, M. (2000) *Industrial Relations Theory and Practice*. London: Financial Times/Prentice Hall.

Tyson, S. and Fell, A. (1986) *Evaluating the Personnel Function*. London: Hutchinson.

Further reading

Hollinshead, G. and Leat, M. (2003) *Human Resource Management: An International and Comparative Perspective*. London: Pearson Education.

Leopold, J. (ed.) (2002) *Human Resources in Organisations*. London: Prentice Hall.

Marchington, M. and Wilkinson, A. (2002) *People Management and Development*. London: Chartered Institute of Personnel and Development.

Maud, L. (2001) *An Introduction to Human Resource Management: Theory and Practice*. Basingstoke: Palgrave.

Newell, H. and Scarborough, H. (eds) (2002) *Human Resource Management in Context: A Case Study Approach*. Basingstoke: Palgrave.

Pilbeam, S. and Corbridge, M. (2002) *People Resourcing: HRM in Practice*. London: Pearson Education.

Pinnington, A. and Edwards, T. (2000) *Introduction to Human Resource Management*. Oxford: Oxford University Press.

Redman, T. and Wilkinson, A. (eds) (2001) *Contemporary Human Resource Management: Text and Cases*. London: Prentice Hall.

Rowley, C. (ed.) (1998) *HRM in the Asia Pacific Region: Convergence Questioned*. London: Frank Cass.

Rowley, C. and Benson, J. (eds) (2003) *HRM in the Asia Pacific Region: Convergence Revisited*. London: Frank Cass.

Torrington, D., Hall, L. and Taylor, S. (2002) *Human Resource Management*. London: Pearson Education.

Warner, M. and Joynt, P. (eds) (2002) *Managing Across Cultures: Issues and Perspectives*. London: Thomson Learning.

CHAPTER 2

Employee resourcing

Introduction

We have so far looked at HRM from such angles as its common aspects, broad coverage, development, the links to strategy and tensions within it. This has given an us overview and framework for the rest of the book. We now shift our focus towards the key initial element in HRM, employee resourcing. How do organisations operationalise and staff their business strategies? This concerns the utilisation of HR planning. A second key aspect of this is employee recruitment and selection.

Overview

HR planning is concerned with the acquisition, use, improvement and preservation of an organisation's employees to match its business plans. It attempts to reconcile HR 'demand' (forecast from extrapolating corporate plans) and 'supply' (forecast by working out the state of HRs available and calculating likely shortfalls and surpluses). It identifies the key characteristics and behaviour of the HR 'stock' and 'sources'. This includes HR age, service, turnover, absenteeism, skills, and so on. Part of this involves so-called 'environmental scanning'. HR planning aims to reduce costs by helping to anticipate or correct HR shortages or surpluses before they become unmanageable and expensive – to 'employ the right number of people with the right skills at the right time'.

HR planning is generally seen to have a valid role, especially in large organisations operating in stable working environments. In contrast, HR planning is perhaps seen as less relevant in small firms and in more volatile contexts. The idea of the so-called flexible firm is one alternative response to this later scenario. In this model, the business has a stable 'core' of employees who are flexible functionally in terms of jobs and skills, and are surrounded by a 'periphery' of other workers who are flexible in terms of their numbers, and who can quickly and easily be expanded or reduced in size to reflect changing business requirements. This second group is seen to act as the 'shock absorbers' of the business, there to soak up variations in demand.

The employee resourcing of organisations is sometimes treated in a manner that has been labelled a 'downstream' or 'third-order' (by Purcell – see Thornhill et al., 2000: 98–100) decision that follows in the wake of business strategy and which HR people implement in a somewhat mechanical fashion. That is to say, sometimes employee resourcing is not considered in decisions until late on and may be taken as not that important or difficult. Furthermore, some actions and decisions in the area of employee resourcing itself may not be internally integrated. There may be management, even political, will to do something, but the implications are not always well thought through.

What might be the problems with the above and what are the influences on resourcing an organisation with people to deliver and fulfil its business strategy? We will explore these here and develop models to look at employee resourcing more coherently. With this in mind, read the cases below and answer the questions which follow them.

Case study 2.1 Health services in the UK

The government is trying to meet its vital targets in the National Health Service (NHS) plan to increase the number of doctors and nurses (by 20,000 full-time nurses) and also to reduce patient waiting times for patient treatment. This strategy has both short- and long-term employee resourcing implications. Higher pay is only part of the solution. With doctors and dentists, the problem is time: it takes so long to train such highly skilled people. With nurses a particular problem is the aging profile of the workforce, as a Royal College of Nurses (RCN) report made clear in late 2000. One in three nurses who currently work in the NHS is aged 35–44, a big bulge given that nationally only one quarter of all women at work are in this age group. Almost one-quarter of nurses are aged 45–54. Since nurses are entitled to retire at 55, this means that the NHS can expect to lose a lot of staff in the next few years. Meanwhile, nursing is no longer the automatic profession of choice that it used to be for so many young women. Projections in the report suggest that many nurses will leave the NHS by 2004 (see Table 2.1). With intakes from nursing education, this will still leave a shortfall if the government is to boost numbers. Filling this gap will be difficult. The government is looking abroad, but in the years 1997–2000, only around 16,000 overseas nurses registered in Britain, and not all of these will work in the NHS. The global market for nurses is tightening. Australia, Canada and America are also facing shortages. If the NHS is to meet its targets it will have to stop older nurses leaving the profession by offering them, for example, more flexible working arrangements. It will need to encourage recruitment by, for example, offering younger nurses clearer career progression. It could offer employment that allows nurses to combine work with childcare. In short, the NHS will have to become a better employer.

Table 2.1 NHS nursing numbers (full-time equivalent)

Current number of nurses	250,650
Nurses due to retire by 2004	90,650
Planned number of nurses in 2004	270,650
Number of recruits needed	110,650
Number of newly qualified nurses by 2004	53,700
Shortfall	**56,950**

(*Source*: Adapted from *The Economist*, 16 December 2000.)

Case study 2.2 Pilots in the UK Armed Services

....

There has been increasing concern about a shortage of trained pilots in the UK armed services. This has been caused by, for example, employee resourcing issues such as retention problems. Another problem is a backlog of training. In a National Audit Office (2000) report, it was reported that the Ministry of Defence (MoD) is producing 45 pilots a year less than the armed services need, and that the shortfall will continue until 2012 even if the MoD meets its targets every year from now on. Some 250 new pilots are needed each year, at a cost of £3.8 million each, excluding operational training. There is no shortage of trainees. However, the time taken for pilots to complete their training and reach the front line and combat readiness rose to nearly six years in 1998, which was double the planned time. This was due to, for example, defence cuts in the 1990s and to shortages of instructors and training aircraft. The MoD says it has taken action to remedy the problem: training time has been reduced to 3.8 years.

(*Source*: Adapted from A. Nicoll (2000) 'Concern over pilot shortfall', *Financial Times*, 14 September, p. 12.)

....

Now answer the following questions:

1. What issues in HR planning do the case studies illustrate?

2. What information would help to form a model in HR planning for a business?

3. What benefits may businesses see from having more strategic HR planning?

....

Following this first section, we will move on to the subject of employee resourcing, that is recruitment and selection. This area has been summarised by some as meeting HR requirements through defining the vacancy, attracting applicants, assessing candidates and making the final decision. This area is one of the key HR policies to achieve key HR and organisational outcomes in some models of HRM.

Once the HR plan has been developed, how is it to be fulfilled? This can be achieved by using a wide variety of quick and simple to long and complex recruitment and selection techniques. Why should businesses bother with sophisticated, but often costly, recruitment and selection? Indeed, there is some evidence that organisations often do not take this area seriously, while others do.

While there are many recruitment and selection techniques, much research indicates that many businesses have often relied on the 'classic trio' of methods – application forms, references, interviews. This is despite evidence of not just a number of problems with these methods themselves, but also their poor reliability as predictors of satisfactory job performance. There is also some interesting variability in the use of recruitment and selection methods between businesses in different countries.

Task 2.1

Think about or undertake the following task: develop an appropriate approach to recruitment and selection for Case studies 2.1 and 2.2.

A very useful collection of short pieces and newspaper articles that cover developments and examples in this area and cast light on them is given in the Further reading section at the end of the chapter. These will repay your investment in time obtaining and reading them.

HR planning

HR planning is seen as providing organisations with the possibility of reaching the ultimate goal of employing the 'correct' number and type of HRs at the right time: neither too few nor too many. In theory, this sounds achievable and not too difficult, requiring HR departments and managers to simply take into account relevant organisational plans and circumstances and then organise the commensurate HRs and actions accordingly. The next section discusses how this might be achieved.

Activities in HR planning

Given the above, it can be seen that there are several main activities and stages in HR planning. These are discussed in the following sections.

Forecasting demand for HRs

HR planning is just one element in corporate planning and cannot be isolated from the planning process as a whole. In order to put into effect the strategic plan, a number of more detailed operational plans need to be produced and reconciled with one another. These include, for example, the following:

- *marketing plans* – specifying which products will be offered and in what quantities;

- *operations plans* – specifying methods of production, distribution and development;

- *financial plans* – specifying how activities will be funded.

HR plans specify the HRs needed to execute these plans. HR managers need to integrate their HR plans with those of other departments, if they are to operate strategically. A demand model is then constructed and data fed in to yield the required HR staffing levels.

Forecasting supply of HRs

HR supply (from both existing and new sources) needs to be examined, calculated and forecast. This involves the use of a range of data and projections. This includes the source (internal or external labour markets) and profiles, characteristics and behaviour of any HRs required and influences on this supply.

Question to think about 2.1

What data might you look at in developing an HR plan for a business?

There is a range of possible data. This includes the following, as noted in Table 2.2.

Table 2.2 Data for HR planning

External	Internal
Demographics	Business plans
Workforce characteristics	HR 'stock': absenteeism, promotion rates, career profiles, skills
Labour market conditions	HR 'outflows': age profiles, turnover, retirements
Location	HR 'inflows': recruitment

Action and assessment

Following the above collection of relevant information, HR action plans need to be developed and implemented to reconcile HR demand and supply and resolve any discrepancies to produce demand-supply fit. This can involve recruitment targets, selection criteria, promotion policies, (re)training, redeployments, redundancies and retirements. This sort of exercise is then monitored and evaluated. The achievements of such goals are assessed and changed to accommodate new conditions and failures. These desires of HR planning can be seen in the various versions of traditional models of HR planning, as outlined diagrammatically in Figure 2.1.

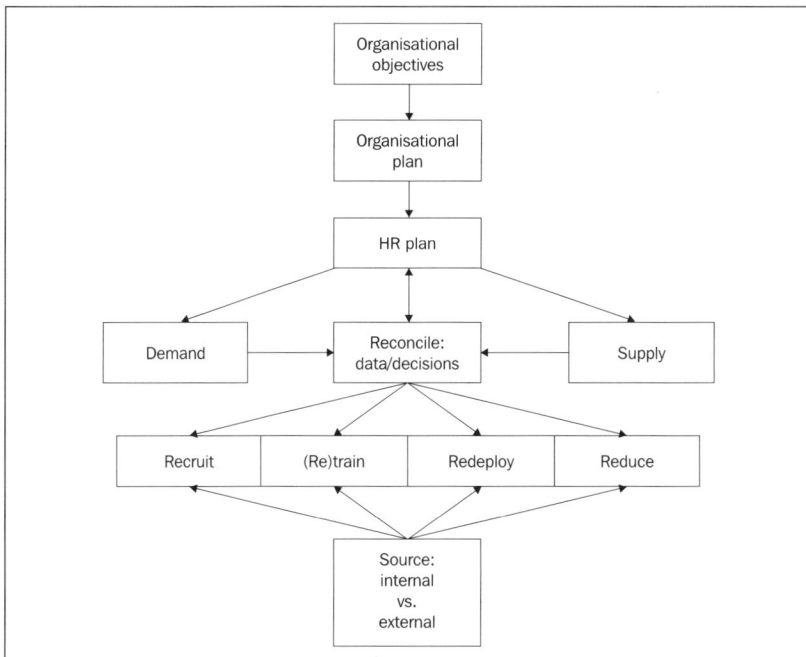

Figure 2.1 Model of HR planning.

By such means it is argued that HR planning will reduce business costs by helping to anticipate and correct HR shortages or surpluses before they become unmanageable and expensive for organisations. Furthermore, such plans can provide a better basis for other areas of HRM, such as employee development, in order to make optimum use of HRs and to improve job satisfaction. In short, this is a planning activity, and through this future problems and organisational requirements may be identified and appropriate actions taken. In sum, HR planning involves many activities and does not proceed in a linear fashion. Rather, there is often backtracking to ensure consistency, coherence and integration.

Methods and data in HR planning

There is a range of possible methods and data that could be utilised in this sort of HR planning. These include the following.

HR databases and analytical software

An initial starting point is any integrated corporate database, a major HR planning resource. Production, salaries and financial files can be drawn upon, as well as HR records containing basic facts in a structured format, records of employee performance appraisals, other reports and so on. These sources can give profiles (such as age, skills and so on) by section of the existing workforce. IT is of importance in HR planning. Larger organisations can use specialist software and sophisticated methods. One example of such a program is by PeopleSoft. In contrast, smaller organisations may meet most of their HR planning needs through the use of general-purpose analytical tools such as spreadsheets.

Work study

One initial question will be, even if 'output' (manufacturing and services) requirements and details of existing HRs are fairly certain, exactly how many, and what type, of people are needed to resource the plan? This is where work study can be used. This sort of approach is useful to compute standard times for different jobs (this area is returned to in the second part of this chapter). Sales and production forecasts can then be used as a basis for HR demand forecasting. This method works for the analysis of existing operations and jobs, but obviously is less useful when new operations and methods of production and services are involved.

Modelling techniques

Another critical area of HR planning is where business outputs, and hence HR requirements, are variable over time. Here, linear techniques and other statistical models can be used in forecasting and to investigate relationships between variables. These can be used to project future demand on previous HR levels and sales or relate employment to a variety of factors, such as how technology or market growth will affect employment. A simple example of this is time series analysis, which can be used to look at previous capacity and resourcing and predict future demand and hence likely commensurate HR requirements. Examples here include organisations that face predictable daily business variations and flows such as retailing or banking, or annual production or service demands such as certain seasonal foods and products, or hotels where staffing will try to reflect occupancy rates.

Key statistics

It is obvious that, to assist in HR planning, various key statistics may be computed by organisations. These are invaluable for HR estimation purposes and include the following, which are also often used as barometers of the 'health' of an organisation and behavioural aspects of work in areas such as job satisfaction, morale, working conditions and so on.

Labour turnover

Labour turnover has a variety of other terms, such as wastage, attrition, quits, leaving, drop-out, exiting and so on. This is a key HR statistic, not least as labour turnover can be costly (but is not always as, for instance, in fast food retailing). Also, some HR planning outputs, such as for redundancies, are radically affected by such rates. For instance, organisations with high rates face different choices if redundancies are required or training is being considered. Importantly for HR planning, a variety of reasons for turnover exist, some of which can be foreseen and hence planned for, such as retirements, although others are less predictable, such as resignations or dismissals. Critically, labour turnover can be measured, to provide an index for comparative reference and some basis for trends. The following shows how this is calculated.

$$\text{Labour turnover:} \quad \frac{\text{Number leaving in a year}}{\text{Average number employed in a year}} \times 100$$

A simple example illustrates this which concerns the labour turnover of clerical officers employed in a local authority. Here the average number employed during the year is 1,000 and the number who left employment during the year was 100. This gives a labour turnover rate of 10 per cent:

$$\text{Turnover:} \quad \frac{100}{1,000} \times 100 = 10\%$$

However, labour turnover is a complex and interactive phenomenon. Therefore problems for management and businesses can result from reliance on using just labour turnover rates.

Question to think about 2.2

What might be some of the problems with reliance on using just labour turnover rates?

These problems are varied. They include the following, as noted in Table 2.3.

Table 2.3 Problems with labour turnover rates

Problem	Characteristic
Confusing	Mixes up leaving and joining.
Undifferentiated	Little insight into patterns and sub-stocks of HRs (grades, departments, skills, age, etc.) experiencing higher levels than others.
Service	Length of service unclear: 50% turnover rate can be: • half workforce replaced over course of a year; • 10% of workforce replaced five times each.
Location	Unclear where leaving from: all in the same job or in many different jobs?

Stability index

Other, more differentiated data can be generated for use in HR planning. This includes a stability index which is used to stop possible short-service leavers from distorting the figures. It is calculated as follows:

$$\text{Stability:} \quad \frac{\text{Number of staff exceeding one year's service}}{\text{Number of staff employed one year ago}} \times 100$$

We can carry on using our earlier example to illustrate this. As you will recall, a local authority employed 1,000 clerical officers but had a 10 per cent turnover rate. However, the number of clerical officers with one or more years' service was 950. Hence, the local authority actually had a stability index of 95 per cent, calculated as follows:

Stability: $\dfrac{950}{1,000} \times 100 = 95\%$

Taken together, an organisation's turnover and stability index can show if there is a problem in a few posts or many positions. This distinction is important and a critical aspect when it comes to HR planning and HRM issues and decisions.

Fringe turnover index

Another HR statistic that may be used by businesses is a fringe turnover index. This calculates the percentage turnover of short-term workers. Importantly, this distinguishes those who join and quit quickly from the overall turnover figure. It is calculated as follows:

Fringe turnover: $\dfrac{\text{Number of staff joining and leaving within one year}}{\text{Average number of staff during the year}} \times 100$

Early patterns of wastage

Other statistics can show businesses when people leave. Research in this area has found that 'phases', according to the three-stage theory of wastage, are common. This is composed of:

1.   *Induction crisis*: initial shock, false expectations, lack of identity.

2.   *Differential transit*: begin to assess organisation and whether one has a place in it.

3.   *Settled connection*: survivor becomes an established employee with commitment.

Absenteeism

Another useful statistic for management and businesses concerns absenteeism, which can be measured in several ways. These include the following:

- percentage of lost working days;

- days lost per working year;

- average length of absence.

Impacts on HR planning

From the above, it seems that HR planning is eminently useful for businesses and management. What then accounts for HR planning's more constrained use in reality? An immediate problem is that organisations do not exist in a vacuum, nor are HRs inanimate objects. Rather, variations in organisational size and changes and trends in environments (internal and external) all have influences. At the same time, humans are complex social beings. All these impact on HR planning. They make the assumptions upon which HR planning is based less than robust, changeable and even somewhat tenuous at times. This can be seen in the following examples of impacts on HR planning.

The impact of organisation

HR planning techniques can vary in sophistication and in their use, for instance between:

* large businesses, which traditionally use sophisticated HR planning and methods (examples include oil companies, public sector groups); and

* smaller and less complex organisations, which use simpler HR planning and techniques, or even ad hoc judgement.

Linked to this organisational variable and factor impacting on HR planning is the operating environment of the business concerned.

The impact of environment

Changes in the external environment have critical impacts on HRM, as we saw in Chapter 1. To minimise the problems from these, organisations can monitor their environments in various ways and use a range of sources. These include surveys, trade associations, news media, journals and so on. HR planning was valuable to large organisations operating in stable environments. A classic example was UK retail banking before the 1980s. HR planning may still be useful in some industries, for example the police force, civil service, local government, education and so on. In contrast, for organisations in more quickly changing environments, such as UK retail banking since the 1980s and some private sector firms, HR planning is more difficult.

Volatility in demand is not a problem per se for HR planning, as this may be predictable, as we noted earlier with the use of time series analysis. However, when consumer demand is volatile and unpredictable, greater problems may arise for HR planning. This problem of the unreliable nature of demand figures on which HR estimates are based can be difficult to manage.

Another problem is that some of the assumptions on which HR planning is based turn out to be wrong. For example, in the UK in the late 1980s there was the so-called 'demographic time bomb'. This predicted a shortfall in younger workers due to falling birth rates and increasing participation in tertiary education, with commensurate negative employee resourcing impacts on those businesses in sectors which normally relied on such age profiles to staff their operations. Examples included UK retail chains. Young people would now have the pick of jobs, with the implication they would choose the 'better' ones. Other problems can still occur, as indicated in the case studies of the UK health service and military recruitment in this chapter.

A flexible response

Given the above factors, some firms have responded by abandoning detailed HR planning in favour of a more flexible response (think back to Chapter 1 and the discussion of flexibility and the flexible firm model). Here, organisations adopt a strategy of retaining a core labour force in permanent employment while having peripheral workers who can be laid off at short notice as required.

However, while pointing out a limitation to HR planning, this flexible approach may not totally invalidate the HR planning process, which need not be rigid. The process can still be used to anticipate and prepare for events. It can also involve thinking critically about existing arrangements and performance. Thus HR planning can help to avoid some mistakes. The following contemporary UK examples clearly show this.

HR planning in practice

We can see the impacts of failure to use HR planning in a range of examples as demonstrated in the following case studies.

Case study 2.3 The UK National Health Service and public sector

....

This provides both an older and a contemporary case. The NHS has been left to cope with the aftermath of the implementation of inaccurate plans. At least two HR planning-related mistakes were made. In the late 1980s, too much new-nurse training was commissioned, at considerable expense to the taxpayer. When it became clear, some years later, that an error had been made and that there would be too many trained nurses, the NHS then over-compensated by reducing the number of training places. A consequent result of this from the late 1990s was a shortage of trained nurses (Taylor, 1998). While this was a problem on its own, particular events and circumstances actually exacerbated it further. For instance, more recently the government's target was to increase the number of

NHS nurses, from 250,650 in 2000 to 270,650 by 2004, during which period the number of newly qualified nurses produced would be 53,700. At first sight, this expansion seems eminently achievable, requiring, it seems, just 20,000 more nurses while many more than this would enter the profession. However, HR planning reveals this to be far from a simple or easy case (as we saw earlier in Case study 2.1), worsened by geographical differential impacts. For instance, hospitals in London had 18 to 20 per cent labour turnover rates and the costs of recruitment agency staff had escalated, more than quadrupling from £154 million in 1997 to over £800 million by 2001 (Timmins et al., 2002).

Similarly, by late 2002 schools in England had a 1.2 per cent teacher vacancy rate, but in London this was 6 per cent, plus another 8 per cent of posts were filled by those without proper qualifications and another 10 per cent by teachers trained overseas (and hence perhaps somewhat transient). In local government, social workers had a 15 per cent vacancy rate, but this was over 30 per cent in some London boroughs (Timmins et al., 2002).

These examples are part of a wider UK public sector problem. Here there is actually an increasing demand in the next few years, for 35,000 more nurses, 15,000 more doctors, 30,000 more therapists and scientists, over 30,000 more school staff and 9,000 more police. This is in a context of an aging workforce. Thus 27 per cent of public-sector staff in 2002 were over 50, with nearly 66 per cent of employers having no one under 21 years old. Add in the effects of differential living costs, and the HR problems become all too apparent.

Case study 2.4 The UK military

In the early twenty-first century the UK armed forces were recruiting 25,000 people per year but still suffered from HR shortages. From 2000, there was more focus on boosting recruitment from the ethnic minorities (then just 2 per cent of service personnel) and also a £12 million package to improve pay allowances in an attempt to reduce premature resignations. However, although recruitment improved, the problem of retaining army troops remains. For example, in 1998 there was a net outflow of 100 per month. While this improved in 1999, with 17,700 recruits producing a net inflow of 24, there was actually a need for a net inflow of 60 for staffing targets to be met. By 2001, the army was 7,000 short of its 19,000 target (Timmins et al., 2002). Similar concern has been expressed about a shortage of pilots in the armed services (as we saw earlier in Case study 2.2).

Case study 2.5 UK train operating companies

The privatisation and break-up of the former nationalised and unitary British Rail has produced a plethora of HR problems (see Rowley, 2002a, 2002b). One of these concerns the lack of train drivers. This has been exacerbated by at least two decisions crucially impacting on HR. First, some train operating companies looked to cut costs. Labour was quickly looked at, especially train drivers, as they were seen as expensive. They were offered early retirement, which many took in the context of the upheaval in their industry. Yet, partly due to this, along with environmental changes (expanding demand with economic growth requiring more services), there was soon not enough drivers for the level of services required. One typical example of this was South West Trains' self-created shortage of drivers in 1997, which led to swathes of cancelled services, disgruntled passengers and poor publicity. Second, and linked to this, there was the collapse of training. The new train operating companies met HR demand by 'poaching' drivers from other, now competing, companies. In the newly fragmented industry, the former long-term investment in training by one overall business had ended and total capacity was increasingly depleted. Individual operating companies are ever more vulnerable to loss by poaching from those operators who did no training and 'saved' on budgets.

....

These examples serve as salutary warnings about the consequences of ad hoc, short-term decisions and impacts on, and from, HRs. These can critically undermine organisations and their business strategies.

Once the issue of HR requirements via HR planning of some form or other has been resolved, one implication may be the need for more HRs. This is the topic of the following sections of this chapter.

Recruitment and selection

With HR planning we can see that job vacancies occur for a variety of reasons. These include both internal growth in the organisation as well as people leaving positions (retirements, resignations, promotions, transfers, dismissals). How does an organisation go about filling any demand with a suitable HR? The case for systematic and effective procedures and methods seems incontrovertible given factors such as:

- the need to comply with laws concerning, for example, discrimination;

- the mass of evidence demonstrating the costs of mistakes;

- the impacts on the image and reputation of the business.

Recruitment is the process of contacting applicants (both internal and external) suitably qualified for a vacant position and encouraging them to apply. Selection is the process of matching the attributes of candidates with the requirements of the job and then choosing the best qualified applicants for the vacancies. Interestingly, even in the early 1990s it was already being argued that the desire for a flexible, multi-skilled workforce in which teamworking was more prominent meant that recruitment and selection was less about matching individual people to fixed requirements of individual jobs at a single point in time. Consequently, immediate skills and background were less important relative to criteria such as willingness to learn, adaptability and ability to work in teams (Beaumont, 1993: 56). There are obvious implications to these ideas for employee resourcing (see below). Furthermore, even such ideas do not totally remove the need for good recruitment and selection.

Stages

There are several stages in the recruitment and selection process involving assessments of both jobs (via job analysis) and candidates (via selection methods). These phases and activities can be seen within a comprehensive recruitment procedure, as outlined diagrammatically in Figure 2.2.

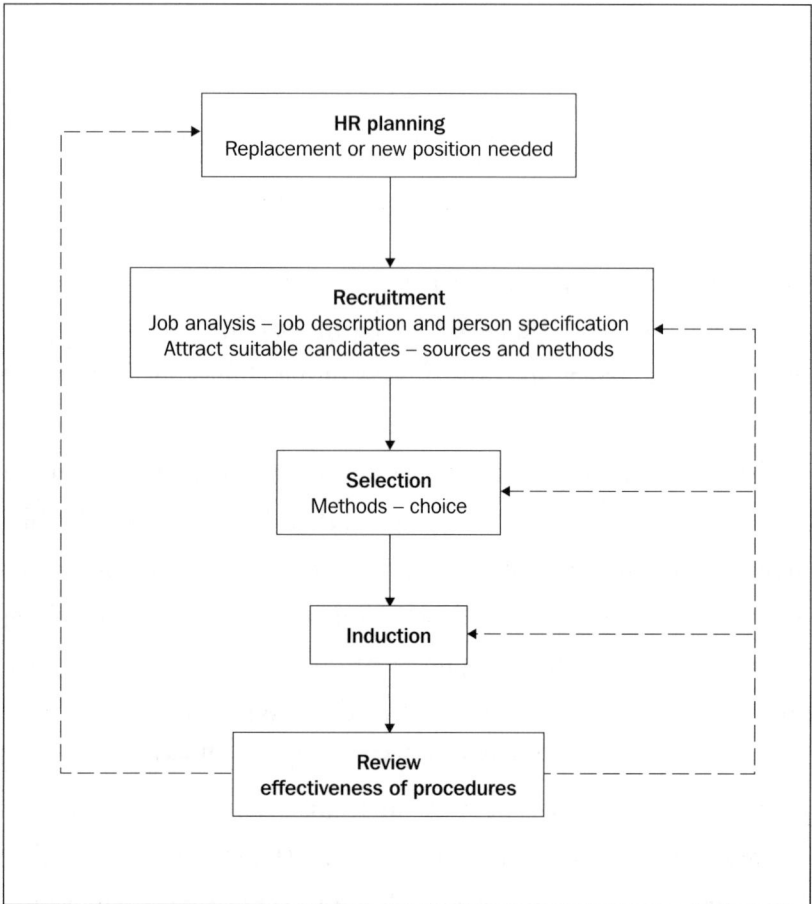

Figure 2.2 A systematic approach to recruitment and selection.

An initial question may be, what exactly is the post that needs filling and what does it actually involve? After all, if we do not know this, how can we judge who might be the 'best' person to fill it? Thus before recruitment and selection begins, key elements about the job are needed. This involves job analysis and its output.

Job analysis

Job analysis is used to elicit what a particular job is about and what it involves.

Question to think about 2.3

How would you discover what a specific job involves?

This can include a range of methods. Some of these are highlighted in Table 2.4.

Table 2.4 Methods of job analysis

Method	Characteristics
Work study	Examine each aspect of job
Questionnaires	Details of what job holder does
Interviews	Ask/check what job holder does
Work diaries	Detailing tasks completed each day
Critical incident reviews	Records kept
Observations	By supervisors
Panels of experts	Ask what might be details of new jobs

One method is work study, sometimes known as 'time and motion' studies, to analyse jobs (as we noted earlier in this chapter). The job analyst, who may be an 'insider' (a generalist or even a specialist from HRM) or an 'outsider', studies selected employees 'on the job', measuring their activities over a sustained period of time. Each task is broken down into individual elements and the way these are carried out is examined microscopically. This is the basis for scientific management and Taylorism. A light-hearted look at such techniques and issues such as employees under scrutiny behaving differently than they would in normal circumstances can be seen in films such as *Modern Times, I'm All Right Jack* and *Spotswood* (see Further reading and background information section at the end of the book).

Questionnaires are another method, and can be specifically designed or standard ones bought in 'off the shelf'. The general approach is to discover the details of what the job holder actually does and what knowledge, skills and abilities they are drawing upon to carry out the job. This is not as simple as it might appear, as many facets of any job may easily be overlooked. One approach is to look at what is involved in the job in terms of the following:

- mental processes – planning, organising, decision making;

- working methods – use of machines, tools, physical activity;

- human relationships – with other employees and customers;

- conditions – hours, physical conditions;

- other characteristics

For example, from the USA, the Position Analysis Questionnaire seeks data on 194 job elements grouped into 27 dimensions and six categories, while the Management Position Description Questionnaire is a checklist of 208 items grouped into 15 sections related to concerns and responsibilities. The Work Profiling System has three overlapping tests, each consisting of 300–400 items analysed by computer to give a job description and profile of the 'ideal' recruit. However, as in much of HRM, there is a trade-off as these methods can be increasingly time-consuming and expensive.

Another method concerns interviews, which have the same purpose as questionnaires and are often used in conjunction with them. They may be used to check questionnaire results and to discover further information about the content, context and requirements of jobs. Interviews may be held with not just job holders, but also with supervisors and subordinates.

Other methods include the keeping of work diaries, with details of tasks completed each day, through to critical incident reviews, where such events are logged and later reviewed. However, if a job is new and does not exist to be analysed, then there is no job holder to investigate. Then the use of panels of experts is of some use as a method to find out what the key tasks and skills of the future job may be.

Job description

From such job analysis exercises, the key elements in the job can be teased out. These elements may then be written up as a statement, i.e. a job description. This sets out what is involved in a job, but does not actually describe the kind of person who might be able to do the job for which a person specification needs to be developed. The possible contents of a job description are varied. They could include the following:

- basic details (title, grade, location);

- responsibilities (both to and for);

- main purpose;

- contacts;

- major duties;

- working conditions;

- general circumstances.

Person specification

This sort of information can now be used to produce a person specification which is a document that lists and defines the assessable attributes, often classified as either essential or desirable, of a person who might be effective and contented in the job. These attributes, obviously, vary according to the job and a disjointed 'wish list' may be produced that is unwieldy, especially when this needs to be put into a recruitment framework. To help in this, the attributes can be grouped into major categories. Two of the most famous are Rodger's 7-point plan and Munro Fraser's 5-fold grading and are listed in Table 2.5.

One example of the significance of the person specification comes from Disney, Paris. This organisation had a very strict code about who it considered to be suitable employees. It did not like people to have visible tattoos, long earrings, more than a single earring in each ear, high-heeled shoes, dyed hair or men with long hair or beards!

Table 2.5 Categories of personal attributes

Rodger's 7-point plan	Munro Fraser's 5-point grading
Physical make-up	Impact on others
Attainment	Acquired knowledge or qualifications
General intelligence	Innate abilities
Special aptitudes	Motivation
Interests	Adjustment or emotional balance
Disposition	
Circumstances	

In summary, businesses and managers should make efforts to:

- see the job and its requirements in all its dimensions;

- compile personal attributes essential to effective performance;

- list attributes which might improve performance as the basis to distinguish candidates;

- be aware of building in prejudices (racial, sexual, etc.) concerning 'suitable' candidates.

Recruitment

How are you now going to recruit the HRs you need? There are several sources, divided into two groups: internal and external (think back to Chapter 1 and the ideas around different types of LMs).

Internal methods

Question to think about 2.4

What types of internal recruitment methods are you familiar with?

There are many common methods. These include the following.

Job bidding

This involves using current HRs. Awareness of employment opportunities can be made by job posting, such as via memos, e-mails, computerised bulletins, newsletters and so on. Interestingly, recent legal changes in the UK will have a role here. For instance, the Fixed Term Employment (Prevention of Less Favourable Treatment) Regulations 2002 may give fixed-term employees a right to be notified of any permanent vacancies within the organsation.

Promotion

Current HR may also be used as part of a promotion system and succession planning to fill vacancies. This includes the idea of being 'groomed', as the 'natural heir', of course.

Both of the above approaches involve employee transfers and are often underpinned by an HR skills database, allowing the identification of suitable existing talent. However, these sorts of routes may simply be transferring the HR demand around, without necessarily actually solving it. After all, who will then fill the transferred or promoted person's job?

Recalls and rehires

Unsolicited inquiries via requests, speculative or cold-call personal inquiries and previous applicants can all be considered as possible sources. Again, an HR database which is regularly updated is useful here. There is a range of reasons for using previous employees. Organisations have had a prior relationship with them and made judgements on them. These people may have left for a variety of reasons, such as personal and family circumstances, retirement or simply at the end of projects or contracts, and so on. Traditionally, this sort of system was very important in seasonal or contract-based work. A good example would be shipbuilding. The excellent television series *The Ship* (see Further reading and background information at the end of the book) displays to good effect the use of such a resourcing method, and its drawbacks, as former employees may no longer be available or may be working for others, even your competitors.

Employee recommendations and contacts

Existing HRs can encourage family, friends and contacts to apply for positions. However, while this may impose a form of 'quality control' check, it can also both create resentment by others and be indirectly discriminatory in its results. Some UK examples prove this. Company A, involved in the production of munitions, historically recruited via families, partly to ease the security checking and vetting of the HRs required. Company B, based in a local LM with a high proportion of staff from ethnic minorities, had a workforce that did not reflect this diversity and remained highly homogenous. As existing HRs were asked to encourage applications for jobs, both workforces were, obviously, often simply replicating themselves. Another example concerns Ford UK's truck drivers at its Dagenham plant using 'father and son' recruitment, even in the 1990s. This meant that despite factory jobs having non-white workers, all the well paid trucking jobs remained with white workers. Indeed, the PR fallout of this affair was so bad that it resulted in the head of Ford flying in from the USA to apologise personally.

External methods

Question to think about 2.5

What types of external recruitment methods are you familiar with?

There are numerous methods. These include the following.

Referrals

These are registers kept by organisations of members seeking employment. Such organisations include trade unions and professional bodies.

Agencies

There are a range of agencies that may be considered for use in employee resourcing. This can include central government provision.

Many countries have these sorts of bodies. The problems with the German system hit the headlines in 2002. In the UK there is a national network of centres acting as agents for potential employers. The obvious possible drawback is that it is only the unemployed, rather than the employed, who are registered. There is also the resettlement service offered to armed forces personnel at the end of their service.

A range of other types of agencies also exist such as outplacement consultants providing help to enforced redundancies. There are also selection consultants and temporary agencies which can be used to reduce employer administration as they recruit and select for positions. Some poor practice (recruits leaving quickly as they are consequently offered other jobs) has led to scepticism with some of these agencies. Another type is the search consultant, or headhunter as they are colloquially known. These organisations often keep track of those likely to be in frequent demand as well as directly approaching promising candidates. While this allows discussions without commitment, it excludes many potential candidates outside the network of the particular consultant used. Again, agency 'sharp practice' can lead to recruits being poached over and over again by the same consultant for different clients.

Educational institutions

Schools and career services can be used in employee resourcing as they can offer guidance and some testing. Others here include college and university leavers, although this tends to be a cyclical, annual process. In countries such as South Korea, Japan, France and Germany, some employers have intimate knowledge of individual universities, departments and even individuals, and focus their attention and recruitment on specific people. However, HR demand may not fit into the annual cycle of the completion of education. This also applies to the traditional 'milk round' by large national employers to university campuses. This was once very popular in the UK, but has diminished somewhat. Indeed, this whole process, with organising, travel, accommodation and costs for both applicants and recruiters who are also on the road for long periods, can be high and the returns to organisations not all they seem to be.

Retirees

At the opposite end of the age spectrum are older workers. In the UK this category became the focus of attention in the wake of all the publicity of the 'demographic time bomb' (as we noted earlier) with falling birth rates and increasing participation in tertiary education. This predicted that organisations would be in intensified competition for the declining number of available young workers, which some sectors had traditionally been very reliant on to staff their businesses. Consequently, such organisations would need to develop alternative employee resourcing strategies. In the UK, one of the most famous of these was that developed by B&Q, the retail chain, which deliberately targeted older workers. Indeed, the commonly raised fears about such workers – their lower productivity, higher absenteeism and ill health – proved unfounded. The actual result was better productivity and especially service, partly as these older workers were more reliable and able to provide product advice as they actually knew about items or had even used them. Similar US examples can also be provided (see *The Economist*, 1998).

Overseas

This is actually an old method of resourcing, for example, in the UK. For instance, recruitment of HRs from the ex-colonies to work in sections of the public sector, such as transport, was common back in the 1950s, even involving the setting up of recruitment offices and facilities in the supplying country concerned. This remains a method of recruitment, and events such as the collapse of the former Eastern bloc and now shortages of HRs in areas such as the health service in many countries have resulted in the tapping into of overseas supplies of HRs (as we saw earlier). This in turn raises all sorts of issues, including the moral and ethical, such as the draining of economies of skilled HRs. This also applies to countries with traditionally very limited immigration such as Japan (*The Economist*, 2000) and South Korea.

E-recruitment

The use of the Internet for recruitment purposes is a significant contemporary development in this area. This is in terms of both employers and people advertising on the web as well as 'cyber agencies'. Hunting for new jobs online is one of the most popular online activities, as companies use electronic recruiting methods.

The advantages of this method are cheapness and speed. Some UK examples of job portals to assist in this are given in Table 2.6.

Table 2.6 Examples of e-recruitment sites

www.monster.co.uk
A 'career network' (with more than 24,000 UK jobs). Easy to search for jobs, create a CV and set profiles for e-mail notification of jobs that match your criteria. Has a career centre with advice on topics ranging from discrimination to redundancy.

www.fish4jobs.co.uk
Simple site to use: asks two basic questions – what job and where – then delivers returns from 29,444 jobs listed. Individual channels – including secretarial, marketing and construction – have trade tips, career centre, with a 'life coach' and 'legal doctor' on hand to help.

www.workthing.com
Dominant in the public sector, education, media, charity and permanent IT positions thanks to its links with the Guardian Media Group. After registration, you can set up a range of different profiles, add your CV for employers to download, and save interesting vacancies. Extras include e-mail notification of suitable jobs (daily or instantly), a salary checker and help on making an immediate impression at an interview.

www.i-resign.com
Originally a entertaining guide to quitting your job, which has expanded to become a fully-fledged jobs portal. Old favourites – including Quit Countdown tips, resignation letter templates and the latest Big Quitters – remain, but with a link to Workthing.com.

www.jobsite.co.uk
One of the UK's biggest online agencies (e.g. 97,000 jobs advertised in one month) and with 35 industries covered. Along with the usual tools, you can create four different covering letters, get advice on how to write a CV and read the latest news on your sector.

www.planetrecruit.co.uk
The best bet for agency-only jobs, which is all it deals with. No thrills and no extra content, but an impressive range of jobs covered (100,000) and a fast search facility.

One recent development to consider involves cases of UK companies using the web to 'check up' on recruits.

Advertising

Another area includes advertising the position, where a whole range of media are available, from the more general to the more specific. This includes press, television and radio, both local and national, and cinema. Recent examples from television recruitment advertising in the UK concern much of the public sector, such as the police service, armed forces and the NHS. Posters, career exhibitions, conferences, brochures, videos and open days might also be considered.

Question to think about 2.6

What are the advantages and disadvantages of internal and external recruitment?

There are numerous methods and advantages and disadvantages to them. Some of these can be seen in Table 2.7. Most organisations follow a mixed strategy, although they differ substantially in their

---

preference for internal and external recruitment. At one extreme are those that promote from within. New recruits are at the entry level for the job grouping. At the other extreme, some organisations advertise all posts externally, although existing employees might apply.

Table 2.7 Advantages and disadvantages of recruitment forms

Advantages	Disadvantages
Internal	
Improve morale/motivation	Not always best person
Chain effect of promotion	Over-promotion
Potential talent not ignored	Disruption from HR mobility
Person knows organisation	No new ideas or skills
Faster/less expensive	'In-fighting' for promotions
Reduces training costs	Favouritism
Better assessment of abilities	Morale of unsuccessful candidate(s)
External	
Larger applicant pool	Expensive
New ideas/contacts	Unknown candidates
Access to clients/'secrets'	Select those who do not 'fit'
Reduces 'in-fighting'	'We did it this way' attitudes
Cheaper than training	Longer adjustment times
Not depleting existing HR stock	Internal candidate morale
Publicity/PR of growth	Publicity/PR of leavers

Selection

Once the closing date for applications is reached, the selection of HRs can begin. This involves deciding whether applicants are suitable and then selecting which are 'the best', ideally by comparing and evaluating them against the yardstick of the person specification. The selection process may conclude with the deliberations of an appointing panel or committee, which reviews the information and reaches a judgement.

Methods

Question to think about 2.7
What selection methods are you familiar with?

There are many methods of selection. These range from the simple and short to the more complex and longer.

Application forms

These forms and questionnaires discover details of background, experience and personal data. This is often simple, assessed subjectively and used to eliminate those applicants seen as unsuitable. There is a vast range of types, length and formats.

References

These are used in support of other methods. They can be used to check the validity of statements made and elicit additional information and testify to character or offer professional opinion. There is an increasing duty of care in this area, with factual evidence and support needed for what is written.

Interviews

A range of types and size of interview formats also exist. These include the following.

Unstructured

This is a commonly used format for interviews. It gives freedom to explore issues in some detail and depth in a free-ranging manner. Also, this type allows interviewers to explore higher-level skills such as conceptual reasoning and so on. However, the use of this format can then mean that comparisons between candidates are difficult.

Structured

These interview formats ask standard sets of questions and record responses. Therefore they allow the production of comparative data between candidates. This will assist in the required 'discrimination' between candidates for the final selection choice.

Mixed

These interview formats allow certain questions to be asked of all candidates. Other questions are specific to the particular individual concerned.

Individual and panel

The interview format may involve just a single interviewer. Alternatively, a small team, commonly three to five interviewers, may be used.

Group

The applicant may be interviewed singly. Alternatively, a number of candidates may be assessed simultaneously.

Telephone

There is some use of telephone interviews. This form can be used as a 'screening' mechanism (see Torrington et al., 2002).

In terms of the conduct of interviews, both sides need to be prepared, on time and professional (much of the following is just as relevant for employee performance appraisal interviews – see Chapter 4). The interview is a two-way process: the candidate is also evaluating the organisation. Furthermore, however difficult it is for some managers, it is the applicants who should do most of the talking, and this may require the development of active listening skills in managers. Also, techniques and skills in areas such as the recording of information during and at the end of each interview and being aware of legal and ethical issues surrounding interviews are required.

Some common perceptions, sequences, protocols and questions in respect of interviews can be noted and put into a pattern, as seen in Tables 2.8–2.10. Despite the de facto importance of interviews, readers may wish to reflect on how closely such a pattern has been followed in their experience. This could be as both interviewer and interviewee.

Crucially, a long and consistent history of research has produced a list of problems with the 'classic trio' of employee resourcing methods. These are application forms, references (both of which present the 'best case' and are open to being 'economical with the truth'), and interviews (biases, subjectivity and so on). Indeed, there has been the development of businesses that check the veracity of content, especially of CVs submitted in support of applications. Following being informed of the use of such companies, a disconcertingly large number of candidates consequently withdraw their applications. Given the enduring popularity (and use of the technique elsewhere, as in employee performance appraisals), it is instructive to note some of these common biases in interviews.

Question to think about 2.8

What problems might there be with using interviews as a selection method?

Table 2.8 Interview guide

Before interview	At interview	After interview
• Who will conduct it? • Is panel needed? Members available and can meet prior to interview? • References dealt with before or after? • Other activities precede or follow? • How many candidates? How much time each?	• Logical pattern • All have clear understanding of conduct • Examine motivation and interest of each candidate • Assess how each candidate is likely to fit in	• How and when will all be notified? • Appropriate arrangements to pay expenses

• Accommodation needed? • Asked to wait for result or notified later? • Information to candidates on job, interview process, etc.? • Who will receive candidates, and have they all been notified? • Is interview room adequate and ensured of no interruptions? • Is a suitable waiting area provided?		

Table 2.9 Interview structure: a recommended pattern

Stage	Objectives	Activities
Opening	• Put at ease • Develop rapport • Set the scene	• Greet by name • Introduce yourself • Explain interview purpose • Outline how purpose will be achieved • Obtain assent to outline
Middle	• Collect information • Provide information	• Structure that makes sense to candidate (biographical, application form areas, competencies) • Listening • Answering questions
Closing	• Close interview • Confirm future action	• Summarise interview • Check no more questions • Indicate what happens next and when

Source: Adapted from Torrington et al. (2002).

Table 2.10 Use of questions and statements in interviewing

Type	Example	Characteristics	Useful when …	Not useful when …
Open	'Tell me about …'	Encourage to talk	Exploring and gathering information on broad basis	Discipline required
Closed	'How old are you?'	Narrow, establish point	Probing single specific points	Gaining data on broad basis or where not well informed
Probing	'What exactly happened next?'	Follows open questions to establish details	Establishing and checking information known or arising from questions	Exploring emotionally charged areas
Reflective	'You feel upset about …?'	Powerful, repeat back statement	Encouraging to continue talking about problems or exploring deeper	Checking information
Leading	'You are sorry now, aren't you?'	Indicates answer looked for/expected	Gaining compliance or acceptance of view	Gaining information about what they think or feel
Hypothetical	'What would you do if …'	Posing a situation	Getting interviewee to think in broader terms about topic	Need time to give reasoned reply
Multiple		Several questions in one	Never	Always

Non-committals ('lubricators')	'Yes', 'Aha'	Listening, encouraging to talk	Indicating you are listening and want them to continue	Keeping talk to a particular point
Inhibitors	'I see', 'Oh!'	Sharp halt	Signalling enough	In normal situations or emotional or frank discussion
Comparison	'Would you prefer weekly or monthly …?'	Realistic and relevant comparisons	Exploring and revealing own needs, values, etc.	Comparisons unrealistic or irrelevant
Summaries	'What we seem to have decided so far …'	Draws together main points	Avoiding discrepancies, gaining commitment	Used prematurely

There are many problems with interviews which revolve around the participants themselves and the biases and effects that may well result. Some of these can be seen in Table 2.11. One example of stereotyping and common misconceptions that can inform selection is the belief that disabled job applicants will suffer higher levels of sickness absence than non-disabled people. In practice, the research and data do not support such a proposition.

Table 2.11 Biases in interviews

Type	Characteristics/impacts
Non-verbal behaviour	Significant impact
Speed	Decisions made very quickly (within a few minutes)
Primacy	First impressions/information assimilated early on
Order of information	Favourable information early/later very influential
'Halo' and 'horns'	Generalisation from one 'outstanding' characteristic (good or bad)
Expectancy	Positive/negative expectations formed from application form
Self-fulfilling prophecy	Questions designed to confirm initial impressions
Stereotyping	Including comparisons with ideal applicant; implicit personality theory as substitute for seeking specific information from applicant; particular characteristics are typical of group members
Prototyping	Favour particular type of personality regardless of job-related factors

Contrast	Preceding applicants create context in which evaluated
Negative information bias	Perceived negative points sought, given undue emphasis over more positive ones
Similar-to-me	Preference to those perceived as having similar background, history, personality
Personal liking	Whether or not they personally like candidate
Information overload	Judgements formed on only a fraction of the data available
Fundamental attribution error	Actions caused by aspect of personality rather than simple response to events
Trait attribution	Past behaviour is a good predictor of future behaviour (omits mediating influences and circumstances)
Temporal extension	Behaviour at interview is typical of general disposition

Source: Adapted from Hakel (1982), Taylor (1998).

Given the above, perhaps greater use of other selection methods should be encouraged? While these may be useful additions to selection, there are some drawbacks that managers need to be wary of with some of these employee resourcing techniques. Despite the weaknesses of the 'classic trio', some other methods are even less reliable. We will note one here.

Graphology

Graphology, the analysis of handwriting, is a popular method in some countries such as France and a few other countries in Europe, whereas in others it is treated with disdain. A possible reason for its use is its apparent 'reliability' as a selection tool (Taylor, 1998). People's handwriting tends not to change to any great extent during their adult life. It is also a 'reliable' method in so far as different graphologists have been found to reach similar conclusions about a candidate's personality when given the same handwriting sample to analyse. However, reliability should not be confused with validity. Research has shown graphology to be a poor diviner of personality traits and thus job performance.

However, not all is lost. Some methods that can be used in selection have been shown to be better predictors of job performance. These include the following.

Employment tests

These seek to measure specific characteristics, abilities and behaviour. The benefits of such methods include the fact that test results can be numerical, allowing direct comparison of candidates on the same criteria and with explicit and specific results. They provide hard data which can be evaluated for their predictive usefulness in later years, i.e. comparing predicted with actual performance. There is a variety of tests to assist in employee resourcing. These include the following.

Ability/work sample

These tests are not particularly new. They involve a range of events. There can be work scenarios and tasks, such as being given a piece of real or simulated work to complete, or team problem-solving. An example from academia would be the need to provide publications, presentations, and so on. Other contemporary examples include Prêt à Manger, the sandwich chain, which used working as a paid employee in a shop for a day as the final leg of its HR resourcing techniques of application forms and structured interviews.

Psychometric testing

These tests are increasingly common. They attempt to determine if the candidate has the 'right' kind of personality for the job (see Clark, 2003, for a good summary). In the UK a survey (2,000) found 54 per cent of companies from a broad sweep of industries said they used such tests (*Financial Times*, 2001). One example is B&Q, the UK retail chain, which receives 200,000 applicants for 15,000 jobs annually and uses an automated system run via their Glasgow call centre. Here initial applicants respond to questions that 'test' their personality to see whether they fit the culture B&Q wants. The system then works out a score and generates letters informing applicants if they are psychologically cut out for work at B&Q, with final selection by face-to-face interviews (Overell, 2002).

Assessment centres

Another, more reliable, selection method is the assessment centre and the battery of tests often used at them. These compare candidates' performance in simulated problems. There can be a range of tests used; indeed, the number of techniques used is an advantage. The use of multiple trained assessors is also beneficial. These allow the pooling of tests and assessors' results. Tests can include, for instance, in-basket simulations where candidates are asked to process and action an accumulation of memos, reports, letters and so on. Others include leaderless group discussions when a group response to a question is required. Individual presentations may also be used, as may assigned leadership exercises. An example of this was the RAF's centre at Biggin Hill where team tasks are set in which each individual takes turns in playing the role of team leader.

Question to think about 2.9

What might be some disadvantages with such tests?

There are several drawbacks with tests. These can be seen in Table 2.12 and are discussed further below.

Table 2.12 Disadvantages of tests

Disadvantage	Characteristics
Responses	Faked to give 'desirable' score (especially where same tests used and practised)
Temporary factors	Produce variable results, i.e. due to anxiety, illness, etc.
Ethnocentric	Often US-based with comparisons (white, middle-class, male, American) as the 'norm' and reference position.
Meaningful	Accuracy (Stagner's research)

A classic piece of research carried out by Stagner in 1958 (reported in Jackson, 1996) is a warning against personality tests. In this, 68 managers completed a personality questionnaire. At the end, each was presented with a written profile summarising the main characteristics of their personalities. They then completed a further questionnaire asking how accurate they believed the profile to be. Some 50 per cent ranked the profile overall as being 'amazingly accurate' and a further 40 per cent as 'rather good'. However, the researchers had tricked the managers by giving them all the same faked personality profile to assess instead of genuine summaries of their own personalities. Thus tests can appear a great deal more accurate and meaningful than they actually are. People may read into results what they want, or expect, to see.

B&Q, the UK retail chain, had to defend its use of psychometric testing in 2001. In this case, a person gained promotion within days of being hired as a sales assistant but was then sacked after the results of a computerised personality test came through. Under B&Q rules, the manager should have waited for the results before offering the job (*Financial Times*, 2001). In the USA there are legal court cases and payouts to people concerning such tests and why certain questions, seemingly irrelevant to the job, are asked. For instance, to what extent is the religious belief or sexual orientation of a person applying for a position as a security guard in a retail store actually relevant to the job?

Recruitment and selection in practice

The use of the so-called 'classic trio' of application form, references and interview remains most common. This is despite research showing these methods are poor predictors of actual job performance. Examples of more sophisticated resourcing can be seen. Japanese car manufacturers in the UK provide a useful example here. Traditionally there had been limited amounts spent on recruitment and selection in the sector. This was then reversed by companies like Nissan. Indeed, recruitment and selection was comprehensive and even stretched to psychological testing in some. The typical sequence was: advertisements placed in press; local job centre handled applications, filtered them and passed on details to the organisation; interview by teams with timed aptitude tests, untimed personality tests, and interview programme; end of day review of information for decisions (from Beaumont, 1993). Likewise, for Toyota in the UK there was a six- to seven-month recruitment process of five-page application form, three-hour testing and orientation, 75-minute targeted behavioural interview, six-hour work sample and final one-hour interview.

International comparisons of resourcing

A useful overview of some international variations in employee resourcing is provided in Torrington et al. (2002). This is reproduced in the text box.

Window on practice

It is interesting to contrast different approaches to selection in different countries. Bulois and Shackleton (1996) note that interviews are the cornerstone of selection activity in both Britain and France, but that they are consciously used in different ways. In Britain they argue that interviews are increasingly structured and criterion referenced, whereas in France the approach tends to be deliberately unstructured and informal. They note that in France the premise is that 'the more at ease the candidates are, the higher the quality of their answer', whereas in Britain they characterise the premise as 'the more information you get about an individual, the better you know him/her and the more valid and reliable your judgement is' (p. 129). Tixier (1996), in a survey

---

covering the EU (but excluding France), Switzerland, Sweden and Austria, found that structured interviews were favoured in the UK, Scandinavia, Germany and Austria. This contrasted with Italy, Portugal, Luxembourg and Switzerland where unstructured styles were preferred.

Bulois and Shackleton identify selectors in Britain as more aware of the limitations of interviews and as attempting to reduce the subjectivity by also carrying out assessment centres and psychological tests; whereas in France these methods were identified as unnatural, tedious and frustrating. Interviews are much more likely to be supplemented by handwriting analysis in France – both methods being identified as valuable, flexible and cheap sources of information. Shackleton and Newell (1991) report that handwriting analysis was used in 77 per cent of the organisations that they surveyed in France compared with 2.6 per cent of the organisations they surveyed in the UK.

Both culture and employment legislation clearly have an influence on the selection methods adopted in any country and the way in which they are used.

(*Source*: Torrington et al., 2002: 205.)

Some businesses, such as in the USA, are increasingly becoming aware of forecast demographic changes which mean they will have to employ more people from different ethnic groups (see also Chapter 1). As a result, companies (such as IBM) are setting up departments to 'manage diversity' among their employees. This includes thinking about new ways of employee resourcing for the future. Some examples of similar developments from the UK include supermarket retail chains and banks.

However, selection may be more ad hoc and reactive than the earlier examples indicate. The level, sophistication, time and cost organisations actually apply to employee resourcing vary. There are instances when these are minimal (fast food retailing) or extensive. The type of selection devices used and the elaborateness of the procedures employed also vary according to the perceived importance of the job to the organisation. For instance:

- Tests and interviews are often sufficient for school leavers applying for entry-level jobs.

- Higher-level occupations may demand more personal and exhaustive approaches.

- Use of psychological tests varies by job: grade, 20 per cent manual, 70–80 per cent management; and type, 90 per cent for graduates (Newell and Shackleton, 1994).

Conclusion

In this chapter we have covered the first key area of HRM – employee resourcing. This was in terms of HR planning and the recruitment and selection this may indicate. The predictions that HR planning makes will be of a conditional nature. This is partly because an unstated assumption in HR planning is that the future has continuity with the past. Yet the influences of environmental volatility, small firms and so on should not be forgotten. These all impact on HR planning. As such, HR planning should be seen not as a highly precise technique, but as a loose collection of ideas and tools which can be applied as necessary to the individual needs and circumstances of a particular business.

In terms of recruitment and selection, several key points were made. Recruitment methods can apply to existing and new HRs, and vary depending on the HR approach of the organisation (flexible firm, etc.), and the level and types of HRs sought. Furthermore, a set of questions quickly arises. These include the following. What is required to perform the job? What selection techniques have predictive validity? Is there a significant relationship between a predictor (for example, interview rating of applicants) and subsequent successful performance in a job? Are these reliable (for example, consistency of the measure over time)? No selection process provides a complete, accurate prediction of performance as jobs change and people develop, while techniques of assessment/measurement are imperfect. Nevertheless, a variety of methods can be used to compensate for prejudice from a single source of assessment.

Evidence continues to suggest that many firms do not treat employee resourcing as seriously as they might. HR planning is rudimentary. Simple application forms and references for pre-selection and interviews for final selection continue to predominate. Many businesses and managers continue to use such techniques, despite a long and consistent stream of research indicating their low reliability and validity as a sole method of selection. Finally, it is important that companies plan their recruitment and selection strategy in advance and in relation to the development of corporate strategy. However, in practice this is usually left to the last minute!

Overview references

HR planning

The Economist

'Can America's Workforce Grow Old Gainfully?', 25 July 1998, p. 77–8.

'Immigration in Japan: The Door Opens a Crack', 2 September 2000.

The Financial Times

Harney, A. (2000) 'Young Japanese Losing Interest in Lifelong Relationship with One Employer', 8 April, p. 9.

Harney, A. (2000) 'Japanese "Job For Life" Starts to Look a Bankrupt Idea', 7 November.

Maitland, A. (2001) 'An Alternative to Early Retirement', 26 June, p. 15.

Maitland, A. (2002) 'A Fresh Start for Older Employees/The End of Early Retirement', 22 January, p. 12.

Mathews, V. (2002) 'Plenty of Life in the Old Reps', 18 October, p. 15.

Recruitment and selection

The Financial Times

Bird, J. (2003) 'Appoint in Haste, Repent at Leisure', 9 January, p. 14.

Donkin, R. (2003) 'Home Grown Talent Can Win the Skills War', 9 January, p. ix.

Dulewicz, V. (2001) 'In Search of the Best Performers', Mastering People Management, Part 5, 12 November, pp. 6–8.

Furnham, A. and Pendleton, D. (2001) 'Psychometric-Speak is Here to Stay', 18 December, p. 19.

Lee, N. (2002) 'An Improved Milkround', 19 August, p. 12.

Pickard, J. (2001) 'B&Q Defends "Brutal" Use of Psychometric Testing', 21 April, p. 3.

Salsback, K. (2001) 'Be Careful Not to Write Yourself Off', 15 August, p. 11.

Tighe, C. (2002) 'Diamonds and Timewasters', Special Report: Inner City 100, 6 November, p. 18.

Yeung, R. and Brittan, S. (2001) 'Beyond the Interview', Mastering People Management, Part 5, 12 November, pp. 2–3.

References

Beaumont, P. (1993) *HRM: Key Concepts and Skills*. London: Sage.

Bulois, N. and Shackleton, V. (1996) 'A qualitative study of recruitment and selection in France and Britain: the attitudes of recruiters in multinationals', in I. Beardwell (ed.), *Contemporary Developments in HRM*. Paris: Editions ESKA, pp. 125–35.

Clark, L. (2003) 'Psychometric testing stays forever Jung', *Financial Times*, 20 June, p. 14.

Economist, The (2000) 'Immigration in Japan: The Door Opens a Crack', 16 December.

Financial Times (2000) 'Concern over pilot shortfall', 14 September, p. 12.

Financial Times (2001) 'B&Q defends "brutal" use of psychometric testing', 21 April, p. 3.

Hakel, M. (1982) 'Employment interviewing', in K. Rowland and G. Ferris (eds), *Personnel Management*. London: Allyn & Bacon.

Jackson, A. (1996) *Understanding Psychological Testing*. Leicester: British Psychological Society.

Newell, S. and Shackleton, L. (1994) 'The use of psychological tests for selection purposes by job grade', *Human Resource Management Journal*, 4, 1: 14–23.

Overell, S. (2002) 'The right personalities in store', *Financial Times*, 5 December, p. 12.

Rowley, C. (2002a) 'Hitting the buffers: labour disputes and British Railways', *Financial Times Mastering Management Online*, issue 10, February.

Rowley, C. (2002b) 'Reversing the engine: using arbitration to solve labour disputes', *Financial Times Mastering Management Online*, issue 12, April.

Shackleton, V. and Newell, S. (1991) 'Management selection: a comparative survey of methods used in top British and French companies', *Journal of Occupational Psychology*, 64: 23–36.

Taylor, S. (1998) *Employee Resourcing*. London: CIPD.

Thornhill, A., Lewis, P., Millmore, M. and Saunders, M. (2000) *Managing Change: A Human Resource Strategy Approach*. London: Financial Times/Prentice Hall.

Timmins, N., Kelly, J. and Odell, M. (2002) 'Recruitment difficulties weigh down public sector', *Financial Times*, 27 November, p. 4.

Tixier, M. (1996) 'Employers' recruitment tools across Europe', *Employee Relations*, 18, 6: 67–78.

Torrington, D., Hall, L. and Taylor, S. (2002) *Human Resource Management*. London: Financial Times/Prentice Hall.

Further reading

For those who want further details, there are links and references given in some of the above titles, while there are many further books which cover similar ground, such as the following:

Albrecht, M. (2001) *International HRM*. Oxford: Blackwell (Part III).

Beardwell, I. and Holden, L. (eds) (2001) *HRM: A Contemporary Perspective*. Harlow: Pearson Education (Part 2).

Hendry, C. (1995) *HRM*. Oxford: Butterworth-Heinemann (Chapters 9–11).

Marchington, M. and Wilkinson, A. (2002) *People Management & Development*. London: CIPD (Chapter 10).

Newell, H. and Scarbrough, H. (eds) (2002) *HRM in Context: A Case Study Approach*, Basingstoke: Palgrave (Chapter 5).

Pilbeam, S. and Corbridge, M. (2002) *People Resourcing: HRM in Practice*. Harlow: Pearson Education (Chapters 1, 4–7).

Redman, T. and Wilkinson, A. (eds) (2001) *Contemporary HRM: Text and Cases.* London: Financial Times/Prentice Hall (Chapter 2).

Taylor, S. (1998) *Employee Resourcing.* London: CIPD (Chapters 1–8).

Thornhill, A., Lewis, P., Millmore, M. and Saunders, M. (2000) *Managing Change: A Human Resource Strategy Approach.* Harlow: Pearson Education (Chapter 4).

CHAPTER 3

Employee rewards

Introduction

We have now considered the initial areas of HRM in terms of resourcing the organisation with people, covering planning requirements for HR and recruitment. One factor that critically impacts on these aspects of HRM concerns employee rewards and their management (see White and Druker, 2000). For instance, HR resourcing difficulties, as with both attraction and retention dimensions, may well link back to employee rewards. Rewards retain their importance for a range of reasons and practices attract widespread media and public attention.

The second main focus of this chapter is concerned with rewards in terms of linking them to 'performance', and how, and to what extent, such aspects can be built into systems. This is also linked, once again, to ideas of HR flexibility and the flexible firm model (see Chapter 1). Indeed, while some forms of such performance-linked reward systems are not particularly new, there is a continuing interest in them from a range of bodies. This includes not just business, but also policy makers; for example, in the UK, such reward systems are seen by some as one way to assist in contemporary public sector recruitment and retention problems. Types of reward system and some related methods and issues will be examined. Rewards is also an area that displays wide variety in practice, not only in the UK, but also internationally. We will also look at some of these issues.

Overview

Employee rewards retain their relevance and importance for HRM for several reasons. First, rewards interact with many other spheres of HRM, for instance employee resourcing, the attraction and retention of HRs and employee relations, with influences on many aspects. Second, rewards also impact on other areas such as business performance, as well as having a possible role in integrating with strategy, reinforcing values (see Wilson, 2001) and enhancing employee motivation and commitment. Indeed, for some commentators, the decline of career systems and commensurate commitment is also important, with the need to focus more on broadly defined rewards to elicit commitment now. However, the situation in this respect is more ambiguous than is sometimes presented. For instance, the average length of job tenure changed little in the 1990s – it went up from 10.2 to 10.5 years across 12 countries (Taylor, 2001). In the UK the average job tenure had risen from 6 years 2 months to 7 years 4 months between 1992 and 2002 (Smith, 2003). There were differences by industry, company size and occupation, of course, but it is largely media reports on related labour market matters that contribute to erroneous perceptions.

Third, overall employee rewards are composed of numerous elements. Putting these together as a 'rewards package' can range from a simple to a more complex mix of intrinsic and extrinsic rewards. A rewards package can thus include pay, benefits, promotion, praise and opportunities for development and training, for instance, together with 'generalised investments' (see Galunic and Weeks, 2001). One framework to assess an organisation's portfolio of rewards can be as follows: salaries/wages; bonuses/incentives; benefits; recognition programmes, seen in two dimensions of cash versus non-cash; and all employees versus some employees, i.e. by performance (Wilson, 2001).

Fourth, rewards can form a large part of the cost basis of businesses, and may even be a method of competing. This reward role does vary, of course. For those organisations operating in highly competitive markets exposed to foreign competition, the minimisation of labour costs could be critical. However, this may be the case less often in other sectors, such as private services, where there are often non-tradable (non-exportable) jobs. For instance, if the price of your haircut goes up due to increases in wages, as via a minimum wage, what would you do, as all other businesses will be paying the same rate? You may try to reduce the number of visits you make, but you are unlikely to go overseas for the service. Businesses may then attempt to compete on the basis of quality rather than (low) cost and hence wages, as this is standardised among all.

Fifth, the area of rewards also attracts much public, institutional and government attention and comment. Debates around both the bottom (i.e. national minimum wage) and top (i.e. top management remuneration) of the rewards spectrum retain their salience and high profile. Sixth, employee rewards remain highly varied internationally. For senior managers there are expectations of very high rewards and large differentials from employees in the USA, whereas in other countries, such as Sweden, Finland, Germany and Japan, this is less so. Then there are ideas of seniority-based pay in some countries, such as Japan and Korea (see Rowley, 2002a, 2002b, 2002c). There is the harmonised annual round of reward increases, such as 'shunto' ('spring livelihood offensive') in Japan, held every year since 1955, although this is now under some stress (*The Economist*, 2003).

Task 3.1

Take a few moments now to reflect on this and answer the following.

What do you think is the best basis for a person's rewards? List any criteria or methods that may be of use to assist in this. To what extent are they applicable for all jobs, organisations and countries?

One aspect of rewards is an increasing, albeit not new, focus on setting levels with a link to performance. This involves trying to causally connect any 'performance' to its generator via a diverse range of schemes, from the simple to the complex. Adding greater performance elements (or 'variable' or 'at risk' aspects) to rewards can create a volatile cocktail of outcomes. The maxim of 'what gets measured gets done' has relevance here. One indicative case came to light in 2002, with the requirement by US law firm Clifford Chance for personnel to put in 2,420 hours of chargeable time to secure lucrative bonuses. This led to accusations of 'padding' and over-billing clients. The resulting PR fallout from this saga also encouraged a move towards a system where associates will in future receive rewards and promotions based on seven categories: respect and mentoring; quality of work; excellence in client service; integrity; contribution to the community; commitment to diversity; and contribution to the firm as an institution.

Performance-based systems require several elements to ensure their success. These include a clear understanding of measures, goals or standards and actions people need to take; challenging but achievable goals (Wilson, 2001); a short, robust and explicit link between performance and reward; and a fit with prevailing personal, organisational and national cultures.

Task 3.2

After considering the above, complete the following task.

As a government advisor, you have been contacted to examine the advantages and disadvantages of the rewards system in the UK public sector. You have been asked to devise and justify a move from national systems to encourage more local flexibility and performance.

Produce your report.

A very useful collection of short pieces and newspaper articles that cover developments and examples in this area and cast light on them are listed at the end of the chapter. These will repay your investment in time obtaining and reading them.

Rewards and integration

The links between business strategy and integration with HRM (as we discussed earlier in Chapter 1) can be seen here in employee rewards. These can be explicit, as demonstrated below and in Table

3.1. Thus, in theory, there can be integrated reward systems, driven by strategy. However, one still needs to remember that contingency theory is important in rewards. In particular, variations can stem from the following:

- organisational strategies and cultures needing different reward strategies;

- the usefulness of reward strategies and practices varying according to context;

- reward practices affecting people differently.

Types of reward

Employee rewards can come in all shapes and forms. There are various components to rewards.

Question to think about 3.1

What different components of rewards are you familiar with?

The broad aspects of rewards can be seen as composed of:

- *money* – salary, incentives, expenses, payments;

- *benefits* – pension, cars, insurance, leave, working time;

- *work* – challenge, autonomy, environment;

- *development* – training, personal development, promotion, employability.

Table 3.1 Integration in rewards

Business strategy	Reward strategy
Achieve added value by improving motivation and commitment	Introduce/improve performance pay plans: individual, team, gain-sharing
Achieve added value by improving performance and productivity	Introduce/improve performance pay plans and performance management processes
Achieve competitive advantage by developing and making best use of distinctive core competencies	Introduce competence-related pay
Achieve competitive advantage by technological development	Introduce competence-related or skill-based pay
Achieve competitive advantage by delivering better value and quality to customers	Recognise/reward individuals/teams for meeting/exceeding customer service and quality standards
Achieve competitive advantage by developing capacity to respond quickly and flexibly to new opportunities	Provide rewards for multiskilling and job flexibility; develop more flexible pay structures (broadbanding)
Achieve competitive advantage by attracting, developing and retaining high-quality HRs	Ensure pay rates are competitive; reward staff for developing competencies and careers in a broadbanded pay structure

Source: Armstrong (1999).

People require compensation for the services they provide for organisations. In taking a job a person must work and forsake time. Therefore organisations compensate for the time lost and the efforts individuals put in to carry out the tasks and duties of a job. The compensations for this may be of two main forms, as follows.

Intrinsic rewards

First, intrinsic rewards. These relate to the inner satisfactions experienced in carrying out the tasks and duties of a job. These satisfactions may be small or large, depending on factors such as the degree of interest in the work, conditions, opportunities and recognition. Intrinsic rewards are not usually sufficient to induce someone to take a job and remain in it, although people may accept fewer extrinsic rewards if the intrinsic satisfactions of a job are obvious and substantial. The classic example of this given in the past was nursing, with it being seen as a 'vocation' and 'career of choice' for some people.

Extrinsic rewards

Second, extrinsic rewards. These have two major aspects. First, there is pay, which can be received in the form of wages, salary, bonuses, commissions, and so on. Second, there is benefits, which can be other rewards that have a notional monetary value but are not paid in cash. There is a vast array of examples here, including cars, pensions, loans, insurance, meals, recreational and childcare services, the use of corporate facilities and resources, and so on.

Reward packages

As can be seen from the above, organisations have many options when putting together the exact details and components of total reward packages. There are some key points to be made on this aspect of rewards. First, there is a trend towards diversity here. For example, employees of the Brazilian company Semco recently had eleven different ways to get paid, ranging from a fixed salary to stock options, royalties and bonus schemes, all of which can be combined in various ways. Second, the proportion of the total cost of reward packages accounted for by benefits varies between (and within) countries, sectors and organisations. Third, recently there has been increasing complexity in types of benefits, especially for senior management. Fourth, the trend has been for the proportion of benefits within packages to rise sharply. For instance, in the USA such benefits have come to account for 25–40 per cent of the total cost of reward packages.

Issues and problems

These sorts of developments in the area of benefits can create problems for management and the business. For instance, people generally do not value some of the benefits components of a package as highly as their 'real' cost. This may be for a variety of reasons. For instance, it may be because they include services which are not needed or which people might not consider appropriate. For example, these could include child and maternity leave for employees with no children, or a company car in a household which has no need of it. Then there is the 'life cycle' question, when different types of benefits have varying levels of attractiveness over the career of a person they are provided for. We can simply note this in terms of the relative importance over a person's working life of benefits such as holidays, pension provision and health care.

A more generic problem has emerged in many economies, such as that in the UK, with a major traditional benefit, pensions.

Developments such as the escalating costs of final salary pensions and high volumes of early retirements in some public sector occupations have forced organisations to look again at this area. Another example would be the escalating costs of healthcare, and thus the price of such benefits, for US businesses.

Responses

One response to the management problem of this 'cost-appreciation' equation in benefits has been to move towards flexible benefits plans, or cafeteria benefits. This system allows employees some choice of benefits and a variable 'pick and mix' within the total. Such a process is aimed at both reducing overall costs and increasing the recipient's awareness of the 'real' costs of benefits. This is an attempt to link benefits more closely to motivation and performance. Thus people are provided with a total benefit budget and a costed benefit 'menu'. From this list, you compose your own total benefits package. For example, to take a larger chunk of your package in up-front benefits (such as pay) vis-à-vis deferred benefits (such as pension) or more of one type (such as childcare) over another (such as a car). This construction of individual, customised benefit packages can be undertaken on a regular basis. However, as with much in HRM, this increasing complexity may well come with costs to the organisation, not least the time involved.

In Europe, flexible benefit plans are still mainly confined to senior executives in large organisations while a survey of 169 of the UK's largest employers across 15 sectors found that 15 per cent offered 'flex benefits' and 69 per cent plan to introduce greater flexibility in the future (Harrison, 2003). One UK example is Lloyds TSB (Harrison, 2003). Its 'Flavours' flexible benefits package was designed, implemented and administered by the consultants Towers Perrin. The scheme allocates 4 per cent of basic pay to Flavours and this can be taken as cash or used to select items from three types of benefit, while existing 'core' benefits (healthcare, holidays) can also be 'sold' or 'traded in' to buy benefits. These groups are:

- 'Health and Wellbeing', e.g. health cash plan, medical insurance, health screening, dental plan;

- 'Protecting Your Future', e.g. pensions, life assurance, critical insurance;

- 'Leisure and Lifestyle', e.g. extra holidays, computers, training, retail and childcare vouchers.

Levels

Reward systems and packages occur at various levels. These range from the collective, such as occupation or industry, company or enterprise, plant, business unit, section or department, down to the individual. These can be negotiated in different ways, as with collective bargaining and agreements covering various periods.

Determinants of rewards

We now move on the complex and emotive area of what actually determines the size of total rewards.

Question to think about 3.2

Compare the reward levels of chief executives, top barristers and professional footballers to that of teachers, nurses and firefighters. To what extent do you think these are 'fair' and 'equitable'?

A perennially problematic area, and one which produces much angst and publicity, is the amount of remuneration given, especially at either end of the reward spectrum. The media is littered with reports of both 'scrooge payers' and 'fat cats', a situation which is even more difficult to handle for the organisation if it is seen as both simultaneously, and also inconsistent in terms of the criteria used to justify reward levels. A classic instance of this would be arguments such as the need to 'pay for the best', while on the other hand, the need to 'pay what the market indicates'. Thus some organisations argue that they must reward senior managers more as the reward level is low in comparison to in the USA. Yet, following the same rationale, as US manufacturing workers are paid on average one-third more than UK workers, why not pay them the same? Also, there is no real market for senior managers; the vast majority remain home-country nationals. For instance, only one in five of US corporations doing business outside the USA actually has a non-US national on the board. There has been a backlash against very high reward levels, even in the bastion of such practices, the USA. For example, even Jack Welch the fêted ex-boss of GEC, has been forced to renounce some of his retirement package (including the use of private jets) from mid-2002. These packages have even included the use of apartments and free dental care for life.

What are such reward levels based on? Is anyone worth the hundreds of millions of dollars paid to some US senior executives? It is worth taking a moment here to jot down the justifications you would use for why you are paid what you are. Can you group these reasons into criteria?

Question to think about 3.3

What general factors do you think help determine reward levels?

These levels often depend on external and internal factors and the relative strength of forces. These include a range of factors, which can be grouped as follows.

Individual characteristics

First, there are the individual characteristics of the person concerned. These include elements such as age and experience, as well as qualifications, skills and performance. However, are rewards given for the 'services rendered' or for the 'value added' by the person concerned? Then there is a person's 'potential' to be considered. These are commonly the first factors used to justify reward levels.

Labour market characteristics

Second, there are a range of LM factors that can come into play at different times. These include not only labour supply and demand,

---

but also interventions. This includes competitive pressures as well as aspects such as cost of living, and so on. The example of professional football players can be used in terms of LM competitive pressures. The higher reward levels in the South-East of England is an example of the cost of living argument. Yet, as we know, LMs are not perfect. They can be sticky and operate imperfectly (see Chapter 1). Furthermore, there can be interventions in LMs. These include both trade unions, with their collective bargaining forcing reward rates higher than would exist otherwise, as well as the state, for example using pay policies, introducing minimum wages and equal pay, or encouraging some reward systems (such as profit sharing).

Job characteristics

Another set of reasons often used to justify reward levels concern the job itself. These include the position's responsibility and skill requirements and also relativities. Differences in levels of pay between different types of employees are known as relativities. These can have both internal (for example, the 'wage-effort bargain') and external comparisons. These can be with other people, in the same or different jobs, inside and outside the organisation and LM, and also social, such as family, friends and relatives, and historical, such as a comparison of these with the past. This is linked to what is called the 'going market rate'. This sets the 'floor' level of rewards for a job. People will begin to leave the organisation if the current rate received is felt to be too far out of line with this. Relativities, like absolute levels of pay, result partly from competitive forces in LMs, interventions on the part of trade unions and governments and administrative decisions within organisations, such as the use of job evaluation.

Job evaluation

A further reason used to justify the size of rewards is job evaluation. One of the fundamentals of a good reward system is that employees believe it to be fair and it is seen to be fair. Rewards should recognise that some jobs are more demanding or difficult than others and the more demanding or difficult the job the better it should be rewarded relative to other jobs in the organisation. Yet, fairness can still be sought. How can this be attained and differences justified? The classic way is to set rewards via job evaluation. This is the process of determining the 'worth' of a job to an organisation. This process internally compares the relative 'value' of jobs. It is used to compare jobs, not to assess a single job in isolation from others. The purpose is to assess the relative difficulty or responsibility of a number of jobs to put them into ranked categories, which might be used as the basis for a reward system which is seen as fair and orderly. Therefore, another way to justify rewards is to say that the level has been set for the job itself and that this has been done objectively as the result of job evaluation. In addition to this, job evaluation has other important roles, such as its use in fairness, and as a defence by businesses in discrimination claims.

Question to think about 3.4

What methods would you use to evaluate jobs for the purpose of rewards?

The following (both non-analytical and analytical) job evaluation methods are some of those more commonly used. They are, as in much of HRM, better seen as systematic, rather than scientific, processes and they range from the more simple and less costly in time and money to the increasingly complex and expensive. As ever, there is a trade-off between cost and sophistication.

Ranking

Ranking is the least systematic method of job evaluation. Here jobs are simply ranked in order on the basis of given criteria. These criteria can include factors such as market value, difficulty, criticality to success, skill required, and so on. These ranked jobs are then divided into grades and a rate of pay is fixed for each grade. However, because this system is subjective and arbitrary, it can create dissatisfaction among those employees who feel that the system is unfair. Also, the extent of differences in criteria such as difficulty and responsibility are not readily established with this method.

Grading (job classification)

Another method of job evaluation is grading (job classification). This approach is similar to ranking except that classes or grades are established first, and then the jobs are placed into these pre-formed grades. Jobs are usually evaluated on the basis of the whole job using one factor, such as difficulty. Although grading is more systematic than ranking, there does remain a largely subjective dimension to the approach, which may cause disgruntlement among employees. Some of the developments in rewards have an impact here. One of these receiving much recent attention is broadbanding. This is an attempt to retain the positive features of traditional pay scales while reducing their less desirable aspects, such as tendencies to focus on promotion over performance, unwillingness to undertake duties associated with higher grades, and inability to offer higher salaries to new employees. Basically, broadbanding involves retaining some form of grading system but with a reduced number of grades or salary bands, and with pay variations within them based on performance rather than the nature of the job. However, there is a general desire to keep a grading system of sorts as this gives order to the structure and helps justify differentials.

Points rating

More systematic methods include points-rating systems, where each job is evaluated according to a standard set of criteria. Such systems can be obtained 'ready made', with consultants such as Hay able to provide generic, off-the-shelf systems. There are many examples of factors and factor plan weightings. A well-known set is that devised for the US National Electrical Manufacturers Association. The International Labour Organisation has also produced a list of factors that are used most frequently. Criteria can include requirements in terms of education, skills, experience, planning and coordinating, initiative, judgement, decision making, and so on. Each of these different criteria might earn a number of points within an established range depending on the level required by the job. The points earned under each of the headings are then added together to give a total for the job. The total determines the grade into which the job is placed. An example is presented in Table 3.2. Points rating is the most commonly applied job evaluation method, as it is seen to be objective and fair. Therefore it is commonly used to assess comparable worth issues in disputes on equal pay because it allows for comparison across job categories and types of employment.

Question to think about 3.5

What might be some of the problems with using job evaluation to set reward levels?

There are various problems with job evaluation to consider and remember. Some of the more general ones can be seen in Table 3.3.

There are also further issues. First, this method may lead to reward systems where pay is determined by administrative rather than LM considerations. One consequence is the danger that rates for some types of HRs may be either inadequate for recruitment, retention and motivation, or unnecessarily high. Second, the specific factors chosen and how they are weighted is critical. For instance, factors may well be biased and even discriminatory, which in the worst-case scenario are self-serving, producing the result that organisations wanted to be achieved, often justifying why some jobs (often done by men) are paid more than others (often done by women). These factors should be replaced by non-discriminatory versions.

Table 3.2 Job evaluation using different job factors

Factors (A)	Maintenance fitter	Company nurse
Skill		
• Experience in job	10	1
• Training	5	7
Responsibility		
• for money	0	0
• for equipment and machinery	8	3
• for safety	3	6
• for work done by other	3	0
Effort		
• lifting requirement	4	2
• strength required	7	2
• sustained physical effort	5	1
Conditions		
• physical environment	6	0
• working position	6	0
• hazards	7	0
Total	**64**	**22**
Factors (B)	**Maintenance fitter**	**Company nurse**
Basic knowledge	6	8
Complexity of task	6	7
Training	5	7
Responsibility		
• for people	3	8
• for materials and equipment	8	5
Mental effort	5	6
Visual attention	6	6
Physical activity	8	5
Working conditions	6	1
Total	**53**	**53**

Note: Each factor is scored from 1–10.
Source: EOC (1985).

Table 3.3 Issues in job evaluation

Issue	Characteristic
Time	Increasingly costly to raise 'objectivity'
Level	Too high or too low
Factor	Which chosen and weights critical

Therefore, the selection of specific job factors, and their weightings, is crucial, not least because it can produce the outcome desired. This can be clearly seen in the examples in Table 3.2. The first example, using factors (A), seems to justify why maintenance fitters should be paid more than company nurses. After all, 'objective' job evaluation has been used in this endeavour, has it not? Given the gender segregation of work, the implications of this are obvious. However, the second example using the same two jobs, but using different factors (B), now indicates that they should be paid the same!

As we saw above, the area of employee rewards, rather than being simple, as initially presented, is often complex and a minefield, with not only legal but motivational and even PR aspects to it. Once we start to delve below the surface of employee rewards, there is little that is totally robust, objective or consistent. To make these matters worse are some of the trends in rewards. One approach taken to attempt to resolve for management some of the issues raised above is to try to link rewards to performance. After all, surely no one will object to those who work harder being rewarded for their endeavours and getting paid more than those who work less hard, will they? This brings us on to the area of performance-related rewards.

Performance-related rewards

There are two basic ways to make rewards. These are as follows.

Time-based systems

The basic wage or salary paid is negotiated on the basis of the actual time spent in attendance on the job or at the place of work. Even today, payment for many jobs is made this simple way. Additional payments can be made at rates above the standard rate for working, for example, overtime, shifts, weekends, unsociable hours and so on. The operation of these sorts of premium can be seen in the television series *The Ship* (see Further reading and background information section at the end of the book), which shows a range of differentially applied payments, such as the esoteric 'cramped working conditions', and so on.

One form of this system is the incremental pay scale. People are paid for the time they spend at work, regardless of the effort they put in and in this case they are also paid an extra amount or increment each year that they work for the employer. This is supposed to encourage employees to stay with the same organisation for a period of time, rewarding long service and resulting in a stable workforce. There is also an implication that people will become more knowledgeable and effective in their job as they work for more years to gain experience. Another advantage is that it is simple and easy to calculate wages. This was the prevalent reward system form for full-time male workers in large firms in countries such as Japan and South Korea, where it is known as 'seniorityism'. This had cultural underpinnings, not least that wisdom is seen to come with age (Rowley and Bae, 2003).

However, an important characteristic of time-based systems is that little about them motivates employees to perform better. Also, employees can sometimes control and manipulate these payment systems to suit their own interests. It can encourage not only clock-watching, but also an overtime culture, as this work is paid at a premium.

Performance-based systems

These sorts of management issues and problems have created fertile ground for the search for alternatives in rewards. The idea of incentives in rewards is not new. Nevertheless, managers continue to seek a method and formula to effectively link rewards to performance. Performance-related pay (PRP) is the topical version of this idea, although with a significant difference, for instance: 'Incentives are used to stimulate performance, while performance pay is to reward it ...' (Torrington and Hall, 1998: 618).

Indeed, there has been a recent shift in payment systems towards providing rewards for some form of performance (or 'variable pay' or 'pay at risk'). Such systems value rewarding individuals, groups or organisational units on their performance contributions. The term 'PRP' has become widely used in the UK private and public sectors, but there remains much confusion as to what it really means. Some take it as a process whereby rewards are determined by reference to performance appraisal and assessment. For others, the letters PRP become confused with profit-related pay. A better approach is to think of performance-related rewards as an all-embracing term which includes rewards which recognise personal contributions and provide employees with the opportunity to participate in the financial success of the organisation.

Performance-related pay schemes

There are a variety of aims for PRP, which (along with the obvious ones of motivating performance and recognising differential contributions) include trying to attain strategic goals and reinforce organisational norms. PRP is based on some form of appraisal of the job holder against inputs (traits, skills) and/or outputs (objectives). This can take a number of forms. The scheme can be related to not just individual, but team, group and plant-wide performance. However, businesses need to ensure that participation in team rewards does not conflict with rewards offered by individual schemes. If there is tension or a conflict, individuals may decide it is more profitable for them to work alone rather than participate in joint team efforts.

Question to think about 3.6

What types of PRP schemes are you aware of?

A variety of PRP schemes exist. These include the following.

Payment by results

Historically, the most widely used incentive scheme rewarded employees according to 'results', such as the number of units of work produced or the time taken to produce them. The more you produce, the more you are paid. One example of this reward system is piecework. Often the incentive is paid for time saved on the 'standard time' in performing a specified operation as derived from work study (which we covered in Chapter 2 and can be seen in films such as *I'm All Right Jack* or *Spotswood* – see list in the Further reading and background information section at the end of the book). Yet there is a need to cater for problems such as external influences depressing output, for example machine failure, raw material delays, demand fluctuations and so on. One solution to such issues is measured daywork. In this reward system, instead of variable rewards corresponding to output achieved, employees are paid a fixed sum so long as they maintain a predetermined and agreed level of working. Again, some of the drawbacks to this form of system are apparent, such as speeding up to achieve the given output in a shorter time. One example might be a large-scale bakery where the speed of part of the line (i.e. the conveyor belt through the ovens) is increased to achieve the required output, but now over a shorter time period, with possible quality implications.

Skills-based rewards

This reward system seeks to reward employees for the skills, or competencies, which they acquire. Its most obvious benefits are to encourage multi-skilling and functional flexibility, while simultaneously indicating the business's commitment to employee development. Most systems of this nature reward people with additional increments to their base pay once they have completed defined skill modules. Obviously, this needs close monitoring and managing to ensure that the skills learned and rewarded are actually the ones needed by the organisation. This form of reward system is more established in the USA.

Performance bonuses

These reward systems include temporary increases to base pay that are tied to specific performance outcomes. There are a plethora of methods here. These include a payment of commission on sales, a widespread method, and the practice of tipping for service. Another common method is whereby organisations set up competitions to achieve particular targets, for instance an increase in sales. This reward system may well have the effect of improving productivity, but unless all feel they have the opportunity to win, some may feel it is not worth the bother of making the extra effort. Rewards also need to be managed efficiently or employees may well end up feeling 'cheated' for the extra efforts made, with obvious effects on their future performance.

Instant bonuses

These reward systems recognise exceptional contributions. These may even take the form of senior managers walking around buildings with an open chequebook to give instant rewards! These bonuses need to be set realistically. If not, employees may well feel that the effort made is not compensated for by the level of reward resulting from it.

Profit-sharing

These systems are not new. In the UK, Rowntree, the chocolate manufacturer (see Chapter 1), introduced a scheme back in 1916. There are a number of ways to link rewards to profit levels. Cash-based schemes are the traditional and most common arrangement whereby employees are paid a cash bonus, calculated as a proportion of annual profits. Gain-sharing is a variant which, importantly, can apply to non-profit-making organisations. Here the bonus relates to costs saved rather than profit generated. This variety of this form of reward system is more commonly used in the USA.

Stock options

Rather than cash, shares can be awarded to employees with these reward systems. This group of rewards is provided in an increasingly complex manner. Some organisations also offer lower-level employees the opportunity to buy shares in their companies at preferential rates. This is seen as a way of encouraging employees to think like owners and, therefore, to work harder to increase the value of 'their' business and their shares in it.

These last systems now lead us on to another area, the role and use of rewards as forms of employee involvement (see also Chapter 5). In the UK, such financial participation plans have been encouraged by favourable tax legislation, which started in the 1970s (in 1978 under the 'Lib-Lab Pact') with the introduction of the approved profit sharing scheme. The area had a significant boost with the post-1979 Conservative governments and their support for such ideas. There followed the approved savings-related share option scheme in 1984 (discontinued in 1996), profit-related pay in 1987, qualifying employee share ownership trusts in 1989, and company share option plans in 1996. In 1992 the EU Council of Ministers adopted recommendations concerning the promotion of 'Participation by Employed Persons in Profits and Enterprise Results'. Initiatives already taken in the UK and France to encourage profit sharing and share ownership have been a continuing influence on these developments in the EU.

Difficulties in PRP

There can be enormous difficulties in introducing, running and managing PRP schemes.

Question to think about 3.7

What problems do you think might arise with PRP schemes?

The choice of scheme and success of such plans is related to the extent to which a variety of factors are met. Some of these can be seen in Table 3.4 and below. Critically, it is often the case of the dictum 'what gets measured gets done' prevailing.

Important aspects here include the freedom and ability to increase performance, clear attribution of the source of any increased performance and a short time to the reward. A key requirement of any contingent reward scheme is that people should have a clear 'line of sight' (see Figure 3.1) between what they do and what they will get for doing it and when. This concept expresses the essence of expectancy theory: that motivation takes place only when people expect that they will get worthwhile rewards for their effort and contribution. However, the time gap between increased performance and any reward may not actually operate like this. For instance, the rewards via shares may be a long time coming, while the size of such rewards may also be small. In profit-related schemes, both the 'ability to influence' and the lag factors come into play. For example, any extra performance may not result in any improvement in share prices, which are affected by many factors other than employee performance. Not only may the individual have very little influence on shares or profits, but the time gap between any enhanced performance and

Table 3.4 Factors to be considered in performance-related pay

Factor	Characteristics
Measure	Level at which performance can be objectively measured
Ability	Change actually results in better performance
Timing	Lag between performance and reward
Cooperation	Extent between individuals or departments
Commitment	Management committed to/able to communicate goals
Involvement	In scheme design, e.g. targets set seen as important
Trade unions	Agree/oppose, e.g. scheme impact on collective goals/ collective bargaining
Acceptance	Employees accept and understand plans
Corporate culture	Not in conflict with organisational culture, e.g. UK public sector
Employee culture	Sensitive to cultural values, e.g. Asian
Calculation	Easy to calculate and direct reward for effort made

reward received for it may well be very long and tenuous. Furthermore, the actual amounts paid out under such schemes may be fairly negligible. All these have obvious implications for motivation.

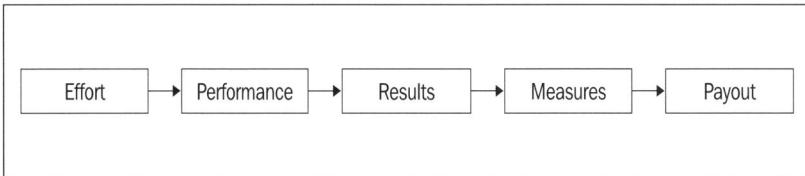

Figure 3.1 The line of sight model. (*Source*: Lawler, 1990.)

The problems of rewarding people using PRP are apparent. Objectively assessing performance remains a perennially difficult task for management in a whole range of HRM areas, from employee performance appraisals to training (see Chapter 4). One possible way forward is to develop a more sophisticated range of criteria. Such an approach is the Balanced Scorecard (Kaplan and Norton, 1996) method. Here measurements are put in place to answer four questions. These are:

1. How should we appear to our shareholders?
    (*financial perspective*)

2. How should we appear to our customers?
    (*customer perspective*)

3. What business processes must we excel at?
    (*internal perspective*)

4. How will we sustain our ability to change and improve?
    (*learning and growth perspective*)

In sum, there are advantages and disadvantages to both main categories of reward system. Neither is a panacea to management and organisational problems. These are compared and contrasted in Table 3.5 below. This again indicates the contingent nature of employee rewards, as is often the case in HRM.

Table 3.5 Advantages and disadvantages of reward systems

System	Advantages	Disadvantages
Incremental	• Simple, easy to calculate • Stable workforce • Experience rewarded	• No incentive to work harder • Slow progress for high fliers • No incentive at top of scales
Results	• Extra effort recognised • Less productive penalised • Encourages performance • Appearance of fairness	• Results must be attributable • Output must be measurable • Needs consistent effort–output link • Subjectivity in measures

Rewards in practice

Employee rewards can be seen in practice in a variety of areas. Here we will give some examples, including strategically related rewards, senior management pay, variations in employee rewards in terms of PRP within organisations and attempts to spread PRP to non-private sector organisations.

Strategic employee rewards

Rewards can be used strategically. One example is at Richer Sounds, the UK hi-fi music equipment retailer (see Case study 3.1).

Case study 3.1 Strategic employee rewards at Richer Sounds

Customer service is seen as the driving philosophy behind this company. Employees are encouraged to help customers buy products rather than go for the 'hard sell'. It argues that the company's basic principles are quality products (branded names), value for money and customer service, and that while the first two can be controlled from head office, the latter is very much in the hands of ordinary branch employees. The company sees rewards very broadly in that there is both a payment and a recognition (i.e. non-financial) aspect to its approach. Pay is above average for the sector, with a basic rate supplemented by commission, profit-sharing and a customer-service bonus. A customer-service index is calculated with individuals being assessed on several indicators, the main one being customer feedback on service quality. Each customer receipt includes a questionnaire, with customers invited to assess the service provided by the salesperson (identified by payroll number). The individual's bonus is related to the feedback, with both additions and deductions totalled monthly. The company also believes that non-financial recognition is important in motivation and has an array of incentives designed to make working satisfying and enjoyable. Staff who perform well receive gold aeroplanes as recognition of achievement, while wooden spoons are given for acts of stupidity. A suggestion scheme does have a small financial component, but the main element is a day trip on the Orient Express for the two best suggestions quarterly. Branches also compete in the 'Richer Way League' based on customer service standards and profit. This provides a Rolls-Royce or Bentley car for a week as a prize for the top-performing branch.

(*Source*: Adapted from Marchington and Wilkinson, 2002.)

Senior management pay

Important aspects of rewards are that employees feel that the system is fair, reasonable and equitable. There is a widespread and increasingly vocal debate about senior management pay. This has led to hostile public opinion and press coverage (using the derogatory term 'fat cats'). The issues revolve around how top management remuneration is set, how it is linked to 'performance' and rewards 'success', and disparities with the rest of the organisation's workforce. Thus in 1997 in the USA the average total direct remuneration was 326 times that of the average employee (compared to 19 times in the UK). Yet, in other countries, such as Japan, Sweden and Finland, this multiple is far lower. According to *Fortune* magazine (in *The Economist*, 2003), in 1970 US real annual compensation averaged US$1.3 million (in today's money) for the top chief executives, which was about 39 times the pay of an average worker. By the end of the 1990s it was US$37.5 million, or 1,000 times. In the UK, this has led to government concern and various committees (such as Cadbury, Greenbury) producing greater disclosure on rewards packages. Even in the USA there has been some backlash, particularly in the post-Enron environment. Senior management pay in the USA has traditionally been far higher than in the UK in general, although with some exceptions, such as (before it was sold) Ben & Jerry's Ice Cream. This company had a similar view on the maximum multiple of workers' salary that could be given to that of UK firms such as Laura Ashley and the John Lewis Partnership.

Use of PRP by type and level of HR

There is also varied use of PRP schemes by employment type and organisational hierarchies. This can be seen in Table 3.6.

Table 3.6 Variations in the use of reward systems (%)

System	Employment type		
	Manual	**Non-manual**	**Managerial**
Performance-related	12.9	32.4	52.4
Profit-related	6.7	12.4	14.8
Profit-sharing	4.8	9.1	9.5
Bonus scheme	24.8	28.6	38.6
Skill-based	10.0	4.8	4.3
Competence-based	3.3	2.3	4.9
Payment by results	2.4	3.3	8.6

Source: Torrington and Hall (1998).

Use of PRP by organisations

Contemporary examples from the UK involve attempts to introduce more performance elements into the pay of both the private sector, such as retail banking, and the public sector, with groups such as health workers, teaching and the police force. While at first sight these may seem eminently desirable, it does not take long to see some of the problems and management issues that may arise. If we take retail banking, how is performance measured? Is it 'sales'? Of what and by whom? Not only may distortions and product misselling occur, but 'churn', i.e. customers only continuing with products for a short period of time and then being switched to other products so the salesperson gets more commission, may arise. Some employees may have no opportunity to achieve sales given the nature of their job.

In terms of the public sector, the same issues arise in the ethos of a 'service' and professionalism. A good illustrative example of the attempt to spread the use of PRP schemes is shown by the UK police force. Part of the Sheehy Report in the mid-1990s recommended the introduction of PRP here. However, there is no practical definition of the tasks of a police officer – and if there were, it would be difficult to check that the tasks had been done. The function of policing is highly varied, often ad hoc and dependent on inspiration for success rather than a rigid industrial-type process and close monitoring. The same characteristics apply to academic work.

International comparisons of rewards

Question to think about 3.8

What variations in employee rewards between countries are you aware of?

There are many differences internationally in rewards (see also White and Druker, 2000: Chapter 9). Reward systems remain varied between countries. We will give a few examples of this. In Japan the 'nenko' system of seniority pay gives greater emphasis to an employee's seniority in the organisation. Likewise, in South Korea a system of 'seniorityism' is prevalent. In China there is a 'one big pot' reward system, especially in large state-owned enterprises (SOEs). While these organisations have declined, shedding 25 million workers between 1998 and 2001, and there were two million private enterprises in 2002, there are still 50,000 SOEs employing 50 million people.

In stark contrast, in the USA it is more common to give very high rewards and bonuses to individual managers (see earlier comments in this chapter). Pay differentials between employees and managers is much greater in the USA and UK than in many Asia-Pacific countries. Equal pay is of much greater concern in the West than in Japan or South Korea, where women employees have traditionally had a separate status to male employees (with a lifetime employment system). Collectively bargained rewards remain more important in some countries, such as Germany, Sweden and Finland, than in others (and also for some sectors such as manufacturing than others such as services).

Therefore, employee rewards are affected not only by individual performance, but also by national criteria. These can include societal expectations such as for high pay among US managers, or collective bargaining in the Nordic countries, or institutions such as government regulation as in Germany which makes labour costs comparatively high. We will return to such themes in Chapter 6.

Conclusion

Employee rewards remain as important and emotive an issue as ever. There are attempts to justify pay levels by reference to a range of factors, including the attempt to be more objective by using more rigorous forms of calculation, such as job appraisal, not least as a defence against claims of bias and discrimination.

There are two basic types of reward system: those in which the key variable is either time or output (these are not mutually exclusive – hybrids are quite common). There are shifts (and fashions) over time in remuneration. Different reward systems may be used for different grades of staff. However, there have been some moves towards paying for performance.

Reward systems vary significantly between sectors and countries. Major issues around pay in recent years have been associated with PRP and equal pay. Also, with the growth of multinational corporations, structuring an equitable reward system for employees from different countries will be a major concern in the future.

Overview references

The following short pieces illustrate issues and developments in employee rewards.

The Financial Times

Bilmes, L. (2001) 'Scoring Goals for People and Company', Mastering People Management, Part 7, 26 November, pp. 10–11.

Conyon, M. and Freeman, R. (2001) 'Firm Benefits from Share Owning Workers', Mastering People Management, Part 4, 5 November, pp. 4–5.

Galunic, C. and Weeks, J. (2001) 'Investments that Build on Human Nature', Mastering People Management, Part 5, 12 November, pp. 10–11.

Taylor, R. (2001) 'The Truth About Work', 25 January.

Wilson, T. (2001) 'Rewards that Work', Mastering People Management, Part 4, 5 November, pp. 2–3.

The Economist

'Japan's Wage Round: Heading Down', 8 March 2003, p. 72.

Mastering Management Online (www.ftmastering.com/resource/ resource.htm)

Rowley, C. (2002a) 'Management in Korea: Background and Traditions', Issue 9, December/January.

Rowley, C. (2002b) 'Management in Korea: Crisis, Reforms and the Future', Issue 11, March.

Rowley, C. (2002c) 'Management in Korea: Employment Policies and Practices', Issue 13, May.

The Sunday Times

Smith, D. (2003) 'Death of Jobs for Life Greatly Exaggerated', Section 3, 22 June, p. 3.

References

Armstrong, M. (1999) *Employee Rewards*. London: CIPD.

Economist, The (2003) 'A survey of capitalism and democracy: pigs, pay and power', 28 June, pp. 7–9.

EOC (1985) *Job Evaluation Free of Sex Bias*. London: EOC.

Harrison, D. (2003) 'Holidays and vouchers with flex appeal', *Financial Times*, 15 February, p. 9.

Kaplan, R.S. and Norton, D.P. (1996) *The Balanced Scorecard: Translating Strategy into Action*. Boston, MA: Harvard Business School Press.

Lawler, E. (1990) *Strategic Pay: Aligning Organizational Strategies and Pay Systems*. San Fransisco: Jossey-Bass.

Marchington, M. and Wilkinson, A. (2002) *People Management and Development: HRM at Work*. London: CIPD.

Rowley, C. and Bae, J. (2003) 'Culture and Management in South Korea', in M. Warner (ed.) *Culture and Management in Asia*. London: Curzon, pp. 187–209.

Torrington, D. and Hall, L. (1998) *Human Resource Management*. London: Financial Times/Prentice Hall.

White, G. and Druker, J. (eds) (2000) *Reward Management: A Critical Text*. London: Routledge.

Further reading

For those who want further details there are links and references given in some of the above titles, and there are many further books which cover similar ground, such as:

Beardwell, I. and Holden, L. (eds) (2001) *HRM: A Contemporary Approach*. London: Financial Times/Prentice Hall (Chapter 12).

Pfeffer, J. (1998) 'Six dangerous myths about pay', *Harvard Business Review*, May–June: 109–19.

Pilbeam, S. and Corbridge, M. (eds) (2002) *People Resourcing: HRM in Practice*. Harlow: Pearson Education, (Chapters 9–10).

Thorpe, R. and Homan, G. (eds) (2000) *Strategic Reward Systems*. London: Financial Times/Prentice Hall.

CHAPTER 4

Employee development

Introduction

We have covered the initial areas of HRM in terms of employee resourcing and employee rewards. One area integrally linked to both of these is employee development. Once the HR plan has been completed and any HRs recruited, how do organisations both develop these HRs and ensure the job is being done? There is a whole set of management and business issues that emerge with this, ranging from the rationale to the amount, type and assessment of employee development. As in much of HRM, there is a range of practices, from the simple to the complex, and these still remain difficult areas. Some acknowledgment of the issues and their complexity is at least a useful start.

This chapter tackles the area of employee development from two major perspectives: first, the area of HR training, its main issues, methods and purposes; second, employee performance appraisal (the measurement of how someone is working, in terms of the methods and issues involved). These two aspects of HRM are intricately linked, and should be seen as such, not least as the latter can be a method of discovering the need for, and evaluating, training.

Overview

Employee development is an important area for HRM in both the literature and in practice. For example, it is one of the key HR policies to achieve key HR and organisational outcomes in HRM models. It is often prescribed that investment here often produces a range of beneficial outcomes, for both employees and organisations.

Investment in employee development is often seen as a 'good thing' in that it is something that the 'best' businesses should do. Linked to this is the area of increasing commitment (especially if career systems are declining) via training as 'generalised investments' (Galunic and Weeks, 2001). Another part of the issue, as in much of HRM, is the need to somehow 'prove' the benefits and results of training expenditure. This issue, which includes the 'when', 'where' and 'how' of evaluation, is a perennially problematic area. Another issue in employee development concerns the fact that it is often a long-term investment with a delayed 'payback'. For some commentators, such as Thornhill et al. (2000: 162), this is especially problematic in economies that may have short-term perspectives. At the same time, organisations may lose trained staff to non-training competitor businesses.

There has been recognition and criticism of the poor training provision in the UK for a very long time, even back to the late nineteenth century. This concerns not only volume, but also that 'academic' qualifications fail to provide the workplace with sufficient skills. There have been numerous initiatives. These include National Vocational Qualifications (NVQs), a national system of vocational qualifications and standards of occupational competence that are narrow and trade-related, with the emphasis on practical skills. There has also been Investors in People, a training standard for investment in HRs (and ongoing commitment).

However, for some commentators, the UK is generally perceived to lag behind international competitors in employee development. At the national or macro-level, limited investment has been criticised and seen as a prime reason for poor economic performance. For commentators like Thornhill et al. (2000: 180), the non-interventionist market force approach has pushed the prime responsibility for training on to employers (the micro-level). Therefore you might expect training to be central to businesses. Yet this may not always be the case. For instance, training may well be peripheral and, rather than invest in their internal labour market, employers may simply resort to the external labout market to 'buy in' the skills needed. How does this compare with the situation in some other leading economies? Training systems in different countries vary significantly. This has implications for the quality of production and competitiveness of organisations.

Traditionally, there has been a high level of continuous training in Japanese companies. It is not unusual for new employees to have one to six months of training on starting with a company. Training tended to be done in-house. Commonly, over 75 per cent of new regular employees and over 50 per cent of non-regular employees received training on starting with a company. There was also a system of pre-employment education for college graduates. This aimed to facilitate the transition from college to work, teach company culture and norms, and cultivate a spirit of harmony and teamwork. Companies recruited managerial talent from elite universities followed by a systematic approach to in-company development.

Traditionally, the German system of apprenticeship training was extensive and developed. Apprenticeship programmes lasted approximately three and a half years. This 'dual system' had theoretical (in vocational colleges) and practical (in workplaces from skilled craftspeople who were trained instructors) training. The system was funded through a mixture of state financing and employer contributions. It was believed that, although costly, this system produced better-qualified HRs, employee loyalty, reduced costs of dysfunctional turnover, and so on. However, there are some concerns that the system is becoming too inflexible.

How do we explain the variations in employee development provision between businesses and across countries? The level of government encouragement of employee development spending by businesses is also varied. We will look at these issues, their implications, and the types of provision and assessment. For instance, to what extent do training approaches suggest a universal model? Why do some businesses use 'internal' ('on-the-job') training while others use 'external' ('off-the-job') training? Consider the above in relation to Case study 4.1 on McDonald's and small businesses.

Case study 4.1 Variations in employee development: McDonald's and small businesses

....

Readers need to develop this case study themselves both from their own experiences and media reports. For instance:

- On McDonald's see C. Adams (2001) 'Work Skills and McJob Training', *Financial Times*, 20 November, p. 21.

- On small businesses, see D. Storey (2002) 'Why Nellie Still Has the Answers', *Financial Times*, 26 September, p. 15; J. Kelly (2001) 'Preaching to the Unconverted', *Financial Times*, 15 February, p. 14.

....

Key questions in employee development include: is simply spending money on training necessarily a 'good thing'? How do businesses know what their training needs are? How is training expenditure justified? Why are training budgets often one of the first areas to be cut? This concerns what is called training needs analysis. Consider this and complete the task set out in Case study 4.2 on ACT.

A very useful collection of short pieces and newspaper articles that cover developments and examples in this area and cast light on them are listed at the end of the chapter. These will repay your investment in time obtaining and reading them.

Case study 4.2 ACT Ltd   COURSE WORK

....

ACT is a small, thriving electronics manufacturing and distribution company. Set up in 1987, the company produces components for the personal

---

computer (PC) assembly market. Growth has been rapid, with a lot of new business won on a reputation for product innovation and high quality. The company currently employs 150 people at a greenfield site in the South-East of England. It is now planning a further expansion of its facility to take advantage of new markets which are opening up in Europe and beyond.

Although the company is a success, the managing director (MD) is feeling uneasy about the way the company is currently managing its human resources. There are two areas in particular that have given him some cause for concern. The first involves the way non-technical training is organised.

The organisation of training

ACT has always invested heavily in training its workforce. Indeed, the MD is convinced that ACT's reputation is mainly attributable to its highly trained workforce. In the past, training was confined to technical areas. However, with the expansion of ACT, it has been necessary to develop the organisation of training to provide additional skills in areas such as administration, finance, marketing, team-building and communication.

There is no HRM department in ACT. Training has always been left to the line managers to organise. With technical training, this was never a great problem. It was always well organised, consisting of mainly 'on-the-job' training and day release courses provided by the local college. However, now that training is extending into non-technical areas, the MD is having increasing doubts about the effectiveness of the training organisation within ACT. A recent incident serves to highlight this.

Walking through the production department a few weeks ago, the MD spotted a memo and a list on the noticeboard. It was written by the department manager and alongside the memo was a very glossy brochure from an external training consultancy advertising a wide range of administration and supervisory courses. The memo invited staff to study the brochure, select a course they felt would benefit them, and add their name to the list. The MD studied the list. Many of the courses that people were applying for actually appeared to the MD to be peripheral to the needs of their job. Then he realised that if everybody who was applying actually went on the courses they had selected, a very serious hole would appear in ACT's training budget! He quickly removed the memo and brochure and made a mental note to have a word with the manager concerned.

As he walked back to his office, he reflected on the incident. There was no doubt in his mind that something would have to be done to ensure that training was organised in a more structured and professional way. The company had to ensure that it obtained a return on its training investment.

The MD's second concern is with the capabilities of his management team.

Calibre of the management team

The management team consists of three board directors, four department managers, and four supervisory staff (see Figure 4.1). With ACT's rapid expansion, emphasis has always been on product design, quality, achieving high levels of output and maximising sales. What has now become obvious is that in the rush to achieve business growth, the development of core management skills has been neglected. Without these skills, the MD fears there will be a real threat to the future survival of the company. A number of examples highlight the MD's concern.

In the boardroom none of the directors seems capable of discussing and dealing with strategic issues. For instance, the other day the MD wanted to discuss the exploration of both new markets in Europe and the sourcing of components from Asia-Pacific to reduce production costs for ACT. But the meeting was quickly taken up with a discussion about the technical details of the latest semiconductor design!

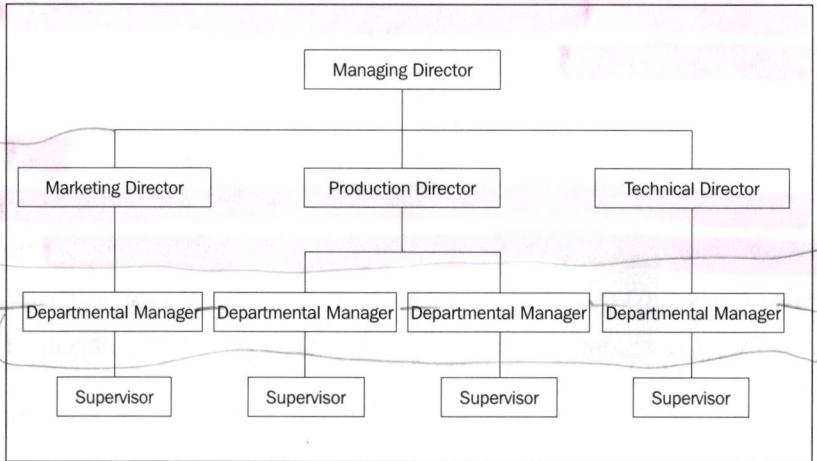

Figure 4.1 ACT organisation chart.

The departmental managers are all good engineers and are respected by the workforce for their technical capabilities. All of them have grown with the company and promotion has largely rested on the possession of sound technical skills. But they seem unwilling to delegate and 'step back' from the day-to-day running of the company. The other day, the MD heard one of the supervisors complaining about the level of interference she was experiencing from her departmental manager. 'He won't keep his nose out. He takes all the decisions, so I just let him get on with it.' The MD has also noticed that some of the supervisors are too laid back with the workforce, while others seem to be managing through a culture of fear and intimidation. *non uniform*

The MD has tried to communicate his concerns at management team meetings, but his managers keep avoiding the issue. When he presses them, they become defensive and withdrawn. The MD is approaching retirement age, and wants to resolve these issues before he retires.

(*Source*: Beardwell and Holden, 1997.)

Task 4.1

COURSE WORK.

Imagine you are a firm of management consultants that has been approached by the MD of ACT for advice and guidance. You have been asked to review the situation and make recommendations that will improve the way training is organised and evaluated, and develop managers to achieve organisational goals.

Produce your report.

Training

Uses

Question to think about 4.1
What purpose can training be used for by businesses?

There are a variety of uses for training. Some of these are indicated in Table 4.1.

Table 4.1 Possible uses of training

Orientation: Into culture, processes etc.	Skills: Fill gaps, update	Alternatives: Recruitment/ redundancy	Preparation: For transfer/ promotion
Motivation: Raise	Efficiency: Increase	Adaptation: To products, services, technology	Flexibility: Functional

Tensions

Training and management development is one of those areas where most people normally agree that it is a 'good thing' and 'the more, the better'. After all, how can anyone argue against such assertions? Yet one needs to take account of several aspects in this area which revolve around the numerous tensions within training and its measurement.

First, there is a tension between 'economic utility' and 'inherent value' in training that needs to be noted and remembered. For some, it is argued that training must be shown in clear and practical ways to meet the needs of the business. Therefore there has been increasing interest in attempts to evaluate the outcomes of training investments. Alternatively, there is much debate on the inherent value of training and developmental opportunities. These take the beneficial outcomes on trust. Obviously, the measurement issue is less of a priority here.

Second, there is also tension between the view that there is a body of knowledge and a set of generic skills which may be taught and the view that the diversity of these skills and knowledge renders them ambiguous. That is, while there is a set of skills which management professionals must have (in the same way as accountants, lawyers, medical doctors, tradespeople and so on), many believe that the wide-ranging variety of management skills and objectives required, which have come about partly as a result of divergent business strategies and partly as a result of changing priorities due to international competition and instability, makes the content of these skills ambiguous. One again this raises issues, not least in evaluation, between the former and the latter approaches.

Third, the degree of 'planning' in training is an important and hotly debated issue. For some, training is seen as a planned process of work-related learning, and can be regarded as the systematic development of the attitude, knowledge, skill and behaviour patterns required by an individual in order to perform adequately a given task or job. For other commentators, training can be less planned and may be informal. Again, issues such as evaluation are dealt with differently in the former compared to the latter approach. This leads us on to the area of management development.

Fourth, there is a distinction and tension between training and management development. We will not go into this in great detail; rather, we will treat them as broadly similar. However, it is worthwhile quickly noting some of the more distinctive features of the latter.

Management development

Management development is concerned with encouraging managers to improve their skills. Particular emphasis is often given in such programmes to important aspects of general management such as leadership, decision making, teamwork, communication, innovation and change. For some commentators, management development improves managerial effectiveness through a planned and deliberate learning process. However, this may over-emphasise the importance of deliberate planning in the process. As we noted earlier, there is a debate about formality versus informality in management development. The relationships between these can be seen in Figure 4.2.

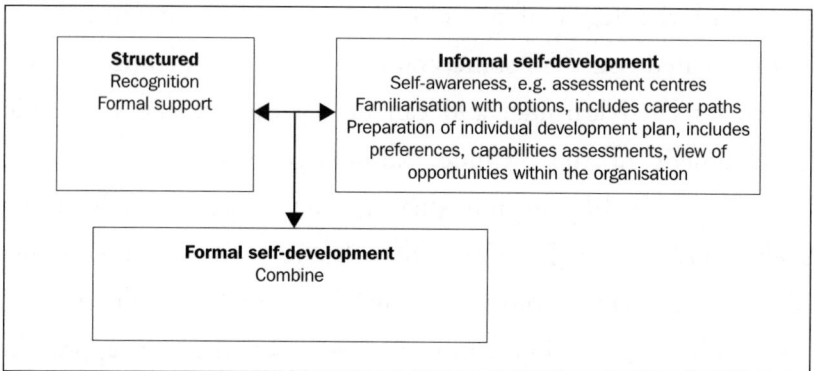

Figure 4.2 Models and techniques in management development.

Formal development

Some see management development as being provided in a formal, top-down and highly structured manner. The emphasis, therefore, is on formal programmes. This sort of approach is associated with such factors as corporate training colleges, training departments, well publicised programmes, an integrated system of appraisals identifying needs and candidates, and so on. Structured learning includes formal, directed, structured methods, for example centrally provided programmes which managers progress through in order to rise up the ranks. Yet there are a number of problems with this approach which include the following:

- Are the courses offered the ones actually most needed?

- Do courses get offered to those who would benefit most from them?

- Is management reluctant to admit 'weaknesses' that need such rectification?

- Do managers argue that they are too busy, that courses are irrelevant or insufficiently practical?

Informal self-development

On the other hand, there is a more informal model of management development. Here management development is decentralised and places greater emphasis on self-development. This is achieved through informal, unstructured ways of learning. Indeed, it has been argued by some commentators that given the varied nature and range of managerial work and an individual's strengths and weaknesses, formal approaches may be inappropriate. Also, informal approaches can be cheaper, with motivational impacts, for example, stemming from devising your own management development plans, 'owning' problems, and so on.

Formal self-development

Another group of commentators has tried to combine the merits of the above two approaches, i.e. self-development plus guidance and organisationally provided support mechanisms. Examples of this sort of approach include mentoring, which consists of using a system of experienced tutors, often senior managers, who take a relatively long-term interest in the development of the specific individual, who guide and provide orientation, and so on. There are many examples of organisations and jobs using such a system, including UK universities whereby a junior or new colleague may be allocated to a specific senior person. This sort of system has obvious advantages, not least in cost-effectiveness and speed of inculcation of the person into the organisation. However, there are the equally obvious, but often overlooked, problems. These include those that revolve around the mentor allocated – they may not have the requisite inclination, skills, training or time to undertake what might turn out to be an onerous role.

A second example of this approach is 'action learning' (Revans, 1972). This has a focus on 'questioning insight' over traditional 'programmed knowledge'. With this, the problem needs to be 'real' and 'significant' to both the learner and trainer, and the main vehicle is often an action project. This is a process of learning by doing. There are a range of approaches here, with a common theme: the view that management is a cluster of practices best upgraded by direct exposure to problem-solving situations. This sort of approach moves beyond debating possible solutions to problems to trying out the more favoured options. Furthermore, learning continues beyond the implementation of solutions through analysis of why something worked as it did. One method here is to organise business exchanges so that a manager experienced in one organisation is planted in another to solve a particular set of problems there by bringing a difference of experience and freshness of approach to bear.

Factors shaping training provision and effectiveness

Several factors are seen to shape the provision and effectiveness of training. These include those outlined in Table 4.2, among others.

Table 4.2 Factors shaping training provision and effectiveness

Factors	Examples
Top management commitment	• Attendance on programmes • Appointment of respected executives to training posts • Allocation of resources to training function • Not first target for cuts
Strategic connection	• Overseeing by senior executives (signal to others) • Seen as based on heavy investment and strategic status allocated, i.e. senior management job to help individual managers
Nature of managerial work recognised	• Extent is 'in tune' with nature of managerial work • Fragmented, large number of disparate activities; prefer action to contemplation, to communicate directly rather than submit ideas to paper; time horizons short
Varied needs and capabilities of individual managers	• Much work is done in teams • Fit in with this and the motivation, needs and potential of individuals
Long-term, ongoing commitment	• Not just seen as a 'one-off' to solve particular problem • Not ad hoc
Systematic	• Allows correct standards to be reached, fewer mistakes, economic use of resources • Right training identified, implemented and evaluated

Further to the formality dimension, management development (and for that matter training) can be viewed within a framework of 'stages'. One of the more useful frameworks here is the six 'levels of maturity' model (Burgoyne, 1988), as shown in Figure 4.3. In brief, these stages are as follows:

1.   No systematic development.

2.   Isolated tactical development.

3.   Integrated and coordinated structural and development tactics.

4.   Development strategy to implement corporate policy.

5.   Development strategy input to corporate policy formation.

6.   Strategic development of the management of corporate policy.

A critical aspect of the area of training is in terms of any evaluation of it, which requires it to have a purpose and objectives to judge it against. There is a host of issues here.

Determining and locating training

One problem is how to foresee what critical new skills will be needed by organisations. A survey of leading international companies (such as Shell, ICI and BMW) on future demands for their management placed emphasis on quality and customer service, internationalisation, commitment and motivation, leadership, corporate culture, and management of change (Barham, 1988). Yet this is a very similar message to that publicised from the early 1980s (see Peters and Waterman, 1982; Kanter, 1984). This phenomenon indicates the difficulties of using practitioners to produce a map of the future – they may simply reflect familiar current concerns.

1. No systematic management development

No systematic or deliberate management development in structural or developmental sense. Total reliance on natural *laissez-faire* uncontrived processes of management development.

2. Isolated tactical management development

There are isolated and ad hoc tactical management development activities of either structural or developmental kinds, or both, in response to local problems, crises or sporadically identified general problems.

3. Integrated and coordinated structural and development tactics

The specific management development tactics which impinge directly on the individual manager of career structure management, and of assisting learning, are integrated and coordinated.

4. A management development strategy to implement corporate policy

A management development strategy plays its part in implementing corporate policies through managerial human resource planning, and providing a strategic framework and direction for the tactics of career structure management and of learning, education and training.

5. Management development strategy input to corporate policy formation

Management development processes feed information into corporate policy decision-making processes on the organisations' managerial assets, strengths, weaknesses and potential, and contribute to the forecasting and analysis of the manageability of proposed projects, ventures and changes.

6. Strategic development of the management of corporate policy

Management development processes enhance the nature and quality of corporate policy-forming processes, which they also inform and help implement.

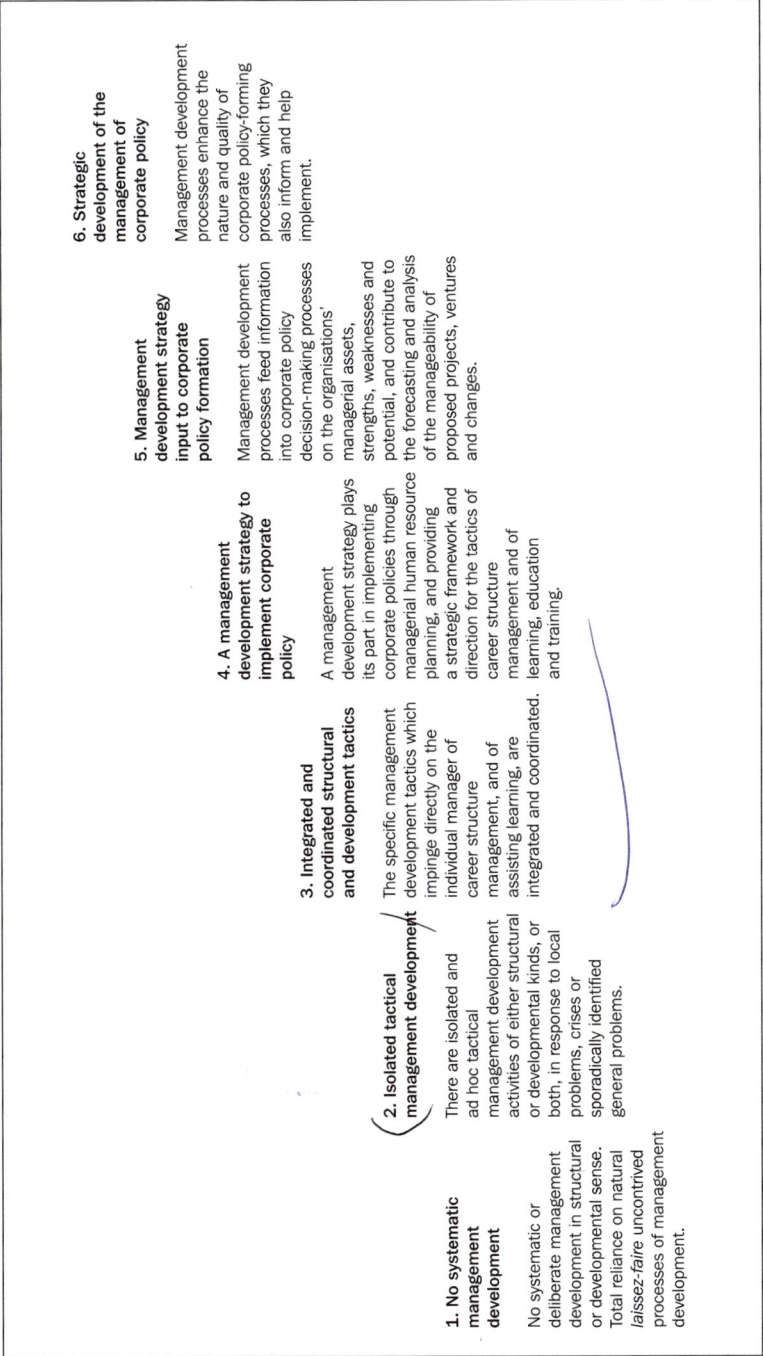

Figure 4.3 Levels of maturity in management development provision. (*Source:* Burgoyne, 1988.)

Furthermore, training does not exist in a vacuum, and can be seen within the following as:

- a 'system' (see Figure 4.4);

- a 'cycle' (see Figure 4.5).

The system can be complex. The cycle is often not followed in its entirety. Think of your own experiences of this area. Which stages were undertaken?

Training needs analysis

Is it good enough just to spend money on training on the assumption that all training is a 'good thing' and must produce some benefit? There are several issues here. Is the training:

- Given and importantly seen as a 'reward'?

- Taken as an implied criticism?

- Simply using up the training budget?

- Needed? This can flow from a so-called 'training needs analysis'.

Question to think about 4.2

What factors might indicate a need for training in an organisation?

These factors include looking at performance and whether any shortfall in this is caused by deficiencies related to training. A useful way of examining training needs is to look at the sources of such requirements. Some of these can be seen in Table 4.3.

External environment   Constant interaction   Organisation

Learning environment

Physical environment   Tutors and instructors   Learners

Learning characteristics

Needs
Perceived training problem
Alternative solutions
Universal and specific needs
Perceived value of training

Design
Objectives
Principles (intrinsic)
Principles (extrinsic)
Method and approaches

Implementation
Level
On or off job
Line, staff or others involved

Evaluation
Methods
Feedback
Commitment
Audit of system
Professionalism of training

Managing training
Roles
Responsibilities
Knowledge and skill

Budgets
Policies
Plans and records

Resources
Commitment

Environmental influences (macro):
political
economic
social
technological
+
Industry norms and expectations, e.g.:
apprentice quotas
competencies
resources
+
Perceived value of training by:
the state
business
trade unions
employees
+
Resources available from:
the state
business
trade unions (grants)
employees (loans)

Output levels - - - ▶ Feedback/ education/ audit loop

Individual, e.g.:
Induction
Specific skill/knowlege/ education
Job role, e.g.:
Supervisor
Technician
Sales manager
Personnel officer
Function or department, e.g.:
Industrial relations
Sales
Marketing
Production
Organisation, e.g.:
Managing change
Efficiency
Effectiveness
Development

Inputs   Transformation processes   Outputs

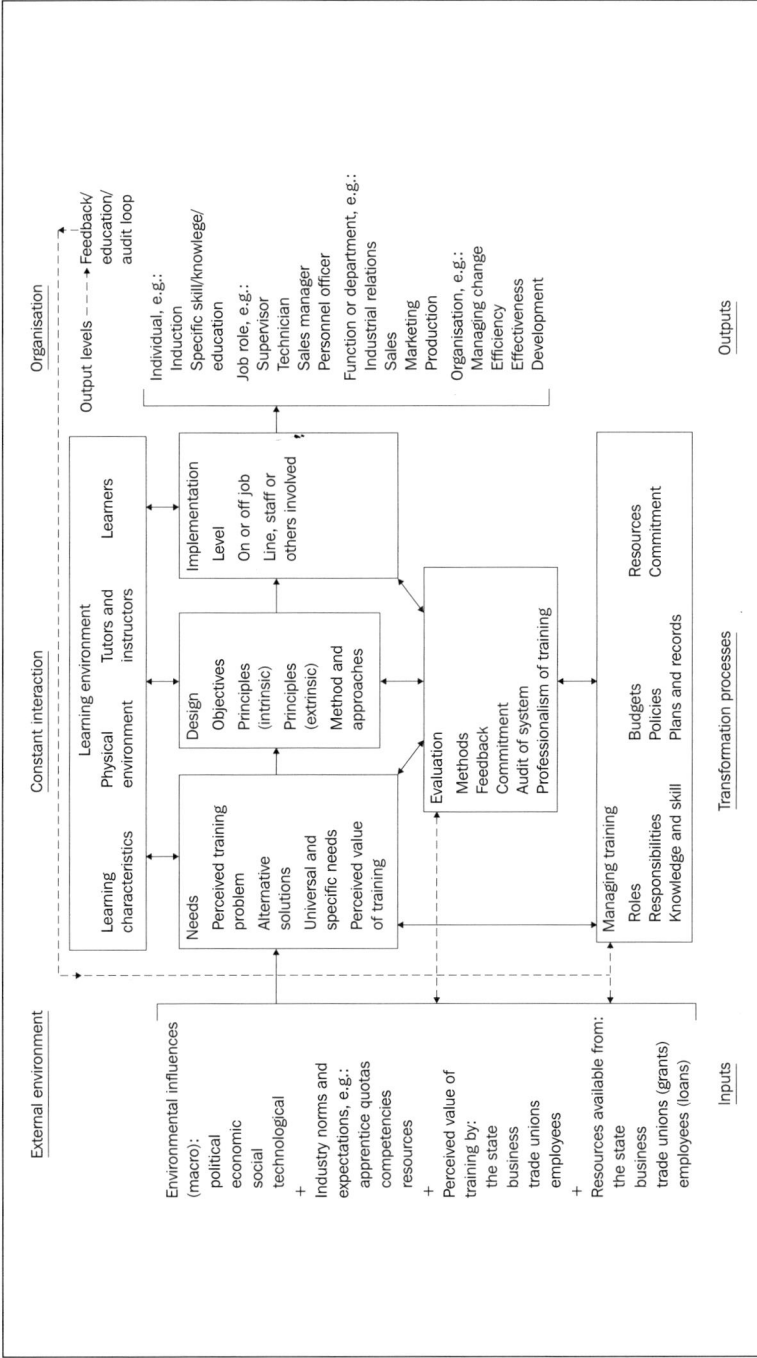

Figure 4.4 The training system. (*Source*: Anderson, 1993: 20.)

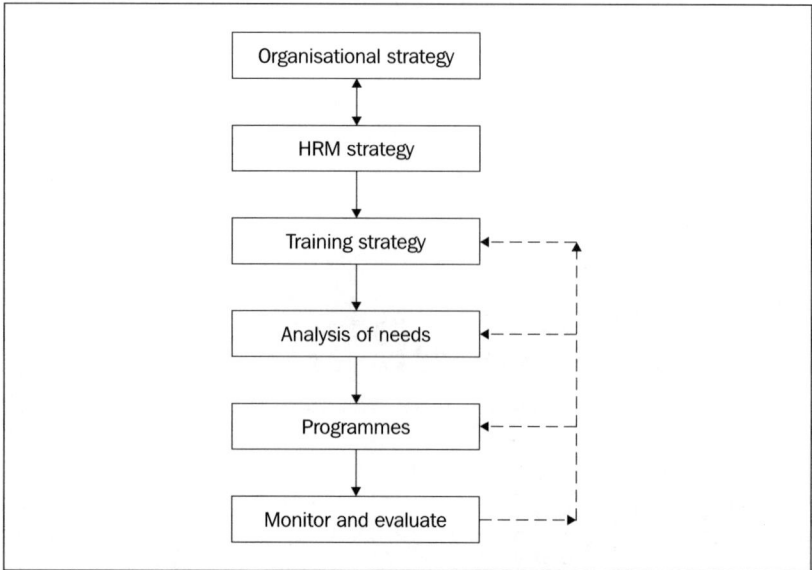

Figure 4.5 The training cycle.

Table 4.3 Sources of training needs

Primary	Secondary
Requests	Workflow and materials
Diaries	Quality and complaints
Questionnaires	Accident rates
Interviews	Employee appraisals
Evaluation of past training	Attitude surveys

In determining training needs, there is a set of questions to think about. These include:

* What types of training are required to achieve organisational goals?

* What jobs and which HRs should be targeted?

- Are skills required simple, basic ones (grammar, maths, technical)?

- Are skills needed more complex (interpersonal, leadership, creative)?

- Are there any trends indicating groups to be targeted (women, minorities)?

Thus organisations first need to determine training requirements with a focus on two levels:

- *organisational* – for example, HR planning, plans for new technologies, products;

- *job* – for example, job requirements (via job descriptions, job analysis, person specifications).

Designing programmes and delivery

Impacts on training design and development come from key factors and variables, for example subject/methods, tutor/learner, resources/ environment, and so on. Questions in relation to this include the following.

- Where should it take place? This can be on-site or in separate locations.

- What types of programmes? These can be provided in-house or by external consultants.

- What type of media? A wide range is possible.

These influences and choices can be located in a framework with two dimensions. This concerns the differing amounts of:

- *direction* – self-directed and participative versus trainer driven and less participative;

- *base* – individual versus group.

Question to think about 4.3

What might be some of the advantages and disadvantages of these different delivery methods?

Each of these dimensions and forms has a set of advantages and disadvantages for delivery. Some of these can be seen in Table 4.4.

Table 4.4 Advantages and disadvantages of delivery methods

Method: • *direction* (more/less) • *base* (individual/group)	Advantages	Disadvantages
Lecture	• Information imparted to large numbers simultaneously • Information prepared in advance	• Lack of participation • One-way
Role play	• Develop interpersonal skills • Confidence in protected environment	• May not be taken seriously • Too nervous/embarrassed to perform

Group discussion	• Exchange of knowledge • Airs varying views/ options	• Wander from subject • Important points not covered
Video	• Real situation • Information to group simultaneously	• Little involvement • One way
Projects	• Scope for creativity/ initiative	• Needs to be of direct interest
Case study	• Examine situation in detail • Removed from work pressures • Opportunities for different views	• Seems too easy • Real life may have other more complex issues to include
Computer-based	• Work at own pace • Immediate feedback • Relearn at convenience	• Nervous of technology • Isolation • Technology
Guided reading	• Work at own pace • Saves time	• Research not encouraged • Availability
In-tray exercise	• Opportunity to experience common issues • Own/directed pace	• Need to be realistic issues • Time needed

Source: Adapted from Foot and Hook (1996).

Implementation and methods

This includes the routine, but crucially important to success, administrative arrangements for training. These range from booking programmes, rooms, accommodation, meals and equipment, through to the event and carrying out the training. This training itself can be categorised into two broad types, as follows.

On-the-job training

First, there is on-the-job training. The British expression 'sitting next to Nellie' sums up some of this approach (see Storey, 2001). The common types here include:

- job rotation

- 'shadowing'

- apprenticeships.

Off-the-job training

Second, there is off-the-job training. The main approaches here include:

- face-to-face – lectures, presentations, workshops;

- programmed or distance learning using manuals/units;

- computer-based teaching and interactive video.

Question to think about 4.4

What are the main advantages and disadvantages of these two types of training that you have experienced?

The advantages and disadvantages of on- versus off-the-job training need to be recognised. These can be seen in Table 4.5. However, the broad methods are not mutually exclusive. Rather, both can be employed in integrated and coordinated programmes.

Table 4.5 Advantages and disadvantages of training types

Advantages	Disadvantages
On the job	
Doing the 'real thing'	Poor abilities, motivation, time of trainers
Experience handed down	Insular, latest knowledge missing
No special facilities needed	Trainees unwelcome – seen as obstacles
Relatively inexpensive	Cover for absent trainers
Trainers know the organisation	Less productive when training
Mixing with others across organisation	Difficulties for trainers settling back into job
Off the job	
Experienced/planned trainers	Relevance/transfer back to workplace
Experienced/planned/latest courses	May not be bespoke, tailored, targeted
Free from workplace distractions/ pressures	'Re-entry', settling back into work
Groups may be cost-efficient	Costly, e.g. accommodation, replacements
Mixing with people from other firms	Seen/treated as a 'jolly'

Trainers

The main roles and responsibilities (line staff) in training can be roughly distinguished as between activities that are:

- *strategic* – for example, corporate plan, HR plan, training policy, training plan.

- *operational* – for example, needs analysis, design, implementation, evaluation.

Trainers fall into categories and require a variety of skills. These include the following:

- consultant/problem solver

- designer/learning expert

- implementer/instructor/teacher

- administrator/manager/arranger.

Aspects of this job are varied. These include the following:

- direct training/instructing

- organising/administrating

- managing element

- advisory service to management.

Evaluation

One of the most important, but often neglected, aspects of training is evaluation. Was it a success? How did the programme succeed in meeting the objectives and goals set? For instance, what improvements have there been? Has any change actually been caused by the programme?

Issues and problems

There has been a shift in emphasis internationally towards 'cost effectiveness', especially in management development activity, and towards the ability to demonstrate quantifiable results from such investments (see earlier in this chapter). Yet it can be difficult to evaluate training, as 'results' may not be observed immediately, and may be more medium or long term. Many note the difficulty in establishing a link between the incidence of training and business performance. Then there is the issue of the counter-factual – how do we know what might have happened without any intervention? This is an area that is often simply neglected.

Question to think about 4.5

How would you assess an organisation's training? What difficulties might you expect in doing this?

Such difficulties are numerous and some are listed in Table 4.6.

Possible routes to evaluation

Some of the questions, and to whom they are addressed, in programme validation can be noted. One of the most famous is by Hamblin (1974) – a multi-level method, composed of different levels of objectives and effects: reactions, learning, job behaviour, organisation, ultimate. Others include the Bee and Bee (1994) version or the whole system (Morris, 1984), which is comprehensive and with three levels. These can be seen in Figure 4.6 and Tables 4.7–4.9. Some of the methods and problems with this have been noted.

Table 4.6 Training assessment methods and difficulties

Assessment	Difficulties
Programme's aims and objectives	• What were the aims and objectives of the programme? • When are these given?
Specific interview/ discussion	• Where is impact expected? • Is it individual's job, department, organisation?
Examine and test	• When is impact expected and assessment timing? • Is it during/end of programme, after return to work?
Observation and note changes	• Who evaluates? • Is it trainee, trainee's manager, tutor?
Performance data and measures	• How to calculate 'costs' and 'benefits'? • Is change the result of programme?
Tutor notes	• Do they have inclination/time to make? • Bias
HRM activities (appraisals)	• Not the focus • Not allocated time or indicates 'weakness'

Training in practice

In the UK there have been many attempts to try to 'fix' the training problem, with recent inquiries again trying to end the long line of failed initiatives designed to raise the prestige and quality of skills training. The woeful lack of training is not a new problem. It has been recognised by policy makers at least since the late nineteenth century. The UK is particularly weak in vocational-type education, especially in comparison to the more academic-type education seen as the route into university and 'better' jobs. This has been linked to a raft of causal factors, from the class system through to seeing vocational qualifications as somehow second class and only pursued if not 'bright' enough for 'proper' qualifications, to the perceived second-rate nature of manufacturing in contrast to sectors such as services and finance. This is often brought into stark contrast by comparing the UK to other countries, which we will return to later.

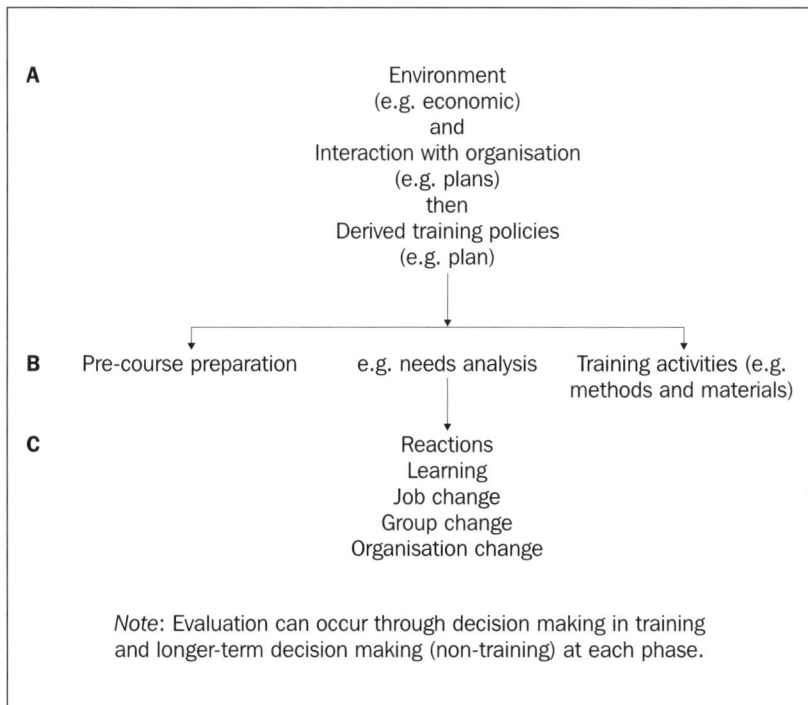

Figure 4.6 Training evaluation: the whole system. (*Source*: Adapted from Morris, 1984.)

Table 4.7 Training evaluation

Objectives	→	Training effects
1. Reactions		Reactions
2. Learning		Learning
3. Job behaviour		Job behaviour
4. Organisation		Organisation
5. Ultimate value	←	Ultimate value

Source: Hamblin (1974).

Table 4.8 Training evaluation: using Hamblin's levels

Evaluation level	Characteristics	Method examples
1. Reactions	• Ask about experience itself, which parts useful/less so • Ask for judgement on speakers, facilities, organisation, improvements	• Questionnaire • Interview and discussion
2. Learning	• Test on what learned as result, e.g. end-of-course • Assess degree to which acquired knowledge, skills, abilities aimed to deliver	• Test • Exercise
3. Job behaviour	• Degree to which knowledge/skills acquired used back in workplace • If no result here, probably deemed failure • Failure may be due to workplace culture or management attitudes against displaying new skills	• Observation • Self-assessment • Questionnaire – manager • Questionnaire – trainee • Interview • Performance appraisal

	• New skills best displayed in environment receptive to change	
4. Organisation	• Effect on functioning of workplace • Improvements in output, quality, productivity, waste, or whatever appropriate for training undertaken • Focus on areas of concern giving rise to training need, and consider extent addressed • Less concerned with behavioural change, more with change in performance measured by key indicators	• Effective indicator • Performance data • Complaints/rejects • Sales/productivity • Accidents • Absenteeism • Labour turnover
5. Ultimate	• Some effect on performance of organisation • Difficult to measure contribution or make judgement as to whether satisfactory	• As above • Difficult

Source: Adapted from Bolton (1997).

Table 4.9 Evaluating the impact of training

Location	Instruments	Stage	Characteristics
Self	Observe behaviour	Reaction	During/end of programme
Line manager	Interviews	Job behaviour	Extent objectives achieved
Department	Questionnaires	Job behaviour	Impact on job performance

Location	Instruments	Stage	Characteristics
Organisation	Performance data	Ultimate	Department or company impact
Designers	Feedback methods	Reaction	Reactive

Source: Adapted from Hamblin (1974), Bee and Bee (1994).

National Vocational Qualifications (NVQs)

There have been numerous attempts in the UK to try to redress the perceived weaknesses of vocational education and their commensurate unattractiveness. One of the main attempts was by the National Council for Vocational Qualifications in the late 1980s. By the early 1980s the UK government had unprecedented centralised control over education, with emphasis on practical vocational skills. A vehicle for this has been NVQs, which are based on assessed competencies. This competency approach was institutionalised with the development of a framework of NVQs. However, there are varied meanings for 'competency'. These include the following:

• Underlying characteristic of a person which results in effective and/or superior performance in a job.

• Ability to perform the activities within an occupational area to levels of performance expected in employment.

• Integration of knowledge and skill, and ability to apply them with understanding to a work activity (assessed via performance).

For Torrington and Hall (1998), the basic idea of competency-based training is that it is criterion-related, directed at developing ability to perform specific tasks directly related to the job you are in or for which you are preparing, and expressed in terms of performance outcomes and specific indicators. With this in mind, we can note the following points about NVQs. They:

- are a national system of qualifications and standards of occupational competence;

- are narrow, trade-related, and designed to be taken in the workplace;

- accredit competencies across organisations so that an individual's performance at work can be taken into account in a qualification;

- confirm that individuals can perform to specified standards and possess skills, knowledge and understanding which make possible such performance in workplaces.

NVQs can be reached via several routes. These include the following:

1. Planned training programme (college, training provider).

2. Assessment only (workplace acquisition).

3. Prior learning (accredit past study and work-based learning).

4. Combination of (1)–(3).

5. Assessed via centres (colleges, providers), 'assessors' and 'external verifiers'.

However, if you are not in employment, how do you gain NVQs? This led to GNVQs (1994) or 'vocational A-levels' (for 16–18-year-olds) to provide a middle path between A-levels and NVQs (for both university and employment entrance). Nevertheless, several criticisms of the system emerged. These include the following:

- extensive bureaucracy;

- weak outside checks on standards;

- too prescriptive and complicated;

- not related to 'real life' requirements;

- too paper-based;

- unsuited to more abstract/conceptual skills as they are prescriptive, task and performance models;

- low popularity;

- poor completion rates.

In short, the system is seen as a flawed model. This is due, first of all, to reliance on the achievement of competences as the measure of success. Yet failure to grasp principles means you can still perform required tasks but not have the underlying knowledge necessary to apply skills to new/varied situations. Second, the system is viewed as a 'quick fix' to produce vocational qualifications with minimum cost and effort, while ignoring the underlying problems of training.

Management Charter Initiative (MCI)

Another initiative was the MCI, part of the broader competency movement. Concerns about the standard of education and training of managers led to the setting up of the MCI in the late 1980s, a government-backed consortium of the Confederation of British Industry (CBI), British Institute of Management (BIM) and Foundation for Management Education. The aim was to give management a greater training profile for it to become a chartered profession. This requires a body of knowledge that could be called 'management' and standards of assessment to be agreed.

Investors in People (IIP)

The White Paper *Employment for the 1990s* (published in 1988) led to another initiative, the IIP scheme. This was designed as a training standard for investment in employees, to encourage companies to attain a recognised level of training. Those aspiring to or holding the award must make an ongoing commitment to training their employees. The IIP Commitment is where organisations:

• make a public commitment from the top to develop all employees to achieve their business goals;

• regularly review the training and development needs of all employees;

• take action to train and develop individuals on recruitment and throughout their careers;

• evaluate the investment in training to assess achievement and improve effectiveness.

As part of the process of becoming an IIP, organisations first have to audit their current training practices and provision. This is done with the assistance of the scheme's survey instrument. Once complete, the organisation takes appropriate actions to meet the standards. Organisations are required to produce evidence of achievements and of training standards and objectives. These are considered by an assessor. Those who achieve the standards are given public recognition and entitled to display the IIP logo on their headed paper and advertising materials.

Yet, despite these numerous initiatives, UK companies are generally perceived to lag behind many of their international competitors. Both the amounts spent and types of vocational education and training provided vary across countries. Thus a survey of more than 1,000 Thai companies, including the country's top 200 largest, in 2000 found that 75 per cent did not train employees to improve their technical capacity (Kazmin, 2003). This variety can also be seen if the UK is compared to other countries. (Much of the country overviews and 'training culture' summaries in the following section is taken and developed from Beardwell and Holden (2001).)

International comparisons of training

UK

New Deal – training for 18–24-year-olds out of work for longer than six months, and training for over 24-year-olds out of work for longer than two years. National Training Organisations – sectoral bodies whose function is to analyse skills gaps using international benchmarking, scenario planning and local focus groups. National Skills Task Force – body composed of government, employees and trade union representatives investigating skill shortages nationally and recommending proposals. Learning and Skills Councils – regional bodies replaced Training and Enterprise Councils (TECs). Colleges of further and higher education. Universities. Business schools.

Training culture: voluntary, finance- rather than industry-oriented; class-based; public/private education.

Japan

There is a high level of training. For instance, it is not unusual for new employees to have between one and six months' training on starting with a company. Training tends to be done in-house. For example, most new regular employees and many non-regular employees receive training on starting with a company. There is also a system of pre-employment education for college graduates. The aims of this are to facilitate the transition from college to work, teach about company culture and norms, and cultivate a spirit of harmony and teamwork. High schools take up to 90 per cent of pupils up to 18 years. Two-year college – vocationally specific training. Four-year university courses. Five-year college of technology courses. Considerable continuous in-company training.

Training culture: directed/voluntary: central and local government set and enforce training standards; meritocratic – top companies take from top universities; lifetime employment and training in large companies; self-development emphasised.

Germany

The vaunted system of extensive and developed training has apprenticeship programmes lasting approximately three and a half years. This is funded through a mixture of state financing and employer contributions. Although costly, this system produces qualified employees, enhances loyalty and reduces costs of dysfunctional turnover. However, some people have expressed concerns that the system is becoming too inflexible. Dual system – in-company training (practical); vocational school (theoretical). Apprenticeships – 319,000 places, though demand is decreasing. Technical colleges. Universities.

Training culture: directed: functionalist; industry-oriented, particularly engineering.

Sweden

Upper secondary school – large vocational content. Technical and specialist universities. Universities. Training in most organisations is strong; heavy emphasis on HR development. Retraining for the unemployed. Labour Market Training Board is very influential. Considerable free adult education. Emphasis on self-development and open learning systems.

Training culture: directed, state uses training to affect labour market policy. Companies are strongly encouraged to train.

France

Much training in the school system. Apprenticeship places – 300,000. University institutes of technology. Universities. Grandes écoles. Law requires employers to spend 1.2 per cent of total gross salaries on training employees.

Training culture: directed: mathematical/engineering orientation; centralised; elitist, e.g. grandes écoles; educational establishment attended often decides career propsects.

USA

Junior or community college two-year associate degree course. Technical institutes. Vocational, trade and business schools. 'GI Bill' with federal loans/grants for four years' higher education after completion of four years' military service. Private schools and colleges. University courses. Apprenticeships increasingly less common and low status. Excellent training by leading companies, but this is not universal.

Training culture: voluntary: anti-federalist in nature with wide variation; uncoordinated, with emphasis on individual effort and individual payment.

So, there is a great variety between countries in their training provision and its underpinnings and support. Part of this is the level of state and government intervention in the training system, and the overall training culture engendered.

Question to think about 4.6

To what extent should training provision be left to the 'free market' and organisations? What might be the long-term implications for organisations and the economy of low training and skills?

The implications of these different levels of provisions and approaches are more than academic. For instance, they have implications in terms of having critical roles in producing different forms of competition and economic performance. Some of these can be seen in Table 4.10.

Table 4.10 Implications of different types of training provision

System	Characteristics	Causes	Implications
Voluntary	• Laissez-faire • Market provides if shortages	• Free markets • Free riders • 'Hire and fire'	• Skills shortages and poaching • Greater numerical flexibility • Competitive downward spiral • Simple, low value-added production
Compulsory	• Directed • Force all to train or contribute	• Interventions • Institutions (state, unions) • Difficult to sack	• Skills provision for all firms • All contribute • Greater functional flexibility • Complex, high value-added production

We will now move on to the second major concern of this chapter on employee development: employee performance appraisal. This will be examined in terms of the methods, techniques and international perspectives in this area.

Performance appraisal

Employee performance appraisal involves several aspects. These include:

- regular assessments determining how well the employee is doing;

- types of processes and procedures of evaluating performance in the job;

- records and discussions of performance levels, both recent and future;

- central HR involvement, control and coordination;

- findings used in other HRM areas (HR planning, training – see Chapter 2 and earlier in this chapter).

However, it needs to be recognised that tensions are apparent in appraisal. First, between measuring past performance versus future potential. Second, between different schools of thought which emphasise the importance of methods, systems and procedures versus the skills of managers. The latter school of thought is gaining some popularity. For instance, skills in appraisals are often now seen as a basic managerial attribute. Third, between the extent to which evaluation issues (such as pay, promotion, and so on) are discussed at the same time as development issues (such as measures to improve performance, objectives, career development, and so on). Fourth, between closed and open systems. Organisations could gather performance data by means such as 'mystery customers', computer monitoring and so on. Are there any ethical issues in this? What about the right to privacy? This is especially important as appraisals are normally seen as being built on trust.

Methods and techniques of performance appraisal

A range of methods and techniques for appraisals exist. With these there is the common trade-off in HRM between more speed, ease and cost versus slowness, complexity and expense.

Question to think about 4.7

What types and methods of employee performance appraisal do you have experience of?

The main appraisal methods include the following. These have some common and specific advantages and problems which we will return to later in this chapter.

Work standards

This is one of the simplest methods. Here the person is judged, for example, by the number of units of output produced over a given period.

Comment boxes

With this method, the appraiser answers questions in a form about the performance of the employee. Often the appraiser is not required to

---

grade appraisees according to predetermined scales, and they are allowed to describe in their own words how the person has performed.

Checklists

This involves the appraiser answering 'yes' or 'no' to questions about the appraisee on various aspects of employee performance.

Ranking

Here the appraiser has less discretion. They must place in rank order, from highest to lowest performing, all those employees being appraised.

Forced distribution

Again, the appraiser's discretion is constrained with such methods. Here appraisers rate people on a forced distribution of categories. For instance, 10% low; 20% low average; 40% average; 20% high average; 10% high. This can be seen in Table 4.11.

Table 4.11 Example of forced distribution

High	Next	Middle	Next	Low
10%	20%	40%	20%	10%
Names	Names	Names	Names	Names

Rating scales

This is one of the oldest, most popular methods used in appraisals. Various attributes of performance are listed, i.e. accuracy, knowledge, quality of work, and the person is evaluated on each of these dimensions individually. A scale is often used, i.e. 1–5 for poor; below average; average; above average; excellent. An overall score is than calculated, so there is some ease of interpretation. An example of a five-point rating scale can be seen in Table 4.12.

Table 4.12 Example of rating scale

Criteria	Scale				
	Excellent	Very good	Good	Average	Poor
Time keeping					
Appearance					
Communication skills					
Relationships with subordinates					
Relationship with seniors					
Organisation skills					

Critical incidents

This method is a procedure for collecting observed incidents that are seen as important or critical to performance. A list (log) of incidents is compiled, with details kept of examples of positive and negative employee performance. High-performing employees are identified as those performing well in many critical incidents. Adequate, but not exceptional, HRs are those involved in few critical incidents.

Management by objectives

This method was traditionally more used for professional/managerial grades. There is commonly a cycle, which may include the following stages:

1. Forms completed: serve as a basis for initial meeting and discussions.

2. Agreement: reached on objectives/goals to achieve during the period.

3. Training and development: needed for achievement of objectives.

4. Modification: due to changed circumstances (e.g. corporate policy, environment).

5. Review: at end of period to see if goals were met and fresh goals set for next period.

Behaviourally anchored rating scales (BARS)

These appraisal methods specify definite, observable and measurable behaviour. The format uses critical incidents to serve as 'anchor statements' on a scale. The form contains defined performance dimensions, each with critical incident anchors (examples of actual behaviour on the job, not general descriptions or traits). The appraiser than rates the person against these predetermined factors identified as important to success. An example of this can be seen in Table 4.13. The advantages of such a method include the following:

- some validity of each of the main duties (obtained from job descriptions);

- agreement over suitable descriptions for each category of behaviour;

- economies of scale if many people have the same job descriptions.

Table 4.13 Example of BARS performance dimension

Performance dimension scale development under BARS for the dimension 'Ability to absorb and interpret policies for an employee relations specialist' (Rated 1–9).		
This employee relations specialist:		
	9	Could be expected to serve as information source concerning new and changed policies for others in the organisation
Could be expected to be aware quickly of programme changes and explain these to employee	8	
	7	Could be expected to reconcile conflicting policies and procedures correctly to meet HRM goals

Could be expected to recognise the need for additional information to gain a better understanding of policy changes	6	
	5	Could be expected to complete various HRM forms correctly after receiving instruction on them
Could be expected to require some help and practice in mastering new policies and procedures	4	
	3	Could be expected to know that there is always a problem, but go down many blind alleys before realising they are wrong
Could be expected to incorrectly interpret guidelines, creating problems for line managers	2	
	1	Could be expected to be unable to learn new procedures even after repeated explanations

Source: DeCenzo and Robbins (1999).

Behavioural observation scales (BOS)

Like the above technique, this method uses critical incident techniques to identify a series of behaviours in the job. However, the format is different in that instead of identifying behaviours exhibited during the rating period, the appraiser needs to indicate on a scale how often the person was actually observed engaging in the specific behaviour under review. An example of this method can be seen in Table 4.14.

Table 4.14 Example of BOS performance dimension

Sample BOS items for the performance dimension 'Communicating with subordinates' (Rated 1–5)						
Puts up notices on bulletin boards when new policies or procedures are implemented						
Almost never	1	2	3	4	5	Almost always
Maintains eye contact when talking to employees						
	1	2	3	4	5	
Uses both written memos and verbal discussion when giving instructions						
	1	2	3	4	5	
Discusses changes in policies or procedures with employees before implementing them						
	1	2	3	4	5	
Writes memos that are clear, concise and easy to understand						
	1	2	3	4	5	

Total performance level:

5–9: Below adequate

10–14: Adequate

15–19: Good

20+: Excellent

Source: Fisher et al. (1999).

Peer ratings

With this appraisal method, colleagues and co-workers at the same level assess each other's performance. This is increasingly popular with businesses as teamworking has been encouraged. One advantage of such a method is that this is based on actual experience of performance in the workplace.

Subordinate ratings

With this method of appraisal, employees are asked to rate their 'bosses'. There have been experiments with this at DuPont, Nabisco, Mobil, GE and UPS in the USA, and BP in the UK. This method is seen as more democratic and also useful in improving the channels of communication.

Self-appraisal

One of the more recent methods to take off in popularity has been self-appraisal. To try to seek more discrimination in rankings with such formats, people can be asked to rank different aspects of their performance relative to other aspects.

360-degree appraisal

This is one of the latest trends in the area of appraisal. This method involves as many different people as possible in the evaluation of a person's performance. This can range from subordinates to peers to managers, customers and clients.

While we have seen that there are many types of performance appraisal, those that involve an interview at some stage are common. Interviews are an important part of the process, not least as they are integral to the communication and feedback that is often involved in the process. Some of the same points as employee selection interviews (see Chapter 2) can be followed as ground rules here, whatever the nature of the particular interview. A possible structure for an appraisal interview can be seen in Table 4.15. However, problems may be encountered when evaluating the performance of an individual, irrespective of the interview.

Table 4.15 Interview structure

Stage	Characteristics
1. Preparation	• Armed with all the facts • Sure how to proceed • Clear purpose and aim
2. Purpose and rapport	• Agree purpose • Agree structure of meeting • Check pre-work is complete
3. Factual review	• Review known facts about performance • Appraiser reinforcement
4. Appraisee views	• Asked to comment on performance • What went well/less well, liked/disliked • Possible new objectives
5. Appraiser views	• Add own perspective • Recognition and constructive criticism • Questions about what has been said
6. Problem-solving approach	• Discussion of differences • Discuss how they can be resolved • Consider developmental training needs
7. Objective-setting	• Agree what actions should be taken • Who takes them

Source: Adapted from Torrington and Hall (1998).

Question to think about 4.8

What problems might there be with performance appraisals and their conduct?

There are numerous potential problems with appraisals, both general and specific to certain methods. These are noted in Tables 4.16 and 4.17.

Table 4.16 Biases in performance appraisals

Issue	Characteristics
Supervisory bias	Range, i.e. race, gender, cultural
'Halo' and 'Horns'	One good/bad event influences whole judgement
Temporal	First/last event outshines all others
Strictness and leniency	Gives high or low marks/ratings
Central tendency	Gives middle marks/ratings

Table 4.17 Problems in performance appraisal methods

Method	Problems
Work standards	• Responsibility not neatly divided between employees • Jobs involve bundles of tasks to disentangle or relate to output
Comment boxes	• Allows bland comments • Difficult comparisons (between appraisers, employees, periods)
Checklists	• Questions pre-set • Merely go down list

Method	Problems
Ranking	• Supervisor bias and halo effect • Difficulties in merging rankings between appraisers • Not helpful in communication, motivation, training
Forced distribution	• A group may not conform to these fixed percentages • Assumes there are good/bad performers in all groups
Rating scales	• Qualitative information not generated • Little value to training, communication, motivation • Biases
Critical incidents	• Demanding – maintaining log may be neglected • Difficult to quantify/interpret log and comparisons
MBO	• Expensive on time and produces uncertain outcomes • May not give comparative data for rewards/HR planning
BARS	• Costly and time-consuming • Long time to agree on descriptions for every job • Takes account of existing performance, not future potential
BOS	• Costly • Time-consuming
Peer	• Rivalry or jealousy • Prejudice, although larger groups may reduce this • Reluctant to express honest opinion • May not know about all aspects of the job • Cultural issues
Subordinate	• Rivalry or jealousy • Prejudice, although larger groups may reduce this • Too frightened to express real opinion • Reluctance to accept views of subordinates • Cultural issues

Self-appraisal	• Difficulty to analyse own performance
	• Unrealistic views of how well/poorly done
	• Tend to overrate themselves
	• Unwilling to admit weaknesses
	• May underplay strengths
	• Cultural issues
360-degree	• Time and costs
	• Willingness of others to complete
	• Above problems

A trend has been for the use of performance appraisal techniques to spread down organisational hierarchies. However, we can also question their use in the traditional organisational structure.

Question to think about 4.9

To what extent are appraisals applicable to all types of HR in organisations?

Some commentators argue that because appraisal sits uneasily with the ethos that characterises the attitudes of most professional groups, it is an inappropriate approach to take if an organisation wishes to maximise its performance (Fletcher, 1997). According to some experts, there is a professional ethos which is in stark contrast with the principles of appraisal, which emphasise wholly conflicting characteristics. These are contrasted in Table 4.18.

Table 4.18 Performance appraisals in professions

Professional ethos	Appraisal characteristics
High levels of autonomy and independence of judgement	Hierarchical authority and direction from superiors
Self-discipline and adherence to professional standards	Administrative rules and following of procedures
Possession of specialised knowledge and skills	Definition by the organisation of standards and goals
Power and status based on expertise	Demand primary loyalty be given to the organisation
Operating and being guided by a code of ethics	Basis of power in one's organisational position
Answerable to the governing professional body	

Source: Fletcher (1997).

In short, appraisals can yield individual level information crucial to HRM and its practices (such as HR planning, training – see Chapter 2 and earlier in this chapter). However, systems require precise planning and meticulous execution to be of value. Appraisals should be approached in a professional manner. They need to focus on performance and be objective, easy to perform, consistent and reviewed to introduce improvements. The appraisee's immediate supervisor or manager is usually the person most often involved in the appraisal process, There are many methods, and these vary in suitability between organisations, HRs and time. Poor, inexpertly or unevenly applied appraisals can lead to a sense of a 'witch-hunt', lapse into tokenism, lose purpose and value, and may be seen merely as a hoop to jump through, creating widespread resentment. Yet, for many managers appraisals are seen as:

- 'owned' by the HR department;

- simply another task forced on them by the organisation;

- of little value and interfering with the real business of running the organisation.

International comparisons of performance appraisal

Question to think about 4.10

What might be some of the issues arising with appraisal systems when used across countries?

Some general problems have been noted by various researchers in relation to multinational corporations (MNCs). These include the following.

In Arabic countries, it is argued, assertive women may receive biased ratings if they are expected to play more 'subservient' roles, especially in public. In Asia, if using 360-degree or peer appraisals where young workers are asked to rate older subordinates, the cultural values of respect and esteem may bias the rating (see Farh et al., 1991; Rowley and Bae, 2003). This can be seen in the following examples. Employees from Taiwan, when compared with similar workers in the USA, are more likely to give themselves lower ratings in self-evaluation forms. American and Western employees usually give themselves higher self-assessed ratings than those given by their bosses; the reverse is true in China (ibid.). One explanation for this is that the more individualist culture in the West encourages higher levels of self-confidence. In more collectivist cultures, there is a greater emphasis on solidarity, interdependence and inter-group harmony. This may lead employees to underestimate their value.

Other research has similarly shown difficulties with appraisals internationally (see reports in Taylor, 1998), for example Singapore Airlines in Thailand where there was reluctance to highlight bad points. Other problems included a Chinese reluctance to assert one's own views directly to superiors; East European countries having a continuing diffidence to appraisals due to the heritage of state-owned enterprise and the rewards of loyalty and political status; and France being uneasy with subordinate involvement.

In sum, the values on which employees are appraised vary between countries. Organisations should be sensitive to this, so as not to underestimate the contribution of various groups of employees. MNCs need appraisal systems that recognise these differences.

Conclusion

Employee development is a key area of HRM which has the chance to make a significant impact on the business. There has long been criticism in the UK about a lack of training and management development. Complaints continue, for example, about the lack of vocational qualifications and an academic focus which fails to give school-leavers sufficient skills for the workplace. Management development has also become the subject of activity and initiatives.

However, there is often a lack of investment, especially in times of recession. We can distinguish between strategic and pragmatic use of training over the long and short term. Despite the need to link training initiatives to corporate strategies, many firms are still a long way behind. Training has tactical links with HR planning and performance appraisals, and is a key instrument in the implementation of HRM. The perennial problem remains evaluation. The importance of training varies across countries. This links to the issue of who should pay for this training:

• organisations – they benefit and the market will provide?

• the state – training given parity with academic routes in terms of funding/esteem and steps taken to reduce poaching?

Employee performance appraisal is expensive, but spreading down hierarchies. Yet appraisals can be a complicated procedure. They need to be seen to be fair and consistently applied to have real value to management and businesses. Methods vary in their suitability:

• simple and easy methods with emphasis on evaluation (rating scales) for some HRs;

• methods with a developmental emphasis (MBO) for managerial HRs;

• culture of organisation (e.g. private versus public sector);

• cross-cultural contexts.

Finally, this work on employee development again links back to Chapter 1. It indicates both the limits to views on universalism and 'one best way' and the importance of contingency and context, as well as the limits to ideas of HRM's strategic input and integration.

Overview references

These short articles and extracts reflect issues in training, types, assessment and comparisons.

The Financial Times

Adams, C. (2001) 'Work Skills and McJob Training', 20 November, p. 21.

Galunic, C. and Weeks, J. (2001) 'Investments that Build on Human Nature', Mastering People Management, Part 5, 12 November, pp. 10–11.

Kelly, J. (2001) 'Preaching to the Unconverted', 15 February, p. 14.

Kelly, J. (2002) 'Clouds Hang Over Labour Policy on Better Skills', 22 October, p. 6.

Latham, G. (2001) 'Training: A Missing Link in the Strategic Plan', Mastering People Management, Part 5, 12 November, pp. 4–5.

Lee, N. (2002) 'Learning How to Make the Best of Workplace Education', 19 August, p. 12.

Storey, D. (2002) 'Why Nellie Still Has the Answers', 26 September 2002, p. 15.

See also:

Beardwell, I. and Holden, L. (2001) *HRM: A Contemporary Perspective*. Harlow: Pearson Education, pp. 343–49.

Thornhill, A., Lewis, P., Millmore, M. and Saunders, M. (2000) *Managing Change: A Human Resource Strategy Approach.* Harlow: Pearson Education (Chapter 6).

References

Anderson, A. (1993) *Successful Training Practice: A Manager's Guide to Personnel Development.* Oxford: Blackwell.

Barham, K. (1988) *Management for the Future.* Ashridge Management College Foundation for Management Education.

Beardwell, I. and Holden, L. (eds) (2001) *HRM: A Contemporary Approach.* London: Financial Times/Prentice Hall.

Bee, R. and Bee, F. (1994) *Training Needs Analysis an Evaluation.* London: IPD.

Bolton, T. (1997) *Human Resource Management: An Introduction.* Oxford: Blackwell.

Burgoyne, J. (1988) 'Management development for the individual and the organisation', *Personnel Management*, June: 40–4.

DeCenzo, D. and Robbins, S. (1999) *Human Resource Management.* Chichester: Wiley.

Farh, J., Dobbins, G.H. and Cheng, B.S. (1991) 'Cultural relativity in action: a comparison of self-ratings made by Chinese and US workers', *Personnel Psychology*, 44: 129–67.

Fisher, C., Schoenfeldt, L. and Shaw, J. (1999) *Human Resource Management.* London: Houghton Mifflin.

Fletcher, C. (1997) *Appraisal: Routes to Improved Performance.* London: IPD.

Foot, M. and Hook, C. (1996) *Introducing HRM*. Harlow: Longman.

Hamblin, A.C. (1974) *Evaluation and Control of Training*. Maidenhead: McGraw-Hill.

Kanter, R. (1984) *The Change Masters*. London: Routledge.

Kazmin, A. (2003) 'A Buddhist boot camp for Thailand's elite', *Financial Times*, 8 January, p. 14.

Morris, M. (1984) 'The evaluation of training', *Industrial and Commercial Training*, March/April.

Peters, T. and Waterman, R. (1982) *In Search of Excellence*. New York: Harper & Row.

Revans, R. (1972) 'Action learning: a management development programme', *Personnel Review*.

Rowley, C. and Bae, J. (2003) 'Culture and management in South Korea', in Warner, M. (ed.), *Culture and Management in Asia*. London: Curzon, pp. 187–209.

Storey, J. (ed.) (2001) *HRM: A Critical Text*. London: Thomson Learning (Chapter 9).

Taylor, S. (1998) *Employee Resourcing*. London: CIPD.

Torrington, D. and Hall, L. (1998) *Human Resource Management*. London: Financial Times/Prentice Hall.

Further reading

For those who want further details there are links and references given in some of the above titles, while there are many further books which cover similar ground, including the following:

Albrecht, M. (2001) *International HRM*. Oxford: Blackwell (Part IV).

Anderson, A. (1993) *Successful Training Practice*. Oxford: Blackwell.

Hamblin, A. (1974) *Evaluation and Control of Training*. Maidenhead: McGraw-Hill.

Harrison, R. (1997) *Employee Development*. London: CIPD.

Marchington, M. and Wilkinson, A. (2002) *People Management and Development*. London: CIPD (Chapters 12–13).

Pilbeam, S. and Corbridge, M. (eds) (2002) *People Resourcing: HRM in Practice*. Harlow: Pearson Education (Chapter 12).

Redman, T. and Wilkinson, A. (eds) (2001) *Contemporary HRM: Text and Cases*. London: Financial Times/Prentice Hall (Chapter 5).

Sisson, J. and Storey, J. (2000) *The Realities of HRM*. Buckingham: Open University Press (Chapter 6).

CHAPTER 5

Employee relations

Introduction

This chapter is concerned with the area of employee relations (ER). Here we make no hard distinction, unlike some other commentators, from the term industrial relations (IR). The area of ER remains as vibrant and relevant today as ever. This continuing importance is the case not just in the UK, but in other countries as well. It is one of the key areas feeding into the development of PM and thus HRM. The area has critical impacts on HRM, for example through the political process and employer and employee organisations, and through LM changes and legislation. This forms the subject matter of the first half of this chapter, with ER dealt with in terms of its early development, definitions, system, strategy, perspectives, partnership and the future.

A key aspect of the ER area, not least as it is seen to be both a 'cause' and a 'cure' for 'poor' ER, is employee involvement. A whole spectrum of practices is often lumped under the rubric of this elastic concept, from industrial democracy through to financial participation. A contemporary guise is the idea of 'workplace partnerships'. However, its use as a panacea to help with business and management problems is often too late and ad hoc, being merely a 'bolt-on' and some sort of organisational 'lifebelt'. This area forms the second major concern of this chapter, with employee involvement dealt with in terms of forms and practices, and the related issues these topics raise.

Overview

Employee relations as a subject often arouses very mixed reactions in people. Why is this? For commentators, attitudes are influenced by a range of factors, including what are termed 'frames of reference' and 'perspectives' in employee relations (see Bacon, 2001: 193–6 and later here). Trying to interpret employee relations issues and events, especially disputes, in terms of the 'facts' of the situation to arrive at an explanation of the causes is not easy. Surely the facts speak for themselves? With sufficient attention paid to collecting detailed information, can we come across objective explanations? We will look at this area.

Employee relations has its origins in industrial relations, which came to the fore in the late nineteenth-century labour problems. On the one hand, there was labour militancy, conflict and economic disruption; and on the other hand, there were issues of poor pay and working conditions. The best solution to this was seen as collective bargaining, to which industrial relations became closely linked. The first public usage of the term was in a US Congressional Committee in 1915, while in the UK it was in a Whitley Committee in 1917. The area remained marked by such pragmatism and its scope largely reflected the practical concerns of management, public policy and governments. From the 1950s to the 1980s the area became almost synonymous with trade unions and strife (reflected in films such as *I'm All Right Jack* and *The Angry Silence*). Managing this was a major, time-consuming concern of both personnel specialists and line managers, as well as the government.

Employee relations draws on a wide variety of theories and data from economics, history, sociology, law, politics and organisational behaviour. It is concerned with all aspects of the employment relationship. The seminal work by the American John Dunlop (1958) developed the idea that in every country there was an employee relations 'system'. This system involved three groups or parties: workers and their organisations; employers, managers and their organisations; government and agencies concerned with work. Every system created a set of rules to govern the workplace. These may take a variety of forms, such as agreements, statutes, custom and practice, but their essential character is to define the status of the parties and to govern their conduct. These rules are of two kinds: procedural – the methods and procedures to be used, such as in settling disputes; and substantive – dealing with, for example, rates of pay and hours of work. These rules may be created in a variety of ways, such as through laws, collective bargaining or unilaterally by one or other of the parties. The parties do not, however, operate in a vacuum, but within an environmental context composed of:

- political, legal and social factors, i.e. power relationships and status of the parties;

- economic factors, i.e. labour markets and product markets;

- technological factors.

If rules were the 'output' of the system, the 'input' was the values and objectives of the parties. The subject matter of employee relations, therefore, involves the three parties of the system and their organisation, objectives and relationships, and their interaction with each other in the environment in which they operate.

Frames of reference and perspectives in employee relations

The suggestion that employees may need some form of collective protection from employers provokes a strong response in many managers. Behind this response is a set of assumptions about the right to manage (frequently termed the management prerogative) and the correct power balance in the employment relationship. These assumptions are a mixture of a complex blend of experiences, predispositions, learned behaviour and prejudice. They combine to create management frames of reference (Fox, 1966, 1974) that capture the often deeply held assumptions of managers towards a labour force… Each of these differ in their beliefs about the nature of organisations, the role of conflict and the task of managing employees. Managers holding a unitarist frame of reference believe the natural state of organisations is one of harmony and cooperation. All employees are thought to be in the same team, pulling together for the common goal of organisational success. The employee relations task of management is to prevent conflict arising from misunderstandings that result if they fail adequately to communicate organisational goals to employees. Any remaining conflicts are attributed to mischief created by troublemakers.

The Management of People

A pluralist frame of reference recognises that organisations contain a variety of sectional groups who legitimately seek to express divergent interests. The resulting conflict is inevitable and the task of managers is to establish a system of structures and procedures in which conflict is institutionalised and a negotiated order is established...

There are no simple methods to assess the frame of reference held by managers – indeed, they usually hold a complex set of ideas rather than falling neatly into a single and possibly oversimplistic frame of reference...

Frames of reference are also important because they underlie the management style adopted in organisations towards the workforce. Many authors have attempted to classify management styles... Whether or not managers recognise trade unions indicates the extent to which a 'collective' approach to managing employees is preferred, and it captures a key factor in distinguishing between management approaches. In addition, the extent to which managers invest in and develop employees indicates the extent to which they stress 'individualism'...

Individualism and collectivism have recently become popular terms in employee relations. In comparison with the traditional management frames of reference, these concepts have 'common-sense' meanings and appear grounded in everyday management vocabularies and thinking about employee relations. Individualism in employment relations is traditionally used to denote non-unionism and/or an HRM-style investment approach to employees... Correspondingly, collectivism in industrial relations in the 1970s is counterpoised with individualism and HRM in the 1980s... The 'collectivism' dimension includes a unitarist position where trade unions are not recognised, an adversarial position of conflict with unions and a cooperative position of partnership with unions. The 'individualism' dimension includes a cost minimisation approach to employees, and a 'paternalist' position of care for employee welfare and employee development.

(*Source*: Adapted from N. Bacon, in Redman and Wilkinson, 2001: 193–6.)

Task 5.1

You can explore this in the following exercise. Read Case studies 5.1 and 5.2 and answer the questions which follow them. Reflect on the structures and groups in the employee relations system.

Case study 5.1 Buses hit by strike over sacked drinkers

Bus maintenance workers staged a wildcat strike in support of three colleagues sacked for drinking on duty. The engineers walked out of Westbourne Park bus garage, forcing more than 100 buses off the road during the morning rush hour. Thousands of commuters were left stranded as key cross-city services failed to run. Many drivers and conductors refused to cross picket lines mounted outside the garage. There were no services on routes 7, 8 and 52A, and few buses on routes 15, 28 and 31. London Buses said the 'unjustified' walkout was causing serious disruption throughout the capital, with 118 buses trapped in the garage. The three engineers – including a Transport Union official – were sacked after being caught in a pub during their shift. London Buses said the men would have had to drive buses on their return to the garage.

(*Source*: Adapted from J. Postlewaite, *The Evening Standard*.)

Case study 5.2 British Airways (aircrew and ground staff) strike

In 1997 the ground staff and cabin crews of BA voted in favour of strike action. This same event was reported in the following ways in a range of newspapers.

The Daily Telegraph

Robert Ayling, embattled Chief Executive of BA, is said to be one of the Labour government's model corporate leaders, just as his former chairman, Lord King, was 'Mrs Thatcher's favourite businessman'. Like his former boss, Mr Ayling is trying to bring about a revolution in BA's competitiveness, and all revolutions call for brutal tactics.

The Times

Regrettable as some of Mr Ayling's tactics may be, BA deserves public support. The alternative is regression to an even unhappier era in the air. Government and industry have a shared interest here – in the recognition by trade unions that a new administration cannot repeal the laws of supply and demand. A 'new mood' in industrial relations which allows unions to frustrate necessary corporate modernisation would be a retrograde step. Amicable agreement between the two sides is desirable.

The Morning Star

Transport and General Workers Union General Secretary Bill Morris authorised the strike after making a last-ditch bid to hold talks with BA. The tough stance followed a briefing between BA unions and the TUC [the trade union national federation] General Secretary, John Monks. Mr Morris, said 'I appealed to BA again this morning to start negotiations with a view to resolving both disputes. However, BA have made it clear they are only prepared to talk about the ground staff issue.'

The Financial Times

Both disputes are essentially about change. The new pay package offered to BA cabin crews is not fundamentally contentious. The dispute, according to the TGWU, which represents the disaffected staff, is over the imposition of a deal without negotiation. The real issue is whether BA, and indeed other British companies, can go through another round of restructuring without the support of the workforce.

The Guardian

Q. Why are the cabin crew striking?

A. BA has imposed sweeping changes to pay and conditions on the majority, who belong to the Transport and General Workers Union – including a 19% cut in basic pay for new recruits. Management did a deal with a breakaway group, Cabin Crew 89.

Q. But are not cabin crew getting big increases in basic pay?

A. Yes, but only by incorporating overtime and other allowances. BA says no existing stewards will have their income cut for three years – which the union believes will become a pay freeze, combined with the likelihood of longer hours. BA says the package will save £43 million.

(*Source*: Adapted from Hollinshead et al., 1999.)

....

Questions

1. Do these cases affect your attitude towards 'wildcat' (unofficial/ unconstitutional) strikes and 'picketing' (workers at workplace entrances encouraging support for the dispute)?

2. What reasons do you think the bus drivers had for going on strike?

3. How far do these BA reports reflect a set of common causal factors?

....

The idea of good and harmonious employee relations is often proposed and is seen as normal. Why does this seem so elusive and the subject of debate? If we look at international employee relations there is even more diversity in structures and practices. The role of employee organisations as one group in the employment relations system has been hotly debated. Yet, in the American HRM model of Beer et al. (1984), trade unions are listed as both 'stakeholders' and 'situational factors'. In the same framework, employee influence is given as an 'HRM policy choice' and 'laws' as another situational factor. Indeed, the idea of employee involvement, and more recently ideas of 'partnership' with labour/trade unions, is not new. The ideas of processes and procedures to reduce or resolve conflict are also long-standing. These can be seen in the recent fire brigades dispute in the UK.

Conciliation

From a unitary perspective, conciliation may be viewed as irrelevant, in contrast to pluralist type approaches. In the human resource management (HRM) area, conciliation may be seen as an assisted continuation of negotiation and related to conflict. An intervention process, conciliation involves an independent, neutral third party acting as interpretor and messenger in identifying the causes of differences and relative significance of issues and positions to develop mutually acceptable solutions. However, agreement to these remains the parties' joint decision, as conciliators do not impose or recommend solutions. There is a long history of support in the UK, including the 1896 Conciliation Act. Conciliation may be provided by private or public facilities. In the UK the best-known is the Advisory, Conciliation and Arbitration Service (ACAS). Conciliation by its full-time staff, almost all civil servants, is voluntary and arises via the parties' request, procedural agreements or its volunteering of its services. In 1999–2000 ACAS received 1,500 requests for collective conciliation (52 per cent over pay and terms and conditions), plus 164,525 cases of individual conciliation (52,791 on unfair dismissal, 36,837 on protection of wages, and 29,053 over breach of contract).

References and further reading

ACAS, *Annual Reports*.

ILO (1980) *Conciliation and Arbitration Procedures in Labour Disputes*. ILO.

Lowry, P. (1990) *Employment Disputes and the Third Party*. London: Macmillan.

Salamon, M. (2000) *Industrial Relations: Theory and Practice*. Harlow: Pearson Education.

(*Source*: C. Rowley, 'Conciliation', in Redman and Wilkinson, 2002: 39.)

Mediation

From unitary perspectives, mediation may be viewed as irrelevant, in contrast to pluralist type approaches. Mediation in the area of human resource management (HRM) may be seen as an assisted continuation of negotiation and as related to conflict. It is an interventionist process involving an independent and neutral third party helping parties to resolve differences and come to some agreement. It is more proactive than conciliation as mediators may suggest their own, non-binding, proposals for settlement, which the parties may accept, reject or alter. However, in practice the dividing line is thin and blurs. The process of mediation may be similar to conciliation, or it may be more formal and similar to arbitration, except with no final binding award. This distinction is reinforced in the UK publicly funded system as mediators are drawn from a list of the Advisory, Conciliation and Arbitration Service (ACAS) arbitrators, who are on the whole academics. In 1999–2000 ACAS completed 595 advisory mediation projects (17 per cent involved collective bargaining arrangements, 13 per cent rewards, and 28 per cent communications, consultation and employee involvement).

There are several issues around mediation. Calling for mediation can be seen as a sign of weakness and undermining authority. Varied amounts of 'compulsion', removing some of the parties' freedom, could be used as it avoids giving third parties power to resolve issues on uncongenial terms. Mediation provides 'public relations' aspects, being used to shift some blame and responsibility for settlements. Yet, reliance on mediation can become addictive; it can 'chill' processes such as negotiation, making earlier settlement less likely. Nevertheless, mediation forces the sides to re-examine cases, making some movement possible, while mediators approach issues with fresh minds and can also bring their own suggestions and proposals for resolutions. The area of mediation will remain an important one for HRM.

References and further reading

ACAS, *Annual Reports*.

Margerison, C. and Leary, M. (1975) *Industrial Conflict: The Mediator's Role*. MCB Books.

Salamon, M. (2000) *Industrial Relations: Theory and Practice*. Harlow: Pearson Education.

(*Source*: C. Rowley, 'Mediation', in Redman and Wilkinson, 2002: 157.)

Among other issues, the earlier case studies illustrate that there may be disagreement in employee relations. If there is, how can we attempt to prevent and resolve it?

You can now attempt Task 5.2 below.

Task 5.2

Develop a system to prevent and resolve disputes.

Employee relations

We can trace the development of ER. It could be said to have existed ever since people have been interacting in the labour process.

Early development of term

Er has its origins in the late nineteenth century and 'the labour problem'. This was seen to have 'two faces', namely on the one hand labour militancy, conflict and economic disruption, and on the other issues of pay and working conditions. The best 'solution' to his problem was seen to be collective bargaining, which should, therefore, be encouraged and supported. It was this area to which ER came closely linked and almost synonymous. The first public usage of the term was by a US Congressional Committee in 1915, and in the UK by the Whitley Committee in 1917. However, it was not until the 1920s that the term caught on. For example, in 1926 a survey for the Board of Trade used the term IR.

The field of ER remained marked by pragmatism and empiricism and its scope largely reflected the practical concerns of management, public policy and governments. It also draws on a variety of theories and data from areas including sociology, economics, history, law, politics, organisational behaviour and so on.

Question to think about 5.1
What do you think IR/ER is concerned with?

Definitions

Some definitions of IR are narrow, for example those of the influential early pioneers in the area, such as Flanders (1970) and others. For these, it was about the institutions of job regulation and the rules governing employment. Thus ER was seen as being about job regulation and collective bargaining, and often about narrow sectors and workers – industrial, male, manual workers and their organisations, trade unions. Yet, this reduces ER to the study of formal bargaining structures and procedures, which is limiting.

In contrast, for some other commentators, the starting point for ER was the 'exchange relationship', the buying and selling of labour. In particular, the disparity between the 'buyer' and 'seller' of labour makes conflict inevitable. For example, for these commentators IR was the process of control over work relations (Hyman, 1975). Yet, while interesting and broadening out the field, ER covers more than just this. For instance, ER involves the study of both structures and actions.

So, there are broader views of ER, viewing it as concerned with all aspects of the employment relationship. It includes the study of individuals, groups, their unions and associations, employers and their organisations, and the environment in which these parties interact. It is this idea of organisation and environment which we turn to next.

The concept of a 'system'

The American John Dunlop (1958) produced his seminal work, which is still used today (see Figure 5.1). Basically, this argues

---

that in every country an IR (or ER) system, a sub-system of the economic and political system, exists and involves three groups or parties: workers and their organisations; employers, managers and their organisations; and government and agencies concerned with the workplace and work community.

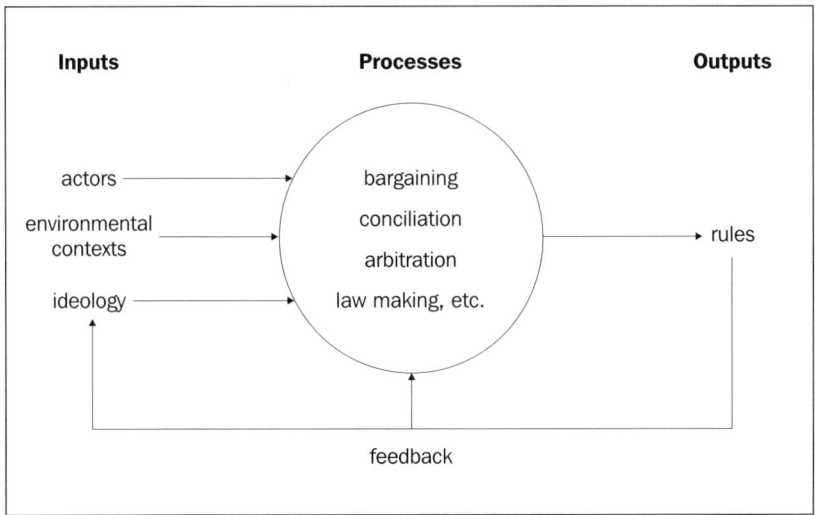

Figure 5.1 The industrial relations system. (*Source*: Dunlop, 1958.)

Furthermore, the concept of an IR system can be applied at different levels: national (i.e. different countries); industry; group, firm and plant (particularly given the importance of multinational corporations).

Question to think about 5.2

What might be the 'output' of such an ER system?

Rules

Every ER system creates a complex of rules to govern the workplace and work community. These rules may take a variety of forms (for example, agreements, statutes, custom and practice), but their essential character is to define the status of the parties and to govern their conduct. These rules are of two kinds:

- *procedural* – methods and procedures to be used, such as in settling disputes;

- *substantive* – dealing with rates of wages, hours of work, and so on.

The system's rules may be created in a variety of ways, for example through laws, collective bargaining, or unilaterally by one or other of the parties.

Question to think about 5.3

What might impact on the operation of an ER system?

Context

The ER parties and the system do not, however, operate in a vacuum, but within an environmental context. This is composed of:

- political and legal factors, i.e. the power relationship and status of the parties;

- economic factors, i.e. labour markets and product markets;

- social factors, i.e. including culture and values;

- technological factors, i.e. types.

If rules are the output of the system, the input to the system is the values and objectives of the parties. The subject matter of ER, therefore, involves the three parties of the system and their organisation, objectives and relationships, and their interactions against the environment in which they operate concerning the employment relationship.

While a classic piece of work, Dunlop, as might be expected, attracted a range of criticisms. Some of this stems from his own 'time and place', of 1950s American pluralism. For example, Dunlop also argued that in each ER system there was an underlying, shared ideology (of consensus) which was expected to lead to stability in the system. However, the emphasis on stability and consensus makes it difficult for the model to explain dynamic change. Thus Dunlop's work was criticised for being:

- too static;

- overly conservative;

- ignorant of behavioural factors;

- more concerned with solving than seeking the sources of conflict.

Nevertheless, the influence of his systems analysis and focus on stability and order in ER was soon evident. This could be seen in the output of leading UK academics, most notably members of the Oxford School of IR and its offshoots, as at the Industrial Relations Research Unit at the University of Warwick (see Rowley, 1998). This had an empirical bias as well as wide-ranging impacts on public policy and practice. Many of the UK's commissions set up by governments to examine ER issues of the day were influenced and staffed by people with such a focus. This influence can still be discerned. More contemporary examples include the Low Pay Commission and the Bain Commission on the fire service.

Strategic choice

Some of the criticisms of Dunlop led his fellow Americans to build on his approach. They introduced into the arena the important concept of 'strategic choice' and the idea of applying it at three levels, as in Table 5.1 (Kochan et al., 1984). These were as follows:

- *Strategic.* This level comprised the strategies, values and structures of parties. Here we may ask questions such as, how does business strategy affect ER? For example, we might compare a business strategy that emphasises product differentiation and innovation with one seeking to minimise labour costs (see Chapter 1).

- *Functional.* This level represented the actual process and results of contract negotiation. The discussion of strikes, bargaining power and wage determination could feature prominently here.

- *Workplace.* This level illustrated the activities in which employees, their supervisors and union representatives engaged in administering the labour contract and adjusting to changing circumstances and new problems on a daily basis. Here there are topics such as managing conflict, motivation, participation and supervision of individual workers, and structuring of work into jobs, groups or teams.

Table 5.1 Strategic choice in industrial relations

	Nature of decisions			
Decision level	*Employers*	*Unions*	*Government*	
1. Macro or global level for the key institutions	The strategic role of human resources: policies on unions; investments; plant location; new technology; and outsourcing	Political roles (e.g. relationship with political parties and other interest groups); union organising (e.g. neutrality and corporate campaigns); public policy objectives (e.g. labour law reform); and economic policies (e.g. full employment)	Macro-economics and social policies – industrial policy	
2. Employment relationships and industrial relations systems	Personnel policies and negotiations and strategies	Collective bargaining policies and negotiations and strategies	Labour employment standards law; direct involvement via incomes policies or dispute settlements	
3. Workplace: individuals and groups	Contractual or bureaucratic and individual employee workgroup participation	Policies on employee participation; introduction of new technology; work organisation design	Regulation of working rights and/or employee participation	

Source: Kochan et al. (1984).

Goals and expectations

Importantly, this model is driven by the goals and expectations of the actors. How the actors go about achieving their goals is through institutional structures and processes. It is through these structures and processes that parties interact and make choices that, together with forces in their environment, determine the extent to which their goals are met.

Options and choice

The model emphasises the range of options that management, labour and government have in responding to environmental changes (such as increased competition or changes in technology). Although the environment is vitally important, there is also, it is suggested, a degree of choice at all three levels.

Another useful addition is the idea of strategic choice and ER decisions being of a 'third order' (Purcell, 1987). This presents ER as 'downstream' of other strategies for organisations. This can be seen diagrammatically in Figure 5.2.

Frames of reference

An important development for ER concerned ideas about the basic structures and roles of organisations.

Question to think about 5.4

How do you personally view the authority structures of the enterprise and management?

Within organisations, are we 'all in it together', part of a team harmoniously pulling in the same direction with similar ambitions, desires, and so on? If so, how do we explain some of the conflicts and issues we have in relation to work? The classic work of Fox (1966) explained that two views may be taken of the enterprise and managerial conceptions of its authority structure, i.e. on the nature, function and legitimacy of trade unions. These are discussed next.

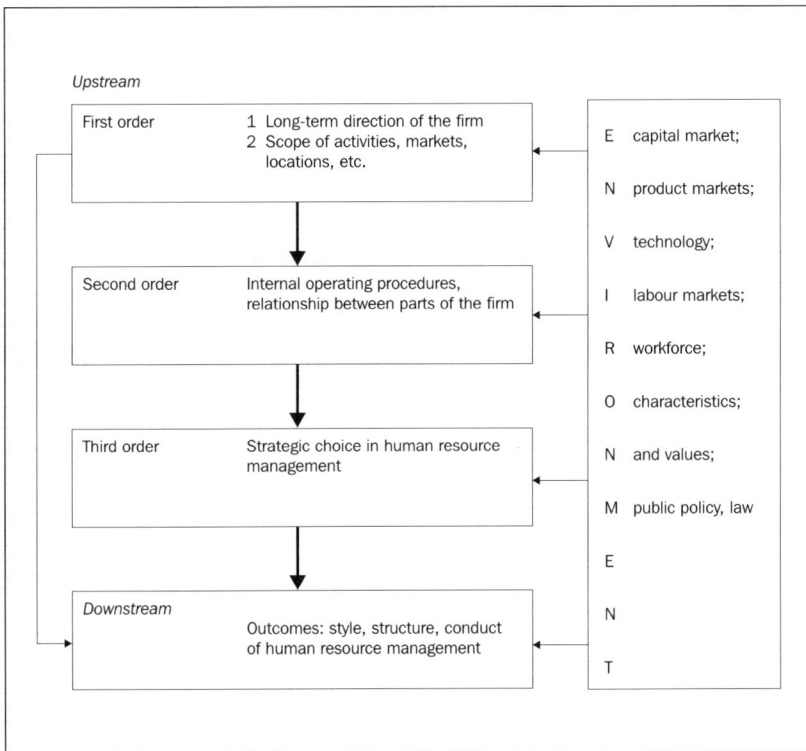

Figure 5.2 Three levels of strategic decision making.
(*Source*: Purcell, 1987.)

Unitarist perspective

In the unitary perspective, the organisation has a unified authority structure with common objectives and values, i.e. there is one source of authority and focus of loyalty – 'a team'. Thus it can be argued here that we '...strive jointly towards a common objective, each pulling his weight to the best of his ability. Each accepts his place and his function gladly, following the leadership of the one so appointed. There are no oppositionary groups or factions, and therefore no rival leaders within the team. Nor are there any outside it; the team stands alone, its members owe allegiance to their own leader but to no other' (Fox, 1966).

Pluralist perspective

In the alternative pluralist perspective, the organisation comprises a coalition of individuals with diverse objectives and values. Here is can be argued that '...the organisation is seen as a pluralistic society, containing many related but separate interests and objectives which must be maintained in some kind of equilibrium' (Fox, 1966). For example, management has to balance the interests of various people, i.e. shareholders, directors, customers, employees: they must sometimes act against the interests of the workforce.

In addition to these, it is worthwhile noting here another possible perspective, a radical view. This is a modification of Marxist analysis. This perspective denies that there can be any common interest in the employment relationship.

To cast further light onto these concepts, the reader needs to reflect and sit back a little. A good way of tackling this is to read a range of different newspapers, such as *The Times*, the *Daily Telegraph*, the *Guardian* or *The Financial Times*, that cover the same employment issue, such as a strike (see Task 5.1 earlier). Was the story covered and reported in the same way in all the papers? If not, why not? Which one was presenting 'the facts'? After all, don't the facts speak for themselves?

With the pluralistic view, it follows that some conflict is inherent in the very nature of ER. It is then as important for management to accept that some conflict of interest is inevitable as it is for unions and employees to accept that there are some common interests (in particular, the success of the enterprise). With its growing acceptance in the early postwar decades of this proposition, collective bargaining became increasingly considered by many as the best method of resolving these differences of interest. It was described as such by the Whitley Committee back in 1917, and repeated over the next 50 years in a plethora of documents and public policy positions. These included the Labour government's Donovan Royal Commission in 1968 and White Paper *In Place of Strife*, in 1969; and the Conservative government's 1971 IR Act and 1972 IR Code of Practice. However, from the 1980s onwards there was a reaction to such views among managers and successive Conservative governments, with a strong movement towards the unitary view. A battery of laws was introduced reflecting this different, unitary, ethos. Post-1997, with the return to Labour governance, the approach changed again. There has been some movement back towards pluralism, but the exact extent of this is blurred and hotly contested. This is partly because there has been both legislative change and continuity.

The primary thread running through ER is that labour is more than a commodity to be exchanged in the open competitive market and more than a set of 'human resources' to be allocated to serve the goals of the firm (Blyton and Turnbull, 1998). Rather, as workers bring their own goals, expectations and aspirations to the workplace, ER is also concerned with how the policies governing ER, and the work itself, affect workers and their interests, as well as the interests of the firm and the larger society (ibid.). Nevertheless, conflicts should be limited in scope and frequency since the parties' goals are interdependent, and common and shared (at least to some degree). The essence of an effective employment relationship is, therefore, one in which the parties both successfully resolve issues arising from their conflicting interests and pursue joint gains in cases where they share common interests (ibid.).

Individualism versus collectivism

There are other useful perspectives to consider in ER. Another way to view ER is in terms of individualism versus collectivism and its variants. By individualism we mean the degree management asserts the individual nature of the relationship with employees in ER. By collectivism we mean the amount of collective focus in the relationships in ER. This also allows the production of a set of ER regimes at societal level.

Furthermore, not only do we find these different perspectives in ER, but their prevalence over time, and across different countries, has varied. This can be seen if we make a quick, broadbrush coverage of UK history over the last few hundred years in order to locate developments and ground the contemporary situation.

Liberal individualism/laissez-faire

Along with industrialisation in the nineteeth century came a belief in liberal individualism or laissez-faire: the belief that everything should be determined by the free play of markets. Thus employment contracts were freely entered into by relatively equal people capable of pursuing their own best interests. Any combination would adversely affect the free market mechanism, which, if left to itself, would ensure the greatest possible good for all.

Liberal collectivism

From the late nineteenth century onwards, liberal collectivism developed. This was 'liberal' in the sense that the role of the state was limited. Simultaneously, this was 'collective' in the sense that parties were free to engage in collective bargaining.

Corporatism

After the Second World War, and particularly during the 1960s and 1970s, a greater degree of government involvement developed in cooperation between the ER parties. This was seen in a range of examples, including incomes policies, the establishment of tripartite mechanisms involving government and employer and employee representatives, and so on, reaching its zenith in the 'Social Contract'. By the late 1970s, such approaches had been undermined. On the one side, opposition grew to the view that unrepresentative trade union 'barons', not elected politicians, were now running the country. This was via 'shady deals', as encapsulated in the phrase 'beer and sandwiches at Number 10', pictures of union leaders leaving Downing Street and even opinion polls listing union general secretaries as more powerful than the Prime Minister of the day. On the other side, some people wanted a return to 'free' collective bargaining and the end of union use in macro economic policy, i.e. to help keep inflation under control via income policies. This tension eventually erupted in the 'Winter of Discontent' in late 1978 with its widespread disruption and very public industrial conflicts. Yet such approaches remained the norm in other countries, for instance the Scandinavian system, South Korea in the 1990s and the succession of social partnership agreements in Ireland since 1987 and in Australia in the 1980s and 1990s (see text boxes below).

Ireland's understandings

Ireland has a long history not only of a centralised approach to wage determination, the first National Wages Policy being in 1948, but also of its integration with a social dialogue between government, management and unions. The First Programme for Economic Expansion (1959) was directed towards the involvement of trade unions on consultative bodies established to plan the development of Ireland's industrial sector and promote employment rather than contain wage conflict.

During the late 1960s Ireland experienced increasing wage conflict and in 1970 an Employer/Labour Conference was established as an alternative to the introduction of a statutory incomes policy. Its objective was to rationalise pay bargaining by setting wage rates across the country. It concluded six National Wage Agreements during the 1970s; up to 1975 this was done on a bipartite basis but from 1975 the government played a more active role (albeit as a part of the employer representation). However, towards the latter part of the 1970s there was increasing pressure from both employers and trade unions to shift the focus of bargaining away from the centralised level. The government responded in 1979 by negotiating a National Understanding for

---

Economic and Social Development directly with employers and trade unions containing sections on employment, taxation and social welfare issues as well as a pay agreement (this was followed by a second National Understanding in 1980).

The Understanding broke down largely because the government was unable to achieve its economic and social policy commitment and employers continued to pressure for decentralisation of pay bargaining. Consequently, there were no centralised agreements for much of the 1980s. However, in 1987 the government managed to gain acceptance, from not only unions and employers but also other interested groups, for a Programme for National Recovery which set out agreed general guidelines for pay and a reduction in hours (to be implemented through local bargaining) and targets for government economic and social policy (including encouraging developments in employee involvement).

A new Programme for Competitiveness and Work was concluded in 1994, followed by Partnership 2000 for Inclusion, Employment and Competitiveness in 1996. The significance of this latter 'understanding' lies in the larger role for other interested groups in the discussions leading up to the agreement (particularly those representing the unemployed and voluntary organisations) and the inclusion of clauses not only allowing for limited locally agreed increases but also committing the parties to promoting industrial harmony (by referring disputes to the Labour Relations Commission, Labour Courts or other third-party mechanism) and developing a partnership approach at the organisation level.

Sources: F. von Prondzynski, 'Ireland: corporatism revived', in A. Ferner and R. Hyman (eds), *Changing Industrial Relations in Europe*, Blackwell, 1998; 'New national pay deal agreed', *European Industrial Relations Review*, no. 277, February 1997, pp. 24–5 and 30–31.

(*Source*: Salamon, 2000: 296.)

The Australian 'Accord'

In Australia an 'accord' was drawn up between the Australian Labour Party and the Australian Council for Trade Unions prior to the 1982 election and encompassed a broad rage of issues including legislation, taxation, social security, investment policy and non-wage incomes as well as wages. After the election the Accord was endorsed by a National Economic Summit Conference which brought together not just government (both federal and state level), employers and unions but also representatives of welfare groups. The Accord moved into its Mark VIII version in 1995.

During the first half of the 1980s the wage part of the Accord provided for wage indexation (linked to increases in cost of living) within centralised awards. Most unions accepted this and those which tried to obtain pay increases outside the Accord were not only unsuccessful but unsupported by the rest of the union movement. However, the government withdrew its commitment to full wage indexation in 1985 (at a time of severe economic crisis) and the wage award increases during the second half of the 1980s became more dependent on unions agreeing to measures which enhanced productivity and performance and improved 'structural efficiency'. During the 1990s the emphasis moved towards the development of enterprise agreements, with the centralised award acting as a 'safety-net' minimum increase.

Whitfield believes that the Accord was more successful than the UK's 'social contract' of the 1970s because there was a stronger link between the political party and the union movement; the Australian unions were facing a worse economic situation and did not have the same confidence as the UK unions following their 'defeat' of the Heath government; and the Australian arbitration system not only provided for a more centralised collective bargaining system but also was able to implement the policy in a more flexible way than had been the case in the UK.

Sources: K. Whitfield, 'The Australian wage system and its labor market effects', *Industrial Relations*, vol. 27, no. 2, 1988, pp. 149–65; K. Hancock and J. E. Isaac, 'Australian experiments in wage policy', *British Journal of Industrial Relations*, vol. 30, no. 2, 1992, pp. 213–36; E. M. Davis and R. D. Lansbury, 'Employment relations in Australia', in G. J. Bamber and R. D. Lansbury (eds), *International and Comparative Employment Relations* (3rd edn), Sage, 1998, pp. 125–30.

(*Source*: Salamon, 2000: 297.)

Individualism/neo-laissez-faire

From the 1980s such corporatism was weakened and swept aside with a return, not so much to liberal collectivism, but essentially to individualism or neo-laissez-faire. Much pro-union support and legislation was repealed and replaced by anti-trade union laws in a step-by-step approach which whittled away union foundations in a 'softly softly' manner. This approach was in stark contrast to the 'big bang' approach of the former attempts at ER changes in the 1970s, which had failed partly because they united opposition against changes. Individual employment protection was also eroded. By 1997 the ER legal terrain was dramatically different than in the earlier period.

Social democratic liberalism/individualism

Since 1997 and the return of the Labour party to government there has been a re-evaluation in terms of ER. On the one hand, there has been much criticism that Labour was all 'style over substance' and little had changed in the ER arena. This was seemingly supported by Labour's pronouncements that the previous Conservative trade union legislation would not be repealed and that the UK had one of the most flexible labour markets in Europe which it needed to maintain. Yet, on the other hand, there was increasing vocal criticism by business interests regarding what they presented as the over-regulation of the economy, part of which concerned employment. However, on balance the welter of employment changes, from individual to collective, from more individual employment protection to the ground-breaking (in the UK context) National Minimum Wage to trade union recognition rights, has noticeably changed the pre-1997 ER legal position. While clearly the Labour government does not want to be seen as 'going back to the future' by being beholden to trade unions, it also needs to put a distance between itself and other political parties on employment issues. This is a tricky balancing act, not least because the trade unions not only founded the Labour party, but have also continued to provide it with members, funds and facilities. While at one time this was seen as a historical anachronism, in the contemporary climate of party funding from wealthy benefactors and the PR fallout, this seems less the case.

Versions of these perspectives can be seen diagrammatically in Figure 5.3. This indicates a range of models using dimensions of varying trade union power and political ideology.

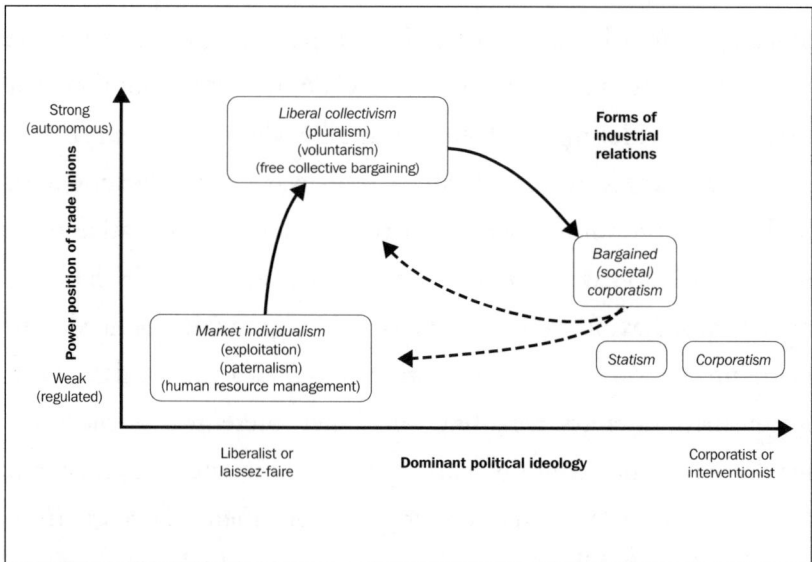

Figure 5.3 Governmental approaches to industrial relations.
(*Source*: Salamon, 2000: 286.)

Partnership

Following Labour's election in 1997 came renewed interest in ideas of workplace partnership and deals. These were trumpeted as the way forward for ER, especially in the context of 'New Labour'. A range of organisations and trade unions signed such agreements, and they received senior political endorsement and encouragement. There had been some developments during the previous 18 years of Conservative rule whereby some businesses and management had tried to change and re-cast 'traditional' ER. This was labelled by some commentators as 'The New IR'.

Such 'New IR' changes involved reconfiguring trade union recognition and bargaining arrangements in order to try to get 'simplification'. For instance, in companies where multiple unions were recognised, there were attempts to move to either 'single-table bargaining' (with all the different unions bargaining together) or single-union recognition (with commensurate de-recognition of the other unions). If the enterprise was new, only single-union recognition would be offered from the start. This union would then represent all in the company, as with enterprise unions, such as in Japan (see text box). This could well be preceded by what was called a 'beauty contest' for management to pick its favoured union. One of the best-known examples of the latter is Nissan's recognition of the AEEU (now Amicus) at its new Sunderland factory on a greenfield site.

Japan – enterprise unionism

Japanese trade unions originated with its industrial revolution in the late nineteenth century and, like their counterparts in Europe and the

---

USA, initially developed as craft and subsequently industrial unions. However, like Germany, the Second World War and immediate postwar occupation had a significant effect. As part of the reconstruction, 'enterprise' unionism became clearly established. Several factors have been put forward for this development:

- Quickest way for US occupation officials to re-establish trade unionism;

- Built on the 'product support organisations' that had been created during the war to enhance the war effort;

- Support from the left wing who saw workplace-level activists providing a counter-balance to the right-wing union leadership outside the enterprise;

- Conforms with Japanese culture and other social structural relationships.

Japan has approximately 71,000 'enterprise' unions (the highest number of unions in any country) encompassing both manual and non-manual employees in a particular company or establishment. However, their membership is limited to 'regular' employees (part-time or temporary workers are not entitled to join) and the level of unionisation in small organisations is low. Consequently, trade unionism is associated with the élite of permanent employees in larger organisations (core employees) – about one third of total employment in Japan. The law prohibits employer domination of unions and does not provide any mechanism for granting *exclusive* recognition – this has arisen from the employers' willingness to agree to a 'union shop'. Unions are dependent, to some degree, on the privileges and facilities provided by the management (including, in some cases, union officials being 'seconded' on full pay by the company to undertake their duties). While this may lead to some unions becoming 'incorporated' into the managerial process, other are clearly 'independent' of management.

The unions have been willing to cooperate with management work strategies because their membership is largely insulated from much of their effects by the surrounding non-unionised, marginal, peripheral workers. Enterprise unionism has, up to now, been supported, at least in part, by the concept of strong internal labour market and 'lifetime employment'. If, as seems possible because of the change in Japan's economic position, employers draw back from this commitment, it may erode the barrier between 'permanent' employees and others in the organisation (they may see themselves having more in common). At the same time, employee attachment to a single organisation may decline if they have to consider moving to look for a new job. This may have the effect of shifting attention more to the inter-enterprise aspects of trade unionism.

It is a misconception that Japanese trade unionism is confined only to the enterprise level. Most 'enterprise' unions belong to one of 100+ national industrial federations. While the enterprise union has a high level of autonomy and is self-supporting and financially independent, nevertheless the industrial federation has a role in coordinating their bargaining activities, dealing with common industrial problems and acting as a political pressure group. In addition, there are a limited number of unions which organise on a craft, occupational or industrial level, for example, *Kaiin* (the Seamen's union).

There are three central trade union confederations: Rengo (the largest, with 60 per cent of all trade union members and covers all sectors), Zenroren (covering the public sector) and Zenrokyo (covering the service sector).

Sources: Y. Kuwahara, 'Employment relations in Japan', in G. Bamber and R. Lansbury (eds), *International and Comparative Employment Relations* (3rd edn), Sage, 1998; J. Benson, 'Japanese unions: managerial partner or worker challenge?', *Labour and Industry*, vol. 6, no. 2, 1995; D. H. Whittaker, 'Labour unions and industrial relations in Japan: crumbling pillar or forging a "third way"?', *Industrial Relations Journal*, vol. 29, no. 4, 1998.

(*Source*: Salamon, 2000: 204.)

Often a key aspect of such single union deals was the idea of what came to be labelled 'no-strike agreements', with compulsory 'pendulum' arbitration. However, not only are such agreements impossible to enforce, they are better seen as 'strike-last agreements'. For instance, how would you actually prevent employees from walking off the job? Ideas of pendulum arbitration have come from the USA. They were a possible method to prevent the 'chilling' of negotiations which occurred as sides simply waited to go to arbitration. Parties were then forced to make realistic demands and offers and reduce the extreme cases that were often made to try to maximise/minimise awards as it was common that positions were split down the middle, making moderate proposals unlikely. In contrast, with pendulum arbitration the most reasonable cases would be presented by both sides, as such 'split' awards were not allowed. It was either the whole of one offer or the other that had to be decided on. So, positions would now be the most reasonable in order to attract the arbitrator's decision (the pendulum).

International comparisons of employee relations

There are difficult issues in the area of conflict resolution (see earlier Overview and text boxes by Rowley). The international diversity in this area can also be seen in countries such as Switzerland, the USA and Australia (see text boxes below).

Australia – compulsory arbitration

The Australian system of compulsory arbitration was developed in the 1890s at a time of extensive and often bitter industrial conflict. It was regarded as a 'bold social experiment' intended to promote greater justice and equality in wage determination. Subsequently, it has become

---

an integral and dominant part of the collective bargaining arrangements with some 80 per cent of employees, public and private sectors alike, being covered by awards or agreements made under the system.

The federal Australian Industrial Relations Commission (AIRC) has power to intervene in 'disputes' which cover more than one state. However, the term 'dispute' does not require the existence, or threat, of industrial action before the AIRC may act, but simply the existence of a difference between a union and employer. The parties are under an obligation to refer a 'dispute' to the Commission or the AIRC may take the initiative to intervene in the 'public interest'. Although the public proceedings of the Commission are relatively formal, the Commissioner may break the proceedings to 'come down from the bench' for informal private discussions with the parties to conciliate a settlement.

In the late 1980s the AIRC was handling some 4,000–5,000 cases a year which can be divided into four categories (3: 102):

- *One-off disputes* about a particular issue;

- *Industry cases* relating to varying a sectoral award;

- *National test cases* concerned with innovations in particular conditions of employment (such as shorter working week or maternity leave);

- *National Wage Cases* which seek a general improvement in wage levels.

It is the *National Wage Cases* (generally an annual event) which have tended to standardise and centralise the Australian wage system and which are important in relation to the government's incomes policy. The government's active participation in such cases (presenting its own evidence of the 'national interest') creates a tripartite rather than bipartite arbitration process. The AIRC's approach to determining National Wage Awards has changed over the years (2: 111–116). In the beginning, in 1907, a 'basic wage' was fixed on 'the normal needs of an average employee … living in a civilised community'. In the 1920s 'margins' were introduced to provide for skill differentials. In 1967, the two elements were amalgamated into a 'total' award.

In the 1970s and early 1980s the primary focus was on restricting 'over-award' payments (increases above the award level negotiated directly between unions and employers) while introducing indexation in federal awards (automatic cost-of living adjustments). The concept of 'comparative wage justice' appears to have been the major guiding factor in AIRC decisions rather than 'capacity to pay' (3: 104).

However, decisions in the late 1980s became conditional on unions and employers discussing measures to improve 'structural efficiency'. In the 1991 decision the AIRC, having previously 'expressed reservations about the ability and maturity of the parties to effectively engage in enterprise bargaining', nevertheless declared itself 'prepared, on balance, to determine an enterprise bargaining principle' (4: 65).

However, the system does not simply replace negotiations between management and unions; rather, such negotiations are carried out within the procedures of statutory tribunals and the framework of their awards. Indeed, the system allows for 'consent' awards (agreements which are registered with the tribunal or commission to confirm and give legal effect to the result of voluntary negotiations).

Sources:

1. K. F. Walker, 'Compulsory arbitration in Australia', in J. J. Loewenberg *et al.*, *Compulsory Arbitration*, Lexington Books, 1976.

2. E. M. Davis and R. D. Lansbury, 'Employment relations in Australia', in G. J. Bamber and R. D. Lansbury (eds), *International and Comparative Employment Relations* (3rd edn), Sage, 1998.

3. K. J. Mackie, 'Lessons from Down-Under: conciliation and arbitration in Australia', *Industrial Relations Journal*, vol. 18, no. 2, 1987, pp. 100–16.

4. R. Lansbury and J. Niland, 'Managed decentralization? Recent trends in Australian industrial relations and human resource policies', in R. Locke, T. Kochan and M. Piore (eds), *Employment Relations in a Changing World Economy*, MIT Press, 1995, pp. 59–90.

(*Source*: Salamon, 2000: 468.)

Switzerland – peace obligation in collective agreements

Switzerland has the lowest incidence of industrial action of any Western industrialised country (generally less than one working day lost per year per 1,000 employees). This may be attributed to three factors:

1. *Industrial structure*: 60 per cent of the working population are employed in the service sector, its manufacturing is primarily high-quality specialised products and it is dominated by small and medium-sized organisations (all factors associated *with lower strike-proneness*).

2. *Political system*: a broad consensual approach involves acceptance that all major political groups should be represented in government and both employers' and workers' organisations are closely involved in the lawmaking process. This is underpinned by the system of direct democracy which allows any group, on presentation of a petition with 50,000 signatures, to challenge legislation through a nation-wide referendum.

3. *Industrial relations*: most collective agreements contain 'peace obligations'.

Collective bargaining is restricted to the private sector and, unlike other European countries, there is a virtual absence of statutory collective labour law relating to trade unions, Works Councils, industrial action or collective agreements. However, under the Code of Obligations (the general law relating to contract and tort), collective agreements are regarded as legally binding contracts and therefore the use of coercion (industrial action) to settle any *dispute of right* relating to matters covered by the agreement is precluded. More importantly, as a consequence of management insistence, two-thirds of collective agreements go further and contain an 'absolute' or 'unlimited' peace obligation which precludes the use of industrial action on any matter during the term of the agreement (i.e. including *disputes of interest* relating to matters not covered by the existing agreement). The peace obligation ceases when the collective agreement expires.

The system of voluntary absolute peace obligations was first introduced in 1937 in the watchmaking and metalworking industries (with government support) as an alternative to the government's measures in the previous year to introduce compulsory arbitration to prevent wage increases following the devaluing of the Swiss franc. The system became more prevalent from the 1950s as part of the general expansion of trade union recognition and collective bargaining following a period of high-strike activity during the late 1940s.

The arbitration tribunals are relatively legalistic in that they are chaired by a judge (accompanied by one union and one employer nominee) and take place in a courtroom. The tribunal may, before making a formal arbitration award, put forward a mediation proposal for the parties to consider and hopefully form the basis of their own settlement. Any breach of the peace obligation may result in a fine (not as a form of compensatory damages but rather to maintain the integrity of the agreement).

Sources: G. Aubert, 'Collective agreements and industrial peace in Switzerland', *International Labour Review*, vol. 128, no. 3, 1989, pp. 373–88; 'Switzerland: the role of arbitration tribunals', *European Industrial Relations Review*, no. 224, September 1992, pp. 22–3; 'Switzerland: industrial relations background', *European Industrial Relations Review*, no. 240, January 1994, pp. 30–3; R. Fluder and B. Hotz-Hart, 'Switzerland: still as smooth as clockwork?', in A. Ferner and R. Hyman, *Changing Industrial Relations in Europe*, Blackwell, 1998, pp. 262–82.

(*Source*: Salamon, 2000: 276.)

USA – compulsory arbitration in essential services

After the comprehensive approach of World War II (during which some 20,000 disputes were handled in five years), the emphasis of compulsory arbitration shifted towards the maintenance of essential services.

In 1947 (following a high level of strike activity) a number of states sought to establish legislation to restrict strikes and provide for compulsory arbitration in a range of essential services such as electricity, gas, water, fuel, etc. However, these industries were in the private sector and became the subject of a series of successful legal challenges based on the Taft–Hartley Act (1947) which applied to all employees other than government employees and which permitted strikes. Consequently, most of these laws failed.

In the public sector it was not until the 1960s that federal and state government employees were permitted to organise and bargain on a collective basis. However, many state legislatures were, at the same time, anxious to maintain a restriction on the employee's right to strike – particularly those employees involved in public safety – and consequently provided for compulsory arbitration in respect of specific groups such as police, firemen, prison guards or, more generally in some states, any essential service or where there was a danger to public health or safety. Thus, effective compulsory arbitration only applies to a very limited range of government employees and, perhaps more importantly, was introduced at a time when trade union recognition and collective bargaining were still in their initial stages of development.

Most agreements in both the private and public sectors provide, ultimately, for arbitration to resolve 'rights disputes'. These decisions have become built up into a quasi-'body of law' which many organisations refer to – whether unionised or not.

Sources: J. J. Loewenberg, 'Compulsory arbitration in the United States', J. J. Loewenberg, W. J. Gershenfeld, H. J. Glasbeek, B. A. Hepple and K. F. Walker, *Compulsory Arbitration*, Lexington Books, 1976; H. N. Wheeler and J. A. McClendon, 'Employment relations in the United States', in G. J. Bamber and R. D. Lansbury (eds), *International and Comparative Employment Relations* (3rd edn), Sage, 1998, pp. 63–88.

(*Source*: Salamon, 2000: 470.)

Classic problems with such processes are as follows. As with other forms of third-party intervention, either side could use this process to opt out of any responsibility for outcomes. The sides lose control over the situation. It means the sides are presented as wholly 'right' or 'wrong'. Yet negotiations are rarely about single issues, but about several. This creates problems for such arbitration.

More recent partnership plans, in some respects, can be seen as a continuation of such trends. However, from 2002 in particular, partnership came to be questioned by some of the former leading lights of the trade union movement, notably Amicus. This was part of a general disillusionment with the Labour government and the election of a new generation of trade union leaders. Ironically, these officials have sprung from the Conservatives' earlier legislation forcing union leadership ballots. These plans came to be presented as 'sweetheart' deals and too employer-friendly, with no time off being allowed for union work and no right to negotiate pay and conditions. They had been concluded after unseemly 'beauty contests' for sole recognition. There are increasing threats within industry to renegotiate these deals, due to changes in union leadership and the perceived failure of agreements to 'deliver'.

The future of employee relations

The area of ER has evolved, as it has always done, partly driven by business and management, as well as state, concerns. As long as there is a labour process then there will be ER and the need to understand where it has come from and what drives its actors. Long-term predictions of a radical change in ER, for example with the demise of conflict and trade unions, have often been unfounded. One of the perennial interests of ER, both in terms of a 'cause' and 'cure', is employee involvement, a flexible and heterogeneous term that can cover a wide range of practices, but each with radically different implications. This has become an even hotter topic, not least driven by practices, ideas and regulations from Europe.

Employee involvement

The importance of employee involvement to ER, and HRM more generally, is often seen as trying to create a sense of belonging and commitment via information about the organisation and its environment. A key management task is to decide if, and how, to share information. This is critical as in many situations management initiate such processes and are critical to their success. Therefore, a lack of action amounts to a decision not to share information, or a lack of interest. It is primarily management's responsibility to create the conditions and establish the policies and practices to promote effective employee involvement.

Question to think about 5.5

Why is employee involvement often seen as a cure for a range of management and organisational problems?

There has been a whole range of reasons for interest in employee involvement. These include those listed in Table 5.2.

It is this great diversity that partly gives rise to a kaleidoscopic concept, exacerbated by the terms employed – 'involvement', 'participation' and so on – used interchangeably, despite the gaps in their implications, such as level, power sharing and so on. Therefore we need to make some broad distinctions from the start. With this in mind, we can see the concept of employee involvement within a framework, as in Figures 5.4 and 5.5.

Table 5.2 Reasons for interest in employee involvement

Factor	Aspects
Efficiency	Improve organisationally
Change	Make more acceptable
Commitment	Enhanced via inclusion
Learning	From employee knowledge and skills
Social	Increased aspirations, reduced alienation
Control	Redefine managerial authority

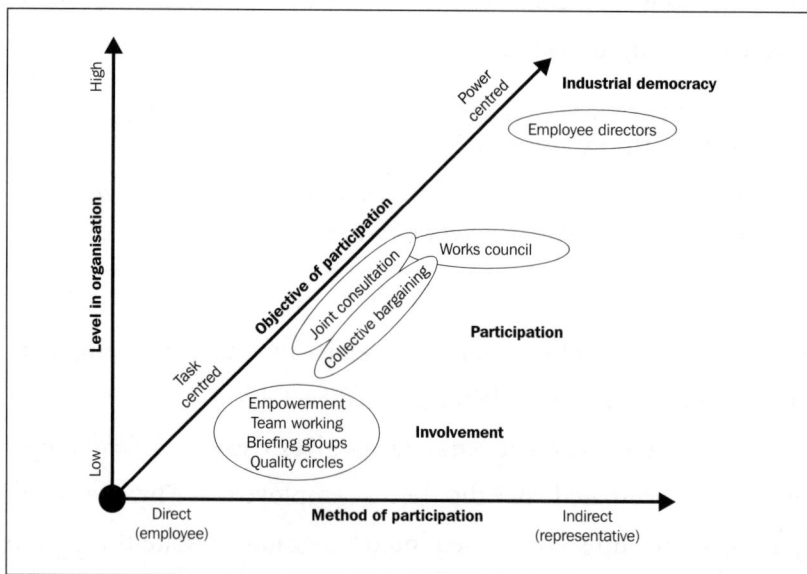

Figure 5.4 Employee involvement framework and forms. (*Source*: Salamon, 2000: 373.)

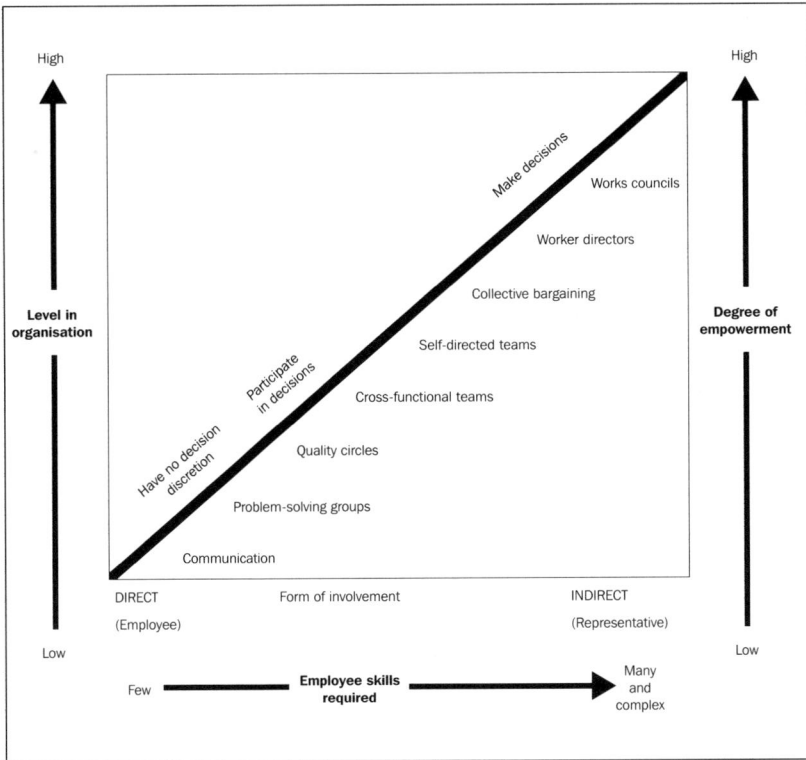

Figure 5.5 Dimensions of employee involvement.
(*Source*: Bratton and Gold, 1999.)

These frameworks usefully and clearly indicate that there are variations in the area of employee involvement, in several dimensions, including method or extent, objective or scope, and level.

Such frameworks also usefully display the differences in forms and types. As Salamon (2000: 374) put it: 'It is the nature and quality of the process of interaction which determines the extent or depth to which employees (individually, in groups or through their representatives) are allowed and able to contribute to and influence organisational decisions (whether operational or strategic).' He goes on, 'This may range from only informing by management though consultation to negotiation and finally co-determination (equal influence in both setting the agenda as well as deciding the outcome or organisational decision making).' Interestingly, he concludes, 'Participation is primarily a philosophy, not a particular institutional form … Therefore, it can take place at any time and in any organisational framework so long as management is genuinely and unreservedly prepared to share responsibility for the decision-making process with employees and/or their representatives.' Nevertheless, to help understanding, some further details will be useful.

Forms of employee involvement

There is a vast array of examples of employee involvement. These have some specific and common advantages and disadvantages.

Question to think about 5.6

What forms of employee involvement have you experienced?

Communication

At a basic level there is communication. Communication can be both one-way and two-way.

One-way communication

With one-way communication, information is given. Its objective is to try to ensure that all HRs know and understand what they and

---

others in the company are doing and why. There is a huge variety of practices here, and these are widespread. They include noticeboards, letters, newspapers, magazines (for example, ICI's staff magazine started in 1927), employee reports, in-company videos, performance appraisals (see Chapter 4), oral presentations, and so on. One of the more commonly reported systems is what is called team briefing.

Team briefing

This is a system of communication, variously labelled, operated often by line management. It is commonly based on leaders and their teams getting together in groups on a regular basis. Information is 'cascaded' down through organisational levels and management tiers via supervisors to small groups. Part of the team brief normally has core information relating to corporate issues. This is supplemented by local news at each stage. Team briefing is not new. It was pioneered in the UK in the 1970s by the Industrial Society, which proposed that team presentations should be relevant to those receiving them: only 30 per cent of information should be related to wider corporate matters, with groups of 5–15 used. Indeed, between 1984 and 1986 it had helped introduce some 400–500 schemes. A survey of 222 large organisations showed that by 1992 some 86 per cent had installed team briefing systems.

Question to think about 5.7

What are the advantages and disadvantages of team briefings?

There are both benefits and problems with team briefing as listed in Table 5.3.

Table 5.3 Benefits of and problems with team briefings

Benefits	Problems
• Reinforces management – allows manager to be seen as a leader • Informs staff – about what they are doing/whether meeting targets • Reduces misunderstandings – weakens grapevine with quick/clean information • Acceptance – understanding of why change is necessary, time to adjust to it	• Can be irregular • 'Dispensable' in times of pressure • Variation between HRs covered • Difference between policy and practice • Top-down and information-giving • Opportunities for feedback, especially on issues not directly related, are limited • Utility of information limited with coverage/ability to use/influence it • Decisions already made

Two-way communications

Unlike simple information-giving, two-way communication attempts to give HRs some 'voice' and feedback. Again, there is a wide variety of methods and practices here. These include the following.

'Speak-out/up' or feedback programmes

Here people can telephone or write, in confidence, to a company representative to raise concerns. They are usually guaranteed a response within a certain period. Examples included large US firms such as Xerox, Caterpillar, Polaroid and IBM.

Open-door programmes

With these, employees can go to see management who are not their immediate supervisors. Examples included firms such as IBM.

'Walking the floor'

Here, senior executives visibly, physically walk around the shop floor and office. This behaviour is both to be seen and to listen, of course.

Sensing groups

With this format, management meet periodically with small random samples of staff. This allows management not only to communicate company policies and goals to the groups, but also to hear employee concerns and suggestions.

Task forces

These groups can be commissioned on various areas and concerns. For example, they can review HRM policies.

Attitude surveys

These are a more systematic means of feedback. This type of survey has spread in usage and can be undertaken either by specialists (for example, NOP or MORI, which conducted surveys in 350 organisations between 1980 and 1990) or in-house. At first sight, this method seems more concerned with measuring commitment than involvement. Yet, research indicates that most staff value opportunities to express their views through such surveys, and see them as a means of having their voice heard. Indeed, some organisations place great store in them. A good example is IBM, which has used surveys regularly since the 1960s. It uses the results to justify its stance on issues such as non-recognition of trade unions. Asda used them for opinions on management and the results were published. The benefits of surveys are numerous. They include the following:

- increased involvement;

- a check that management's perception of the firm's position corresponds to HR's;

- an assessment of the extent to which policies are having the desired effects;

- simply asking for views increases morale.

Suggestion schemes

The history of such practices goes back to the nineteenth century. Dunlop's scheme from 1958 was called 'Bright Spark'. Such systems were given a boost in the 1980s in the UK by the Industrial Society. Often suggestion schemes are seen as only applicable to large manufacturing firms and manual workers, but they are also to be found in the service industry and for white-collar staff, for example banks, building societies and retailing, such as Asda's 'Tell Archie' scheme. With suggestion schemes, staff are invited to submit ideas to improve aspects of organisational performance, for which they are rewarded. There can be several types of award, such as the following:

- 'Encouragement', for effort even if not implemented;

- 'Valued', for a measure leading to clearly quantified savings (fixed amount or percentage of savings);

- 'Special', for savings not easily identified (i.e. health and safety).

Question to think about 5.8

What are the advantages and disadvantages of suggestion schemes?

Both benefits and problems are associated with suggestion schemes. These can be seen in Table 5.4.

Table 5.4 Benefits of and problems with suggestion schemes

Benefits	Problems
• Cost savings • Encourage climate of change • Identify those with creative thinking skills • Innovations • Bypass obstructive management in non-confrontational manner without undermining authority • Opportunities to practise skills of evaluation/implementation of ideas	• Administration, delays in evaluating/rewarding ideas • Small rewards • Practical running, e.g. eligibility (who and what ideas), type of awards, etc. • Conflict – is constant improvement a normal part of job or something to receive extra rewards for? • Disillusionment if not acted upon

Task and work groups

Employee involvement can also occur at a different level and in a different form, as in task and work groups. These have a long history, deriving from the famous Human Relations experiments of the 1920s.

From the 1960s, ideas of job enlargement and enrichment, introducing elements of responsibility into tasks, also developed. The pace in such areas was set by some Scandinavian organisations, such as Saab and Volvo. Examples of such developments include the following.

Autonomous work groups

In 1972 Saab Scania's factory abolished the classic, Fordist mass-production single assembly line moving at fixed rates past workers. In its place were six separate assembly areas, and workers divided work among themselves. Similar experiments occurred at Volvo at its Kalmar and Uddevalla plants. These plants have since closed, but there was debate at the time as to the causes for the closures, including currency movements, and the relative role of forms of working within the decision.

Quality circles (QCs)

Typically these groups are small, with 6–12 members led by a supervisor or team leader in the area. Variously labelled, they are voluntary, meeting regularly in paid (sometimes leisure) time. They identify, select and analyse work-related problems, collect data, present findings and propose solutions for approval and then implement them. Post-1945 came the development of this American idea (set out earlier by people like Deming and Juran) in Japan, where there were over 10 million workers in QCs by the late 1980s. In the 1970s QCs were 'rediscovered' by leading US firms such as Lockheed, and they became more relevant. By the 1980s they had become extremely popular, for example in the UK and Europe (France's Aerospatiale had 30 in the late 1980s) and elsewhere. For instance, in the UK, Ford's search for the elixir of Japanese company success in its 'After Japan' programme led to it focusing on QCs as a chief ingredient. The common requirements for such QCs include the following:

- management convinced of benefits, long-term commitment and resources;

- involvement of middle managers;

- facilitator for administration and development;

- training for leaders and members;

- recognition and publicity of activities to maintain interest.

Question to think about 5.9

What are the advantages and disadvantages of QCs?

There are a range of benefits and problems with QCs, as noted in Table 5.5. There was also the emergence of total quality management (TQM), partly as an alternative means of addressing quality issues. However, TQM is a more integrated approach, with harder objectives, i.e. performance first, rather than involvement.

Teamworking

This has its origins in the UK in its present guise in the practices of Japanese companies such as Komatsu, Hitachi, Nissan and especially Toyota. Post-1990s, teamworking has become more popular.

Table 5.5 Benefits of and problems with quality circles

Benefits	Problems
• Improve quality/reliability of product/service • Cost savings • Increase interest in and commitment to job • Enhance supervisory authority and leadership skills	• Sustaining, have short life/high failure (UK: one in three suspended within three years) • Time/expenses in running, training, disruption, etc. • Challenge notions of authority, seen as criticisms of management • Disinterest – middle management responsible for overseeing, but denied authority, e.g. voluntary, own agenda, not obliged to follow priorities

Empowerment

This term has become fashionable since the 1980s, although it was linked to earlier movements such as the 1970s Quality of Working Life approach. In essence it is about providing the right opportunities and structures (and, of course, the culture) so that HRs can contribute to the organisation. The onus is on management to 'empower' staff (see Rowley, 1999). This is individual, direct involvement in work. A range of benefits flow from this method, such as the need for less direct control, with greater HR autonomy, albeit within certain bounds.

Financial

For some commentators, employees also obtain involvement through particular financial arrangements. This is not a new idea (see also Chapter 3 on employee rewards). Indeed, there are examples from as far back as the early nineteenth century. Nevertheless, a large rise in popularity in the UK took place in the early 1980s, partly with government encouragement (via favourable tax legislation). Arrangements include share ownership: employees gain a direct share in the company they work for; and profit sharing: employees receive a cash bonus from the revenue surplus.

Success of involvement

Several important elements in the success or otherwise of employee involvement have been identified. These can be seen in Table 5.6.

Table 5.6 Elements in the success or failure of employee involvement

Elements	Reasons/characteristics
Management commitment – more than just initiation	Many schemes time-consuming to properly run
Support – throughout the management system	Middle- and lower-level managers often pivotal to implementation
Advance consideration and exposition of objectives	Avoid confusion and conflict between schemes
Training of all those involved	Show commitment, ensure competence and review regularly
Regular monitoring of schemes	Measures set against specified objectives
Problems and shortcomings typical	Should not be unexpected, not least due to concept diversity

International comparisons of employee involvement

There are widespread variations internationally in the meaning and practice of employee involvement. This includes the ideas of industrial democracy, workers on the board, co-determination and works councils. These are more common in European countries, especially Sweden and Germany. There are examples of company councils, such as in the UK, while the idea of works councils has been driven by the EU (see text box and Table 5.7), as have the notions of 'social dialogue' and information and consultation rights.

Northumbrian Water Ltd – Company Council

Northumbrian Water was privatised in 1989 (with most employees becoming shareholders) and, with the abandonment of national-level multi-employer bargaining in the industry, it introduced radical changes in its industrial relations. The objective was 'to move towards an "us" rather than "us and them" approach to employee relations, with one "big team" pulling together' and to model employee representation on the 'democratic parliamentary system' (Company Personnel Adviser) (1: 14).

Before 1989, the company recognised eight unions (NALGO and NUPE (now merged), AEU and EETPU (now merged), GMB, TGWU, APEX and UCATT) and negotiated within three bargaining units (manual, craft and non-manual staff). The initial aim was to replace this with a single union in order to support the development of harmonisation and single-status. However, following union protests, the company agreed to recognise the unions jointly as a Confederation of Northumbrian Water Trade Unions (CNWTU). At the same time, a Northumbrian Water Ltd Employee Association (NWEA) was formed to represent the 17 per cent of the workforce who were not union members.

Management introduced a 'council' system of employee representation to deal directly with employees (rather than through unions) and to integrate negotiation and consultation.

Employee Councils were set up in each operating area for 'constructive discussion' of local issues and to act as an information and discussion channel between the Company Council and employees. The employee 'councillors' were elected by secret ballot in functional 'constituencies' of about 20 employees regardless of job or status.

A *Company Council* was introduced comprising seven 'company councillors' (one for each Employee Council) and four management representatives (including the Managing Director – who chairs the Council, and the Human Resource Director – who acts as secretary). CNWTU and NWEA each had only an 'advisory' seat, although the Council quorum required that one had to be present. The functions of the council are as follows:

- To 'discuss, negotiate, amend and agree' terms and conditions of employment, procedures for grievances and discipline, health and safety and other company-wide issues;

- To consult and advise on 'company-wide issues concerning employee relations';

- To do this within a framework which recognises that 'the development and maintenance of harmonious employee relations is vital to ensure the prosperity of all employees and the company' and which promotes 'trust, care and cooperation in the development and improvement of employee communications, recognition and reward'; and

- All company councillors are expected to 'conduct themselves in such a way as to promote harmony and progress of employee relations'.

The role of the Company Council includes receiving communication of decisions already made by management (information), discussions to provide information prior to a management decision (consultation) as well as discussions to secure Council agreement (negotiation) – the management 'aims for as many items as possible to fall into this category' (2: 15). A sub-committee of the Company Council also acts as the final stage of the Grievance Procedure. Minutes of the Council meetings are put up on notice boards but it is up to the employee councillors to decide whether there should be any further feedback discussion with their constituents.

It is perhaps significant that, in 1991, the first pay negotiations under this new process resulted in backing for management's 'final' offer by the 11 members of the Company council but rejection by the employees in a ballot. Management then brought in an academic consultant to review whether the offer was 'reasonable', following which an improved offer was made and accepted by a majority of the employees.

Sources:

1. 'Industrial relations developments in the water industry', *IRS Employment Trends*, no. 516, July 1992, pp. 13 and 14.

2. 'A question of involvement', *IDS Study*, no. 561, September 1994, pp. 13–15.

(*Source*: Salamon, 2000: 401.)

Conclusion

The area of ER remains as important, but as changeable, as ever. While the focus of the area has shifted, partly reflecting the practical concerns of business, management and governments, the concept of a system of actors with different perspectives remains a useful framework in the understanding of ER. The different actors may wax and wane in their relative influence and power, but their interactions and perspectives remain crucial, not only to the functioning of an economy, but also its competitiveness and types of production (see points on flexiblity in Chapters 1 and 2 and training in Chapter 4).

The area of employee involvement is a diverse and elastic concept, seemingly allowing everyone to support it. It also has a range of benefits for organisations and HRs. Some of the key ideas and practices are not particularly new, although fashions do come and go, as witnessed by

Table 5.7 European Works Councils: examples

	International Service System (Denmark)	United Biscuits (UK)	BP Oil (UK)	Honda Europe NV (Netherlands)
Title:	Council for European Social Dialogue	European Consultative Council	Europe Employee Forum	Communication & Consultation Group
Employee signatories:	FIET (International Federation of Commercial, Clerical, Professional & Technical Employees)	GMB (on behalf of ECF-IUF: the European food industry committee affiliated to ETUC)	Elected employee representatives from 11 BP oil companies	Representatives 'on behalf of' Honda employees in Europe
Aim:	Information and consultation on matters relating to ISS Group: • structure, economic and financial situation; • probable trends in employment and investment; • changes in organisation, work methods, training and safety; • mergers, closures, cut-backs or collective redundancies Committee: 3 employee representatives to be informed and consulted on any plans relating to acquisitions, mergers, relocations or collective redundancies which affect the interests of employees beyond the boundaries of one country	• Joint understanding of the performance of the business, of its operating environment and the marketplaces, and of other matters of genuine mutual concern; • Exchange of information and views between management and employees with the aim of establishing a transnational dialogue	Information and consultation on: • performance and strategy of group; • transnational matters which may have serious implications for interests of employees Link Committee: 5 employee representatives to maintain communication between central management and Employee Forum and to agree Forum agenda (may initiate items)	• The presentation, clarification and understanding of information regarding issues of European activity and/or influence; • The exchange of views and establishment of dialogue over European business subjects which shall be taken into consideration within the company decision-making process.
Frequency of meetings:	Annual plus extra-ordinary meetings	Annual half-day (within one month of announcement of annual results)	Annual 1 day	Annual 2 days (first day communication, second day consultation)
Selection of employee representatives:	(a) elected worker directors (b) elected by enterprise committees or works councils (c) appointed by management in consultation with local unions	Nominated by national trade unions or works councils	In line with national law and practice with the proviso that they must be elected by employees or by members of forums elected by employees	Nominated and elected according to local law and custom and practice
Qualification of employee representatives:	Permanent employees for 1 year	3 years' service	*No information*	Full-time permanent employees
Trade union involvement:	Up to 2 representatives of FIET or any associated union	• 1 UK GMB full-time officer (also representing the ECF-IUF) • 2 other UK union full-time officers (USDAW and TGWU) • 1 non-UK union full-time officer	No direct union involvement	No direct union involvement
Employee side pre-meeting:	Half-day	Half-day	Allowed for	No provision
Dissemination:	(a) Via enterprise committees or works councils or similar body; or (b) To be jointly decided by local subsidiary management and Council employee representative	Joint statement of key points circulated to all sites for briefing to all employees	Report prepared by secretary (Director of Human Resources) and Link Committee chair to be circulated to participants and business managers (to be conveyed to as many employees as possible)	Relevant manager and employee representatives report back together to all employees in their unit

Sources: 'EWC agreement at ISS', *European Works Council Bulletin*, Winter 1995, pp. 13–15; 'The first UK European Works Councils', *European Industrial Relations Review*, no. 251, December 1994, pp. 20–22; 'European Works Councils update – trends and issues', *European Industrial Relations Review*, no. 256, May 1995, pp. 14–22.

Source: Salamon (2000: 405).

ideas of 'industrial democracy' in the 1970s versus 'empowerment' more recently. This also varies internationally, with much development coming via the EU. Yet its various forms have radical differences in their implications for management and businesses.

Overview references

The following short articles illustrate issues and developments in employee relations.

The Financial Times

Bradley, D. (2002) 'Social Planning Comes to Britain', 2 September, p. 13.

Fairclough, M. and Birkinshaw, C. (2001) 'Employee Rights and Management Wrongs', Mastering People Management, Part 7, 26 November, pp. 4–5.

Overell, S. (2002) 'Milestone or Millstone?', 11 October, p. 13.

Sherwood, B. (2002) 'No Firings Without Consultation', 28 October.

These short articles illustrate issues in international differences and conflict resolution.

The Financial Times

Atkins, R. (2001) 'Inspecting the Works Council', 12 January, p. 16.

Bradley, D. (2001) 'A Lesson in Management from a Bowl of Lemons', 3 December, p. 16.

Durr, B. and Cheng, L. (2002) 'How UPS Delivered a New Deal', 1 August, p. 10.

Fenton-O'Creevy, M. (2001) 'HR Practice: Vive La Difference', Mastering People Management, Part 7, 26 November, pp. 6–8.

Fenton-O'Creevy, M. (2001) 'Seeking Success by Involving Workers', Mastering People Management, Part 3, 29 October, pp. 4–5.

Johnson, R. (2002) 'Ireland's Beautiful Marriage Shows Signs of Strain', 12 June, p. 13.

Sacks, M. and Lewis, A. (2001) 'Turning Disputes to Corporate Advantage', Mastering People Management, Part 7, 26 November, pp. 2–3.

Taylor, R. (2001) 'A Bridge to Work's Future', 30 August, p. 14.

See also *Mastering Management Online* (www.ftmastering.com/resource/resource.htm):

Rowley, C. (2002) 'Hitting The Buffers: Labour Disputes and British Railways', Issue 10, February.

Rowley, C. (2002) 'Reversing the Engine: Using Arbitration to Solve Labour Disputes', Issue 12, April.

Rowley, C. (2002) 'Conciliation', in T. Redman and A. Wilkinson (eds), *The Informed Student Guide to HRM*. London: Thomson Learning, p. 39.

Rowley, C. (2002) 'Mediation', in T. Redman and A. Wilkinson (eds), *The Informed Student Guide to HRM*. London: Thomson Learning, p. 157.

References

Beer, M., Spector, B., Lawrence, P., Quinn Mils, D. and Walton, R. (1984) *Managing Human Assets*. New York: Free Press.

Blyton, P. and Turnbull, P. (1998) *The Dynamics of Employee Relations*. London: Macmillan.

Bratton, J. and Gold, J. (1999) *Human Resource Management Theory and Practice*. London: Macmillan.

Dunlop, J. (1958) *Industrial Relations Systems*. New York: Holt.

Flanders, A. (1970) *Management and Unions: Theory and Reform of Industrial Relations*. London: Faber & Faber.

Fox, A. (1966) *Industrial Sociology and Industrial Relations*, Royal Commission Research Paper No. 3. London: HMSO.

Fox, A. (1974) *Beyond Contract: Work, Power and Trust Relations*. London: Faber & Faber.

Hyman, R. (1975) *Industrial Relations: A Marxist Introduction*. London: Macmillan.

Kochan, T., McKersie, R. and Capelli, P. (1984) 'Strategic choice and industrial relations theory', *Industrial Relations*, Winter.

Purcell, J. (1987) 'Mapping Management Styles in Employee Relations', *Journal of Management Studies*, 24, 5: 534–48.

Rowley, C. (1998) 'Allan Flanders', in M. Warner (ed.), *IEBM Handbook of Management Thinking*. London: Thomson Business Press, pp. 195–200.

Rowley, C. (1999) 'HRM in the service sector', *Personnel Review*, 28, 5/6.

Salamon, M. (2000) *Industrial Relations: Theory and Practice*. Harlow: Pearson Education.

Further reading

For those who want further details of any topics covered in this chapter, there are links and references given in some of the above titles, while there are many further books which cover similar ground, such as those listed below.

Albrecht, M. (2001) *International HRM*, Part V. Oxford: Blackwell.

Beardwell, I. and Holden, L. (eds) (2001) *HRM: A Contemporary Perspective*. London: Financial Times/Prentice-Hall (Chapters 10–11, 13–14).

Gennard, J. and Judge, G. (1999) *Employee Relations*. London: CIPD.

Hollinshead, G. and Leat, M. (1995) *HRM: An International Perspective*. London: Financial Times/Prentice Hall (Chapters 3–7).

Hollinshead, G., Nichols, P. and Tailby, S. (eds) (1999) *Employee Relations*. Harlow: Pearson Education.

Keithley, D. (2002) 'Arbitration', in T. Redman and A. Wilkinson (eds), *The Informed Student Guide to HRM*. London: Thomson Learning, pp. 11–12.

Leat, M. (2001) *Exploring Employee Relations*. Oxford: Butterworth-Heinemann.

Marchington, M. and Wilkinson, A. (2002) *People Management and Development*. London: CIPD (Chapters 14–15).

McColl, P. (2002) 'Advisory, Conciliation and Arbitration Service (ACAS)', in T. Redman and A. Wilkinson (eds), *The Informed Student Guide to HRM*. London: Thomson Learning, pp. 4–5.

Pilbeam, S. and Corbridge. M. (2002) *People Resourcing: HRM in Practice*. London: Financial Times/Prentice Hall (Chapters 15–17).

Redman, T. and Wilkinson, A. (eds) (2001) *Contemporary HRM: Text and Cases*. London: Financial Times/Prentice Hall (Chapters 7, 11).

Rose, E. (2001) *Employment Relations*. Harlow: Pearson Education.

Sisson, J. and Storey, J. (2000) *The Realities of HRM*. Buckingham: Open University Press (Chapters 6, 12).

Storey, J. (ed.) (2001) *HRM: A Critical Text*. London: Thomson Learning (Chapters 4, 8, 10).

Thornhill, A., Lewis, P. Millmore, M. and Saunders, M. (2000) *Managing Change: A Human Resource Strategy Approach*. Harlow: Pearson Education (Chapter 8).

CHAPTER 6

Conclusion

Introduction

Over the course of this book we have looked at the key areas of HRM from the perspective of the common tensions inherent within it (see Figure 1.1 in Chapter 1). These differences have implications for perspectives in HRM (see Table 6.1). This includes tension between the common desire to seek universal, simple answers to perennial HRM issues versus the contingent and complex reality of working life and the management of people. Then there is HRM's implicit and inherent long-term time frame versus the common short-termism of many businesses (especially those in an Anglo-American context). For instance, think of the 'payback' from sophisticated recruitment and selection, training and involvement. Furthermore, there is tension between HRM's use by specialist practitioners or line managers, with impacts on areas such as training and time, for the latter, as well as consistency and strategy. There is a further tension in HRM – between espoused versus actual policies and practices. The rhetoric of much management is about the value and importance of people as 'our greatest asset'. Yet this is combined with a continuance of working systems which do not seem to indicate support in practice of this platitude.

Table 6.1 Tensions in HRM perspectives

Tension	Perspective
Universal versus contingent	Implication for best practice
Short versus long	Time frames
Specialist versus line	Delivery
Espoused versus actual	Reality

Therefore, over the course of this book we have examined the key areas in HRM, along with their issues, theories and practice. This has been undertaken in terms of broad areas:

- employee resourcing: in particular, HR planning, recruitment and selection;

- employee rewards: specifically, remuneration and performance-related rewards;

- employee development: in particular, training and employee performance appraisal;

- employee relations: especially the ER system and employee involvement.

Key points

This has resulted in the emergence of a set of key points and conclusions. These include the following.

How is HRM different?

The management of people has a long history, which we broadly traced (Chapter 1). HRM can be seen as either simply the latest twist in this, or a turn that has produced a radically different concept.

Question to think about 6.1

What, if anything, is different between HRM and earlier forms of people management? To what extent is it simply the latest incarnation of people management?

There are supporters of both camps. This is the idea of 'old wine in new bottles' for some commentators. In contrast, for some others, HRM is actually a '… distinctive approach to employment management which seeks to achieve competitive advantage through the strategic deployment of a highly committed and capable workforce, using an integrated array of cultural, structural and personnel techniques' (Storey, 1995: 5). If we take some credence from the latter camp, how is HRM different? We can attempt to make distinctions in terms of three aspects of HRM, which concern its:

- integration

- strategic input and

- line responsibility.

Yet, what is the evidence and likelihood of HRM as conceptualised in this form actually being in existence or developing? It seems the answer to this is 'not a lot'. For instance, much research shows that the take-up of HRM-type initiatives and this strategic quality is not always new, nor proved. This is for several reasons, which include the following.

Conflicts

There are conflicting tendencies and tensions within HRM. Some of these may be mutually exclusive and so actually make the adoption of the 'whole package' somewhat difficult. For example, to what extent can management expect both high commitment and large investments in employee development consistent with high (numerical) flexibility from the same workforce?

Opportunities and constraints

There are HRM-type changes in people management. Yet these reflect pragmatic responses (as has commonly been the case in the area of people management) to opportunities and constraints in the socio-economic and political environment (see Legge, 1995).

Reasons

The reasons for this failure to develop a strategic approach within HRM is due to a set of factors. However, it '… is not just a question of will or conviction, but of deep-seated features' (Storey and Sisson, 1991: 174).

Question to think about 6.2

What might be some of the factors that might help to explain the limited role of HRM in business strategy?

There is a range of possible reasons. These include those noted in Table 6.2. A classic element within this is that there are not many 'true' owners in the UK or US context because: 'The vast majority of shareholders are either small retail investors, or huge pension funds, mutual funds and insurance firms that manage diversified holdings through investment managers ...' (*The Economist*, 2003: 10). These are, in the apt, pithy phrase used in an earlier report, 'punters, not proprietors' (ibid.). These constitute a group of impediments which are mutually reinforcing. Therefore, 'Hopes that HRM would lead to a more strategic approach to the management of human resources have been largely frustrated' (Sisson, 1995: 105).

Table 6.2 Constraints on the development of HRM

Factor	Characteristics
Management composition	• Dominance of financial function • Weakness of HRM at senior levels
Ownership patterns	• Role of institutional investors • Not tied to long-term development
Organisational structures	• Importance of diversification • Multidivisional pattern

Dynamism

The emergence and development of HRM indicates the inherent dynamism and changeable nature of the area of employment and its management. We examined some main practices, methods and implications, and the issues and problems that may arise here. This indicated the need for a questioning approach for dynamism will continue. A PEST (Political, Economic, Social, Technology factors) analysis shows important influences and impacts on this. Thus, management need to be aware of, and keep up with, changes that impact on HRM. Some of the main types of change include the following:

- employee resourcing: workforce diversity and flexibility;

- employee rewards: performance pay and disparities;

- employee development: measurement and the need for long-term perspectives;

- employee relations: partnerships and participation.

Universal recipes or specific ingredients?

One reason that this dynamism is important is that it impacts on ideas of 'best practice' in this field of management. Yet, for one group of commentators the argument remains that if we look hard enough, there are universal panaceas to some of the key issues and practices in people management. This involves the commonality or peculiarity of HRM, the transferability or specificity of its practices. While these are not new issues, they have taken on powerful resonance in the twenty-first century. Part of this has been due to areas such as developments in the European Union and ideas of 'common' employment rights or a 'level playing field', as well as globalisation. This area has been looked at from two perspectives.

Universalism

For this camp, HRM is universal, and this can be over time, sector and place. It is only a question of learning what these HRM techniques are, and then transferring and applying them for maximum impact and benefit. Even if these may have varied before, in an increasingly globalised and swift-changing world they vary less and less.

Contingency

In contrast to this approach, some view management, especially HRM, as specific and unique to its location and context. This is neatly indicated in the following quote: 'Many aspects of management work can be developed into a science: successful personnel management is an art' (Torrington and Hall, 1998: 696). What underpins this 'art' of people management? Factors include both culture (norms, values) and institutions (state, trade unions), which retain salience to and influence on the HRM system (Bae and Rowley, 2001).

International comparisons of HRM

These points can be seen and highlighted if we look at HRM comparatively and internationally. As we have seen throughout the book, there are many differences in the use of HRM internationally between different countries (see examples in Rowley, 1998; Rowley and Benson, 2000; Rowley and Benson, 2003). Japan is a good example here (see first text box). This variability can be seen in one indicative dimension, conflict, as in Asia (see second text box).

Japan: changing strategies of HRM

Many organisations and countries have regarded Japanese HRM practices as an important element in its economic success. However, the HRM practices that organisations have sought to emulate are themselves undergoing re-evaluation and change in Japan – particularly in non-manual areas where productivity has lagged behind that of most Western countries. Morishima argues that 'the Japanese model of HRM is premised on the assumption that firms recruit candidates with the largest learning potential, provide them with continuous training opportunities, and reward them according to the degree to which they have acquired internally relevant job-related skill' (1: 625).

1. *Educational credentialism.* Success in higher education, through limited highly competitive access, is assumed to guarantee the ability and characteristics of future employees (schools and universities compete to select the 'best'). This is often supported by a strong relationship between individual organisations and certain educational institutions (a dependence on and trust in the recommendations from those educational institutions). Consequently, there is a reliance on the educational system, rather than the organisation, to make the 'right' initial selection of people.

2. *Long-term employment.* The concept of 'lifetime employment' (from school or university to retirement with one organisation) has frequently been perceived as a central plank of Japanese HRM practice. Long-term employment (job security) is supported not only by management values and HRM practices but also by the following:

   • Legal protection which inhibits redundancy among 'regular-status' (core) employees without the employees' or union's agreement;

- Government policy supporting job security by subsidising up to two-thirds of the wages of employees laid off temporarily rather than made redundant;

- Trade union policy of accommodation (particularly on wage issues) in return for 'job security'.

Estimates of the consequent 'overstaffing' or 'hidden unemployment' range from 1 to 5 million employees and affect nearly 75 per cent of organisations (1: 626). At the same time, demographic factors have produced a bulge in the middle management ranks resulting in a 'career collision' between the early career plateau of many older managers and the lack of promotion opportunities for younger aspiring employees.

3. *Embedded organisational training.* Once recruited, employees are expected to undertake extensive, continuous specific 'on-the-job' training and development activities interspersed with periods of more general 'off-the-job' training at progression points in their career development. An occupational category may contain seven or eight skill grades within each of which an employee may take three to four years to demonstrate his or her competence before moving up to the next grade – a total of 20–30 years.

4. *Assessment and reward.* Pay and promotion is closely tied into the 'skill-grade' system of progression and reflects *capability* and *seniority* (skill acquisition derived from programmed on-the-job training) rather than *performance* (individual ability and contribution). The effect of this has been to limit the wage gap between people in the same category (or cohort of entrants) and to establish a strong link between an individual's wage level and his or her length of service with the organisation. The underlying concept of pay fairness is based on 'giving a piece of the cake, big or small, to all members of the group who took part in the collective undertaking' (2: 618) with only limited recognition of variability in the individual's performance or contribution, an important element in the integration of individual and corporate objectives.

5. *Information participation.* Japanese work practices are often based on the decentralisation and devolution of decision-making responsibility. This requires not only sharing information (between different levels and parts of the organisation) but also the individual employee exercising judgement. The model also encompasses the concepts of continuous improvement (of product, individual and organisation), the integration of quality assurance into all aspects of work and teamworking involving consensus or collective decision making.

However, now 'a worldwide competitive environment requires a shift of Japanese industry from an enterprise-centred to a more market oriented approach' (2: 617). This presents a dilemma for HRM practices: while some believe that 'it is precisely during hard times that companies have to act responsibly *via-à-vis* the works, i.e. in respecting the unwritten personnel obligations of job and career security', others see the future lying in 'radical change' through 'the development of a pay for performance system for managers without any guarantee of job security in case of underpar performance' (2: 618).

Two different change strategies can be identified:

1. *Externalisation of employment.* Within the legislative constraints, the concept of 'job security' has moved away from the simple 'employment with the same organisation until retirement', first, to transfer placement to a related organisation and, then, to transfer placement with an unrelated organisation (i.e. outplacement guarantee). Perhaps more importantly, some organisations have started to recruit contingent mid-career employees. These tend to be specialists introduced into the organisation as 'innovators and pace-setters of new management practices' (on fixed term contracts with clear performance reward criteria) and represent an ad hoc response to competitive pressures. The creation of this third 'specialised abilities' group within the Japanese labour market (between the long-term core and short-term flexible peripheral groups) has been acknowledged by Nikkeiren (Japanese Employers' Federation) (3: 297).

2. *Competitive appraisal and reward.* Japanese organisations have introduced a number of changes aimed at assessing and recognising individual performance. The introduction of management by objectives has been linked to increasing the range of reward variability (within any given hierarchical level) dependent on the individual's performance in meeting his or her objectives. Similarly, promotion based on 'seniority' may no longer be guaranteed and younger people (with shorter length of employment) may be promoted over longer-service employees. In the opposite direction, some organisations have introduced systems of 'status destitution' for poor performers (2: 619).

Morishima's survey of 1,600 organisations in the early 1990s (1: 635) showed that while 57 per cent appeared to be following the 'traditional' pattern of HRM, 33 per cent had sought to introduce a more competitive appraisal and reward strategy (these tended to be the larger, unionised, manufacturing organisations) and 11 per cent had sought to introduce both strategies (these tended to be smaller, less unionised, service organisations).

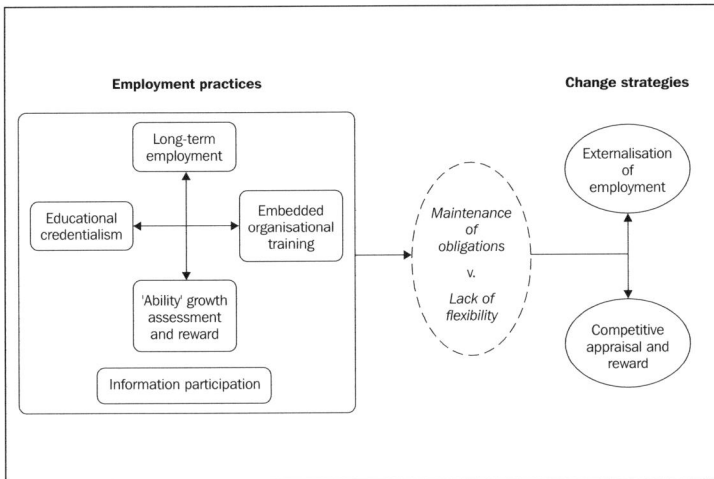

Figure 6.1 Japanese employment practices and strategies for change.

These developments in HRM introduce a degree of uncertainty into the relationship between management and unions. The previous integration of the enterprise-based union with the organisation was based on the management guaranteeing job security and investment in training and development in return for the union ensuring cooperation by their members. Greater individualisation of the employment contractual relationship is leading more middle managers to organise to defend their interests and seek increased codification and standardisation of HRM practices: 'they do not accept or do not consider relevant anymore the complex rites of interaction, the unwritten, informal and diffuse rules governing the appraisal, promotion and reward system that were traditionally the cement of the management system and of the cohesion of Japanese firms' (2: 620).

Sources:

1. M. Morishima, 'Embedding HRM in a social context', *British Journal of Industrial Relations*, vol. 33, no. 4, 1995, pp. 617–40.

2. P. Debroux, 'Recent changes in human resource management practices in Japan', Conference proceedings: *Creating management synergy in Asian economies*, Asian Academy of Management, Penang, December 1995, pp. 616–35.

3. T. Grønning, 'Whither the Japanese employment system? The position of the Japan Employers' Federation', *Industrial Relations Journal*, vol. 29, no. 4, 1998, pp. 295–303.

(*Source*: Salamon, 2000: 261–3.)

Industrial action in south-east Asia

The pattern of industrial action in south-east Asian countries appears to be affected by a variety of factors:

- The adversarial conflictual nature of industrial relations (as demonstrated by the use of industrial action) is, it is often argued, alien to the cultural values of deference to authority, teamworking and consensual decision making, hence there is a preference for resolving any disputes through conciliation, mediation and arbitration rather than industrial action.

- Trade union density is relatively low, collective bargaining less developed and management style often autocratic or paternalistic (with a consequent reluctance to share power with employees and a frequent strategy of obstructing the activities of trade unions).

- Government policy and legislation is driven by concerns to maintain 'industrial peace' and limit wage costs in order to secure economic development and, in particular, inward foreign investment. Furthermore, the political environment in some countries has been non-democratic and/or involved periods of martial law.

The extent of industrial action appears to be relatively low (see Table 6.3). However, a distinction is often drawn between *disputes* and *strikes*. The figures for both Taiwan and South Korea refer to the number of registered disputes rather than strikes. Similarly, during 1985–9, there was an annual average of 1,490 strike or lock-out notices filed in the Philippines but only an average of 357 strikes actually took place each year, while in Malaysia there was an annual average of 985 recorded disputes but only 17 strikes per year.

It appears that there is a fairly extensive use of other forms of industrial action, rather than the strike: sit-ins, hunger strikes, demonstrations, union meetings during working time or, as in the case of service industries in Thailand such as banks and hotels, the wearing of black mourning dress while at work. The use of forms of industrial action which do not involve actual withdrawal of labour may be due, in part, to the legal restrictions placed on strike action and, in part, to the employees' insecurity derived from low wages, the absence of strike benefit from their union and the surrounding high level of unemployment. The use of 'hidden conflict' forms of action such as group resignation from the organisation may, also, be a reflection of both the employees' unwillingness to be seen to confront management directly, through the threat of collective industrial action, and the relative undeveloped and restricted nature of collective bargaining.

In most of the countries, strikes are illegal in many parts of the essential services and public sector and any dispute is subject to compulsory arbitration. While in Singapore the restriction is limited to gas, electricity and water (with other defined essential services required to give 14 days' notice of strike action), in other countries the restriction is broader and may include transport, petrol-refining, hospitals and medical services, banking and telecommunications, or even tourism (Thailand) and export-oriented industries (Philippines) – industries which form a significant proportion of waged employment in these countries. In Malaysia, the only restriction on strikes in essential services is that 21 days' notice of such action has to be given. Furthermore, in both Singapore and Malaysia political strikes (intended to coerce the government) and sympathetic strikes are illegal.

In other industries, legislation often restricts the use of strike in favour of a requirement to use conciliation and/or arbitration. In most countries, strikes are illegal if the dispute is referred to arbitration (although in Taiwan a strike may take place before arbitration has commenced). In Thailand strikes (but not other forms of industrial action) are prohibited during the period of collective agreement, during negotiations and during the five days allowed for conciliation (all disputes must be referred to conciliation). Perhaps most significantly, in Singapore, Malaysia and South Korea important areas of managerial prerogative (hiring, promotions, transfers, dismissals, etc.) are excluded from collective bargaining and, consequently, cannot be a matter for 'dispute' and therefore any industrial action is illegal.

Even in the apparently more stable democratic countries (Singapore and Malaysia) penalties for illegal industrial action can include fines and imprisonment and unions may be deregistered if they undertake illegal acts. For example, the last two significant cases of industrial action in Singapore resulted in action against the unions involved: a strike at Metal Box in 1977 by the non-NTUC Metal Workers' Union resulted in its deregistration and replacement by an NTUC-affiliated union and the 1980 work to rule by SIA Pilots' Association resulted in its deregistration and prosecution of both union officers and members.

The impact of the political environment can be clearly seen in some countries:

- *Philippines*: Martial law was introduced in 1972, following increased social and industrial disturbances, and for a short period all strikes were, in effect, banned. The lifting of martial law in 1981 was followed in 1986 by a change in government and the introduction of a constitutional guarantee of the right to organise, collective bargain and undertake strike action. Later legislation, in 1989, has sought to encourage the use of voluntary (as opposed to compulsory) arbitration.

- *South Korea*: The South Korean constitution, introduced in 1948 and influenced by US occupation, guaranteed basic trade union rights of association, collective bargaining and collective action. However, until 1987 it was generally 'ignored, suspended or abused by government and management actions' and dispute settlement involved 'overt government intervention, often with total disregard for workers' civil rights and personal safety' (Rauenhorst (1990) quoted in 1: 141–2). The change to a more democratic government in 1987 resulted in a sharp increase in disputes primarily concerned with wage increases (from 276 in 1986 to 3,749 in 1987, although they declined in subsequent years).

- *Taiwan (ROC)*: The abandonment of martial law in 1987 (after 40 years during which strikes were illegal) came at a time of the emergence of a more assertive, independent and confrontational union movement and consequent increasing industrial disputes (over 1,400 per year in 1985 and 1986 compared to under 500 per year throughout the 1970s). The change also saw a substantial increase in the number of employees involved in such disputes.

Sources:

1. S. J. Deery and R. J. Mitchell, *Labour Law and Industrial Relations in Asia*, Longman (Melbourne), 1993.

2. A. Verma, T. A. Kochan and R. D. Lansbury (eds), *Employment Relations in the Growing Asian Economies*, Routledge, 1995.

(*Source*: Salamon, 2000: 449–50.)

Table 6.3 Industrial action statistics (annual average)

	Singapore		Malaysia		Philippines[1]		Thailand		Taiwan (ROC)[2]		South Korea[3]
	No	WDL[4]	No	WDL	No	WDL	No	WDL	No	WDL	No
1960–4	67	230,429	n/a	n/a	n/a	n/a	n/a	n/a	30	n/a	n/a
1965–9	12	30,369	n/a	n/a	110	783,000	n/a	n/a	29	n/a	n/a
1970–4	6	6,774	n/a	n/a	110	1,142,510	190	168,609	244	n/a	n/a
1975–9	2	1,811	48	57,588	55	144,500	93	254,679	444	n/a	109
1980–4	0	0	24	11,619	183	678,402	28	87,521	900	n/a	178
1985–9	0	0	17	17,760	357	1,957,646	5	52,162	1,558	11,913	1,556

1. Philippines: Strikes were banned under martial law between October 1972 and November 1975, therefore figures for 1970–4 are averaged over three years (1970, 1971 and 1972) and figures for 1975–9 are averaged over four years (not including 1975).

2. Taiwan (ROC): Figures relate to the number of 'disputes'; strikes only became legal with the lifting of martial law in July 1987, therefore figure for working days lost in period 1985–9 is annual average for three years (1987, 1988 and 1989).

3. South Korea: Figures relate to the number of 'disputes'.

4. WDL = Working days lost.

Source: Salamon (2000 : 449–50).

Question to think about 6.3

What might be some of the uses for management of knowledge of HRM practices elsewhere?

Comparative views are useful for a range of reasons. These include those noted in Table 6.4.

Table 6.4 Usefulness of comparative views

Element	Result
Ethnocentrism	Reduced, ground views
Own system	Put in perspective
Public policy	Examples provided
Research/views	Ground/test results
Overseas operations	Understand more

Question to think about 6.4

How would you explain variations in HRM practices between countries?

These differences may result from several factors. They can be explained by those noted in Table 6.5.

Question to think about 6.5

How would you go about examining HRM practices in different countries?

A range of options is available. These can be seen in Table 6.6.

Table 6.5 Reasons for differences in HRM

Approach	Characteristics	Issues	Problems
Convergence	• Process of industrialisation and use of technology move all towards similar political and economic systems • Are universal truths applicable everywhere?	• Some countries remain at different stages • Even with same technology, implementation of practices varies	• Fail to understand that the way practices are interpreted and implemented differs between countries
Contingency	• Recognise practices affected by factors • Common variables were organisational size, technology, environment	• Contingent factors still impose rational logic of administration and organisation • So still 'best way' given contingencies	
Culture	• Collective programming of mind of group • Reflected in particular assumptions, beliefs and norms • Much made of differences in cultures	• Can all differences be explained in terms of people's attitudes? • Emphasis on history and individuals' perceptions, but little account of how values change over time	• Fail to recognise that a divergent and contradictory range of practices may exist within one society and static views

		• Values on their own not enough; need to be rooted in social and economic structure of a given society	
Institutional	• Understand social and economic institutions supporting values and practices • Cannot examine separate aspects of system without locating in its specific societal context	• Static view of national industrial order • Little attention paid to role of the state	

There are some different ways to examine HRM. However, it remains important to consider some of the issues in more detail. This can be illustrated by using the example of conflict.

Task 6.1

Look at Figure 6.2a for a few moments and then consider which countries you would rank from 1 to 22. Afterwards, turn to Figure 6.2b and compare how your ranking reflects this. What explains any differences between the two? For instance, think back to Chapter 5 and the ideas of perspectives and the exercises given there. Also, now turn to Table 6.7 for further reasons (relating to definitions and collation) why the 'official' rankings are less robust than they might at first sight seem.

Table 6.6 Discovering HRM in other countries

Method	Characteristics	Issues
Large-scale data sets Secondary analysis	• Nationally representative • Establish changes and trends over time • Cheap if already generated • 'Representative'	• Cannot give reasons why or causality • Definitional difficulties • Problems of inadequate data • Data may be filtered and generated for other purposes
Questionnaires	• Popular in employment research • Generate standardised data • Relative cheapness • Provide some breadth	• Obtain superficial evidence • Questions predetermined • Unexpected findings difficult to integrate • Susceptible to ethnocentrism
Case studies	• In-depth interviews, observational methods, working • See realities of how work is organised at a closer level • Pick up unforeseen issues • Examine why practices are used	• Time-consuming • Knowledge of society/language • Difficult to generalise • Lose objectivity and independence – 'go native'

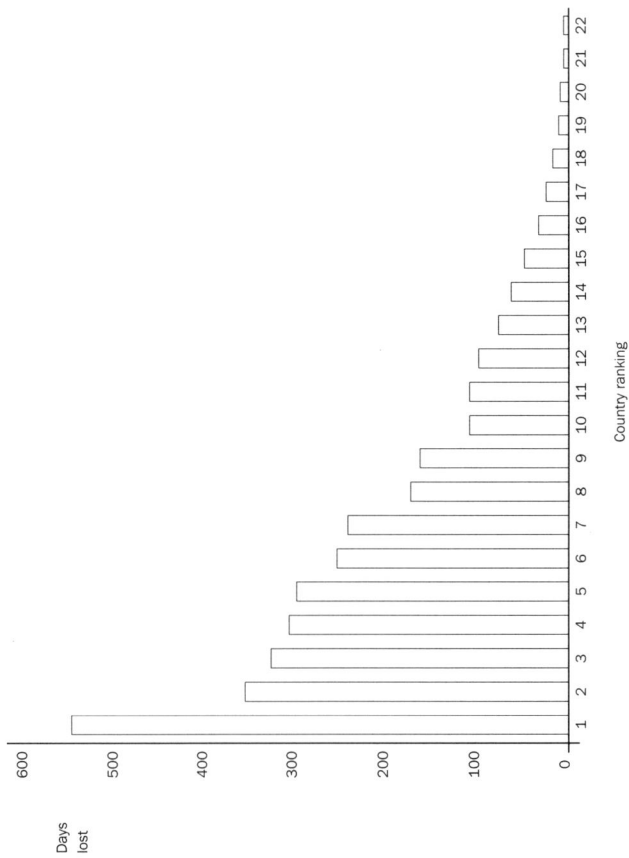

Figure 6.2a Working days lost (per 1,000 employees in all industries and services).

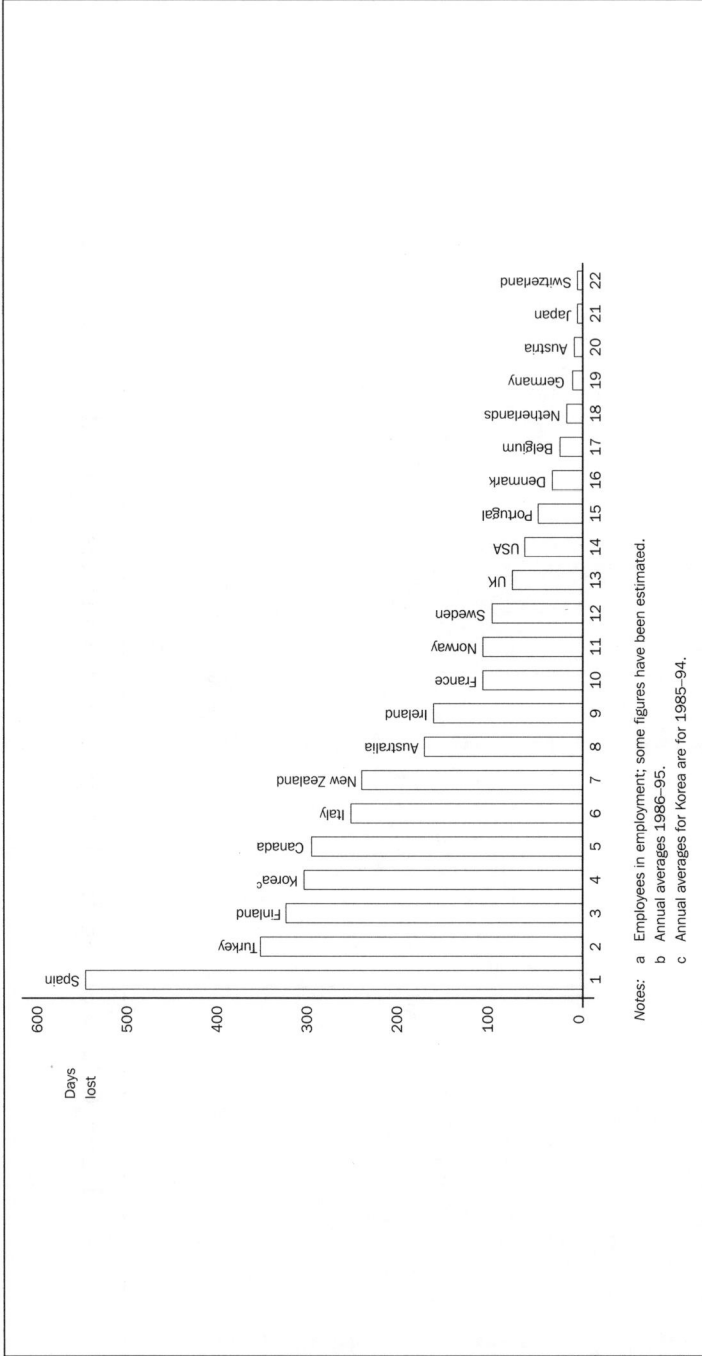

Figure 6.2b Working days lost (per 1,000 employees[a] in all industries and services[b]). (*Source*: Ross et al. (1998: 362), based on Sweeney and Davies (1997) using ILO, Statistical Office of the European Communities (SOEC) and OECD data; Korea Labor Institute (1995).)

Notes: a   Employees in employment; some figures have been estimated.
        b   Annual averages 1986–95.
        c   Annual averages for Korea are for 1985–94.

Table 6.7 Labour disputes: comparisons of coverage and methodology

Country	Minimum criteria for inclusion in statistics	Are political stoppages included?	Indirectly affected workers included?	Sources and notes
Australia	Ten or more workdays not worked	Yes	Yes	Bureau of Statistics surveys firms identified through press reports and contacts with the IR parties and government departments
Canada	At least half-a-day in duration plus at least ten workdays not worked	Yes	No	Manpower centres, provincial labour departments, conciliation services and press
France	Al least one workday not worked; however, agriculture and public sector excluded	Yes	Yes	Labour inspectors
Germany	More than ten workers involved and of at least one day in duration or more than 100 workdays lost	Yes	No	Compulsory notification by employers to local employment offices
Italy	No restrictions on size	Yes	No	No information
Korea	NA	NA	NA	NA

Country	Minimum criteria for inclusion in statistics	Are political stoppages included?	Indirectly affected workers included?	Sources and notes
Japan	No restriction on size, excluding unofficial reports	Yes	No	Legal requirement to report to Labour Relations Commission
Sweden	At least one workday not worked	Yes	No	Information gathered following press reports
UK	Ten workers involved and one day in duration unless 100 or more workdays are lost	No	Yes	Employment Service Jobcentres make reports for Office of National Statistics which also checks press, unions and large employers
USA	More than one day or one shift in duration and more than 1,000 workers involved	No	Yes	Reports from press, employers, unions and agencies

NA = Not available.

Source: Ross et al. (1998: 360), based on Sweeney and Davies (1997), using ILO data.

The future of HRM

Several organisational trends will have impacts on the development of HRM. These include the following.

HRM as a subject

HRM as a subject faces a healthy future in terms of both academia and teaching as well as research. The increasingly popularity of business and management qualifications at different levels has helped to drive this. Within these courses, the study of people management is covered in a variety of ways and from a multitude of aspects. Much research in the area is also durable and is conducted, although the focus of this continues to change and develop. Thus there is less work on 'conflict' and more on HRM's contributions to the performance of businesses and economies, for instance.

HRM as a function

HRM as a function faces a different set of issues. For some commentators, it may lead to a decline, although others see greater continuity. A range of developments will have different impacts on the HRM function.

Question to think about 6.6

What might be some of the impacts on the decline or continuity of HRM as a function?

The impacts are numerous and varied. These factors include those in Tables 6.8 and 6.9.

Table 6.8 Impacts on HRM as a function

Developments	Impacts	Results
Business decentralisation	• Centre involved in strategy • Divisions involved in operational issues	• Inconsistency/ variability in policy and practice within/ across organisations • Strategic role, input and integration of HR issues impacted on
Decentralising HR specialists	• From corporate to business unit • Within business unit to departmental level	
Devolving HR activities to line management	• Use of non-specialists • Line management variability	
Outsourcing	• Dedicated call centres • Use of external consultants	

Source: Developed from Sisson (1995); Hall and Torrington (1998).

Thus while the management of people will remain, it seems that who does it, where and how may change. One of the most recent trends is to outsource either the whole of the HRM function or certain aspects of it, from recruitment to rewards, to specialists. What then for ideas of HRM and universal frameworks?

Conclusion

The area of people management is not new. It has evolved and been labelled and relabelled in several ways. However, for some people HRM is a break with this past as it contains some elements that 'old' PM simply did not possess or even claim to be interested in. This sort of hard distinction is not proven in the UK. Nevertheless, that should not distract businesses from the fact that HRM remains critically important. Furthermore, while HRM is crucial, the introduction and use of textbook practice by organisations varies. We have examined this through the prism of context which has shown variability, and have explored some of the many reasons (sector, size, location) for this kaleidoscopic picture.

Table 6.9 Decline and continuity of HRM

Decline	Continuity
In recessions, fewer people resourced, rewarded, developed	In recessions, still deal with redundancies, retaining, even recruiting
Trade unions more docile, less 'troubleshooting'	Trade unions remain, alternative sanctions, i.e. overtime bans, PR campaigns
Routine administration reduced with automation, i.e. pay, records	Heterogeneous workforces requiring management of diversity
Subcontracting out of functions, i.e. resourcing, rewards, development	If economic boom, it is key to attract/retain sufficient quality HRs
Rise of 'macho management' reasserting managers' 'right to manage'	Myriad laws require careful consideration, i.e. increasing need to consult workforces over changes

This variability in HRM needs to be remembered when faced with the often naive nostrums and platitudes of many proponents of the latest 'fashion' to solve all organisations' HRM problems and issues. If it was that simple, it would have been solved already! The management of people needs to be put in context and viewed through this lens.

References

Bae, J. and Rowley, C. (2001) 'The impact of globalization on HRM: the case of South Korea', *Journal of World Business*, 36, 4: 403–28.

Economist, The (2003) 'A survey of capitalism and democracy: beyond shareholder value', 28 June, pp. 9–12.

Hall, L. and Torrington, D. (1998) *The HR Function: The Dynamics of Change and Development*. London: Financial Times/Pitman.

Legge, K. (1995) 'HRM: rhetoric, reality and hidden agendas', in J. Storey (ed.), *HRM: A Critical Text*. London: Routledge, pp. 33–59.

Ross, P., Bamber, G. and Whitehouse, G. (1998) 'Appendix: employment, economics and industrial relations: comparative statistics', in Bamber, G. and Lansbury, R. (eds), *International and Comparative Industrial Relations*. London: Routledge, pp. 328–66.

Rowley, C. (ed.) (1998) *HRM in the Asia Pacific Region: Convergence Questioned*. London: Cass.

Rowley, C. and Benson, J. (eds) (2000) *Globlalization and Labour in the Asia Pacific Region*. London: Cass.

Rowley, C. and Benson, J. (eds) (2003) *HRM in the Asia Pacific Region: Convergence Revisited*. London: Cass.

Salamon, M. (2000) *Industrial Relations: Theory and Practice*. Harlow: Pearson Education.

Sisson, K. (1995) 'HRM and the personnel function', in Storey, J. (ed.), *HRM: A Critical Text*. London: Routledge, pp. 87–109.

Storey, J. (1995) 'HRM: still marching on, or marching out?', in J. Storey (ed.), *HRM: A Critical Text*. London: Routledge, pp. 3–32.

Storey, J. and Sisson, K. (1991) 'Looking to the Future', in J. Storey (ed.), *New Perspectives on HRM*. London: Routledge, pp. 167–83.

Torrington, D. and Hall, L. (1998) *HRM*. London: Prentice Hall.

Further reading and background information

Further reading

Further reading titles have been noted in the relevant chapters. The following represent only a selection of the vast amount of further material available.

Armstrong, M. (1999) *Employee Reward*. London: IPD.

Armstrong, M. and Murlis, H. (1994) *Reward Management – A Handbook of Remuneration Strategy & Practice*. London: Kogan Page/IPD.

Bach, S. and Sisson, K. (2000) *Personnel Management: A Comprehensive Guide to Theory and Practice*. Oxford: Blackwell. (Recent research and theory-based text covering the practice, and difficulties, of managing people.)

Blyton, P. and Turnbull, P. (eds) (1992) *Reassessing HRM*. London: Sage. (A well-written collection of sceptical pieces on numerous aspects of HRM.)

Bolton, T. (1997) *HRM*. London: Blackwell. (A general text.)

Bramham, J. (1994) *HR Planning*. London: IPD. (Text on manpower planning.)

Bratton, J. and Gold, J. (1999) *HRM: Theory and Concepts*. London: Macmillan.

Brewster, C. and Harris (eds) (1999) *International HRM: Contemporary Issues in Europe*. London: Routledge.

Cook, M. (1993) *Personnel Selection and Productivity*. Chichester: Wiley. (Recruitment and selection text.)

Cornelius, N. (2000) *IIRM: A Managerial Perspective*. London: Thomson Learning Business Press. (From the perspective of a practising line manager whose job involves HR responsibilities.)

Cowling, A. and James, P. (1994) *The Essence of PM and IR*. London: Prentice Hall. (Simplistic introduction to the area.)

Cowling, A. and Mailer, C. (eds) (1998) *Managing HRs*, 3rd edn. London: Arnold. (Introductory text.)

Dressler, G. (2000) *HRM*, 8th edn. London: Pearson Education. (Comprehensive review of concepts and practices.)

Fitzgerald, R. and Rowley, C. (eds) (1997) *HRs and the Firm in International Perspective, Vol. I, Vol. II*. London: Edward Elgar. (Comprehensive collection of historical works in the area.)

Fletcher, C. (1993) *Appraisal – Routes to Improved Performance*. London: IPD. (Training and development.)

Foot, M. and Hook, C. (1999) *Introducing HRM*. Harlow: Longman. (Standard introductory work.)

Hall, L. and Torrington, D. (1998) *The HRM Function: The Dynamics of Change and Development*. London: Pitman.

Harrison, R. (1992) *Employee Development*. London: IPD.

Harrison, R. (1993) *HRM: Issues and Strategies*. Harlow: Addison-Wesley.

Herriot, P. (1991) *Recruitment in the '90s*. London: IPD. (Recruitment text.)

Legge, K. (1995) *HRM: Rhetorics and Realities*. London: Macmillan. (Important critical analysis of HRM.)

Leopold, J. (ed.) (2002) *Human Resources in Organisations*. London: Financial Times/Prentice Hall.

Mabey, C., Skinner, D. and Clark, T. (eds) (1998) *Experiencing HRM*. London: Sage. (Fascinating and important collection of actual impacts of HRM on employees.)

Mabey, C., Salamon, G. and Storey, J. (eds) (1998) *HRM: A Strategic Introduction*. Oxford: Blackwell.

McBeath, G. (1990) *Practical Management Development – Strategies for Management Resourcing and Development in the 1990s*. Oxford: Blackwell.

McGovern, P. (1998) *HRM, Technical Workers and the MNC*. London: Routledge. (Fascinating case studies of the impact of HRM in hi-tech firms in Ireland.)

McKenna, E. and Beech, N. (1995) *The Essence of HRM*. London: Prentice Hall. (Simplistic introduction to the area.)

Marchington, M. and Wilkinson, A. (2002) *People Management and Development: HRM at Work*. London: CIPD.

Maud, L. (2001) *An Introduction to HRM: Theory and Practice*. London: Palgrave.

Molander, C. and Winterton, J. (1994) *Managing HRs*. London: Routledge.

Mumford, A. (1990) *Management Development – Strategies for Action*. London: IPM.

Newell, H. and Scarborough, H. (eds) (2002) *HRM in Context: A Case Study Approach*. London: Palgrave.

Patrick, J. (1992) *Training – Research and Practice*. London: Academic Press.

Pickford, J. (ed.) (2003) *Mastering People Management*. London: Financial Times/Prentice Hall. (Good, but variable, collection of up-to-date articles on some of the key areas.)

Pilbeam, S. and Corbridge, M. (2002) *People Resourcing: HRM in Practice*. London: Financial Times/Prentice Hall.

Pinnington, A. and Edwards, T. (2000) *Introduction to HRM*. Oxford: OUP. (Covers main elements, concepts, issues and contemporary developments in HRM.)

Poole, M. and Warner, M. (eds) (1998) *Handbook of HRM*. London: ITP. (Very comprehensive and readable collection on HRM.)

Price, A. (1997) *HRM in a Business Context*. London: ITP. (Introductory text.)

Prior, J. (ed.) (1991) *Handbook of Training and Development*. Aldershot: Gower/IPD.

Redman, T. and Wilkinson, A. (eds) (2001) *Contemporary HRM: Text and Cases*. London: Financial Times/Prentice Hall.

Redman, T. and Wilkinson, A. (eds) (2002) *The Informed Student Guide to HRM*. London: Thomson Learning.

Reid, M. and Barrington, H. (1994) *Training Interventions*, 4th edn. London: IPD.

Rowley, C. (ed.) (1998) *HRM in the Asia Pacific: Convergence Questioned*. London: Cass. (Eight-country comparison of HRM.)

Rowley, C. and Benson, J. (eds) (2000) *Globalization and Labour in the Asia Pacific*. London: Cass. (Sixteen-chapter, ten-country comparison of globalisation and employment.)

Salaman, G. (ed.) (1992) *HR Strategies*. London: Sage.

Scott, A. (1994) *Willing Slaves? British Workers Under HRM*. Cambridge: CUP. (Case studies of managerial change and shop floor trends in IR historical context.)

Sparrow, P. and Marchington, M. (eds) (1998) *HRM: The New Agenda*. London: Pitman.

Stedwick, J. (2000) *An Introduction to HRM*. London: Butterworth-Heinemann. (Practical and theoretical aspects with running case study.)

Storey, J. (ed.) (1991) *New Perspectives on HRM*. London: Routledge. (Excellent collection of articles on HRM.)

Storey, J. (1992) *Management of Human Resources*. Oxford: Blackwell.

Storey, J. (ed.) (1995) *HRM: A Critical Text*. London: Routledge. (Excellent collection of contemporary pieces on HRM.)

Storey, J. and Sisson, K. (1993) *Managing HRs and IR*. Milton Keynes: Open University Press.

Taylor, S. (1998) *Employee Resourcing*. London: IPD.

Towers, B. (ed.) (1996) *The Handbook of HRM*. Oxford: Blackwell. (Multi-authored collection on key debates.)

Tyson, S. and York, A. (2000) *Essentials of HRM*. London: Butterworth-Heineman)

Warner, M. and Joynt, P. (eds) (2002) *Managing Across Culture: Issues and Perspectives*. London: Thomson Learning.

Contemporary developments

To assist in keeping up with the rapid changes in HRM, it is strongly recommended that the quality journals and broadsheet newspapers are read. Particularly good in this respect are *The Economist* and *The Financial Times*. These also give very useful contemporary international and comparative insights and examples.

There is also a good range of journals, aimed at both academics and practitioners, providing HR-related information. These include the following.

Asia Pacific Business Review

British Journal of Industrial Relations

California Management Review

Employee Relations

Employment Gazette

Employment Relations Record

European Industrial Relations Review

European Journal of Industrial Relations

Human Resource Management

Human Resource Management Journal

Incomes Data Services

Industrial Relations

Industrial Relations Journal

Industrial Relations Services (10 journals)

International Employment Relations Review

International Journal of HRM

Journal of General Management

Journal of International Business Studies

Journal of Management Studies

Journal of World Business

Labour

People Management

Personnel Review

Personnel Today (5 magazines)

Work, Employment and Society

'Lighter' things

The importance of work and the management of people can readily be seen in popular culture. This includes the 'social realism' art of the former Soviet Union and the photographs of working-class reality such as by Bill Brandt from the 1930s. A range and variety of music, television series and programmes, 'docusoaps', 'docudramas', films and books indicate the historical and contemporary salience of aspects of employment issues, in various fashions, guises and ways. Indeed, many popular 'sitcoms' are set in the workplace. These forms include, among others, the following, with a short synopsis of their location and content in relation to the work cited.

Music

Employment, work and related issues appear in popular music. This can be heard in songs from artists ranging from Pete Seeger, Woody Guthrie and folk musicians to Merle Travis, Merle Haggard, Billy Bragg and Bruce Springsteen, among many others. In the late 1950s were the highly influential 'Radio Ballads', eight programmes on the Home Service in which working-class people and their toil were set to music by folk singers Ewan MacColl and Peggy Seeger.

Television programmes, series and documentaries

The Life and Times of Rosie the Riveter (1981)
Documentary on women working in American industry during the Second World War.

Final Offer (1984, Toronto)
UAW twists and turns to negotiate with both the UAW International and GM.

Collision Course (mid-1980s, USA)
Rescue and ultimate collapse of Eastern Airlines following deregulation, unitarism, workers' participation.

Manufacturing Miracles (late 1980s)
Postwar story of Japan's Mazda, with women workers, company unions, quality circles, pay.

Roger and Me (1989) with Michael Moore
Life and times of GM in Flint, Michigan; political documentary, insightful and funny.

The Factory (1995, Channel 4)
Work and life in Robinson Willey, a Liverpool gas fire factory.

People's Century (1995, BBC)
Episode 'On The Line (1924)' on development and impacts of assembly line and mass production in range of industries (cars, radios, biscuits) and countries (US, UK, France, Italy, Germany) up to mid-twentieth century.

The House (1996, BBC)
Covent Garden, especially on negotiations on agreements.

Red Base One Four (1996, Channel 4)
London Ambulance Service's attempts to introduce new technology and change working practices.

The Ship (1996, Channel 4)
Management, work and employment relations at Swan Hunter shipyard in North-East England.

When Rover Met BMW (1996, BBC)
The area of recruitment and induction is especially interesting.

Hotel (1997, BBC 1)
The Adelphi hotel in Liverpool; employment and management.

Airport (1999, BBC 1)
Behind the scenes at Heathrow airport.

Airline (1999, ITV)
The workings of the easyJet airline at Luton airport.

Back to the Floor (1999–2001, BBC 2)
BAFTA award-winning series of job swaps within different sectors, e.g. Prism Rail/WAGN, Gardner Merchant, PGL, Sainsburys, Wedgwood, Raddison Edwardian.

Troubleshooter (2000, BBC 2)
Sir John Harvey-Jones returns to earlier businesses.

Bubble Trouble (2000, BBC 2)
Episode on Japanese management practices and changes in Japan, the US, UK, e.g. Toshiba, Matsushita, Nissan.

Startup.Com (2001)
Documentary charting the rise and fall of an online firm and its workforce.

The Office (2001 and 2002, BBC 2)
Mock fly-on-the-wall documentary, BAFTA award-winning comedy on life/management at a Slough-based paper materials company.

The Secret Life of the Office (2002, BBC 2)
Work at Holiday Autos call centre under the close direction of the boss.

The Richard Taylor Interviews (2003, Channel 4)
Spoof recruitment for a range of jobs, including management consultants, security staff, bar managers, cabin crew, event organisers, etc.

Trouble at the Top (2003, BBC 2)
Latest run in the series of a range of sectors and industries.

I'll Show Them Who's Boss (2003, BBC 2)
Gerry Robinson acts as a management consultant to a range of small businesses, including a Nottingham lace-making and dyeing firm.

So What Do You Do All Day? (2003, BBC 2)
A single day in the work life of a range of business people.

Apply Immediately (2003, BBC 2)
Series following individuals as they seek new career paths.

Television dramas

The Scar (1997) with Charlie Hardrick
Drama of working-class life in decimated Durham mining community in north-east England.

Dockers (1999) Jimmy McGovern
Co-written by 14 of the participants in the Liverpool docks dispute.

The Navigators (2001) Ken Loach
Effects of rail privatisation on a group of track workers, management and contractors in 1995.

The Battle of Orgreave (2002) Mike Figgis
Recreation, with many veterans, of pivotal coking plant conflict during 1984 miners' strike.

Clocking Off (2003, BBC 1)
Latest run of the series set in a factory.

Don't Drop the Coffin (2003, ITV 1)
Series about a family firm of undertakers.

Films

Labour's Reward (1925)

The Passaic Textile Strike (1925)

Metropolis (1927) with Birgitte Helm
1920s vision of city and work conditions in 2000.

A Nous La Liberté (*Give Us Our Liberty*) (1932)
Satire of the assembly line in a gramophone factory, with tyrannical managers and timid workers.

Black Fury (1936) with Paul Muni (originally banned in several US states)
Pennsylvanian miner forms breakaway union, taking on owners and strikebreakers.

Modern Times (1936) with Charlie Chaplin
Classic, light-hearted view of Taylorism and parable of the industrialised world.

Stand-In (1937) with Leslie Howard
Efficiency expert and accountant sent to assess failing Hollywood studio.

How Green Was My Valley (1941) with Walter Pidgeon
Hardships in Welsh mining family, community and work at the turn of the nineteenth century, involving a labour dispute and challenging greedy mine owners.

The Devil And Miss Jones (1941) with Jean Arthur and Charles Coburn
Rich boss, sensing union unrest among retail workers, goes back to the shop floor.

Millions Like Us (1943) with Patricia Roc

This Land Is Mine (1943) with Charles Laughton
Propaganda piece against Nazism also radical in the way it attacks capitalism.

The Most Beautiful (1944) directed by Akira Kurosawa
Group of women in wartime factory producing lenses for Japanese planes.

Fame Is the Spur (1947) with Michael Redgrave
Labour politician's story, 1870s to 1930s, covering Peterloo, strikes, hunger marches, economic depression.

Chance of a Lifetime (1950) with Basil Radford and Kenneth More
Workers in an agricultural machinery factory set up a cooperative;
currency crisis destroys credit.

The Man in the White Suit (1951) with Alec Guiness
Connivance of management and unions to perpetuate inefficiencies
and halt technology.

On the Waterfront (1954) with Marlon Brando
Union boss corruption on New York's docks in the 1940s with
'D&D' (deaf and dumb) code of longshoremen.

Hell Drivers (1957) with Stanley Baker
Driver rebels against employer's practices and dangerous schedules
in the world of trucking.

Cairo Station (1958) with Youssef Chahine
Labourers' lives, and achieving unionisation during change in Egypt.

I'm All Right Jack (1959) with Peter Sellers
Classic satire on unions and management practice in postwar
British employment.

The Angry Silence (1960) with Richard Attenborough
Worker defies 'wildcat' strike in Midlands factory, becoming a
'blackleg' and being 'sent to Coventry'.

The Apartment (1960) with Jack Lemmon
New York insurance clerk's relations with bosses, ideas of an
Orwellian workplace.

Saturday Night and Sunday Morning (1961) with Albert Finney
Nottingham engineering factory worker, alienation and pay systems (piecework).

The Molly Maguires (1970) with Sean Connery
Factual; Catholic miners fight Protestant employers over working conditions in nineteenth-century Pennsylvania.

Blue Collar (1978) with Richard Pryor and Harvey Keitel
Oppressive factory jobs, car workers exploited by their own union.

Norma Rae (1979) with Sally Field
US textile worker turns union activist.

All Night Long (1981) with Gene Hackman
Frustration of demotion from company's HQ to night manager at a 24-hour drugstore.

Kentucky Woman (1983) with Cheryl Ladd
Discrimination, role of laws in USA as a woman fights to be accepted as a coal miner.

Congratulatory Speech ('Shukuji') (mid-1980s) with R. Saotome
Satirical film of 'salaryman's' supreme dedication when asked to give a speech at the wedding of the VP's son.

The Killing Floor (1984) with Damien Leake
Narrative of struggle of trade unionism birth in slaughter and packing houses of First World War Chicago.

Brazil (1985) with Jonathan Pryce
Classic, satirical and comic look at bureaucracy.

Gung Ho (1986) with Michael Keaton
Classic, xenophobic view of work and employee relations in a Japanese car plant in a US town.

Matewan (1987) with Chris Cooper
Labour, ethnic and racial troubles, violent clashes with striking miners in 1920s Virginia.

The Secret of My Success (1987) with Michael J. Fox
View on 1980s yuppies with mailroom worker in large corporation establishing a second identity as a wheeler-dealer company executive.

Tin Men (1987) with Richard Dreyfus and Danny de Vito
Classic film about the rivalry between unscrupulous aluminum-siding salesmen in Baltimore in 1963.

Big Business (1988) with Bette Midler and Lily Tomlin
Two sets of identical twins mismatched at birth meet again years later on opposing sides of a property development battle.

Prejudice (1989) with Grace Parr
Discrimination; impact of legislation in Australia; gender in newspapers; ethnicity in healthcare.

Other People's Money (1991) with Danny DeVito and Gregory Peck
Sharp satire on a ruthless asset stripper trying to profit from taking over a family-run firm.

Spotswood (1991) with Anthony Hopkins
Efficiency expert examines work practices in a Melbourne shoe factory.

Hoffa (1992) with Jack Nicolson
History of (in)famous leader of the US Teamsters union.

Glengarry Glen Ross (1992) with Al Pacino and Jack Lemmon
Classic view of work, teams and motivation via a day in the life of real-estate salesmen.

Teamster Boss: The Jackie Presser Story (1992) with Brian Dennehy
One of the USA's political power brokers uses bribery, blackmail and murder to achieve his ambitions.

Of Mice and Men (1992) with John Malkovich
Steinbeck's tale of itinerant labourers working the fields of California during the Depression.

Barbarians at the Gate (1993) with James Gardner
Power struggles in takeover bid against American conglomerate Nabisco in 1983.

Germinal (1993) with Gerard Depardieu
Drama about man who tries to help oppressed miners.

Philadelphia (1993) with Tom Hanks
Organisation dealing with AIDS in the workplace.

Rising Sun (1993) with Sean Connery and Wesley Snipes
Investigation of a death, and Japanese etiquette in a conglomerate in the USA.

Disclosure (1994) with Michael Douglas and Demi Moore
Power politics and sexual harassment in the workplace.

Daens (1996) with Jan Decleir
Priest tries to improve working conditions in nineteenth-century Belgium textiles industry.

Brassed Off (1996) with Tara Fitzgerald
Local communities set against the backdrop of the UK miners' conflict and pit closures.

The Full Monty (1997) with Robert Carlyle
Changes in workforce gender composition and unemployment in Sheffield steel industry workers.

Among Giants (1998) with Pete Postlethwaite
Camaraderie among gang of Northern cash-in-hand workers painting electricity pylons threatened when a backpacker joins them.

Antz (1998) with the voices of Woody Allen and Gene Hackman
Animation about a neurotic and insecure worker ant struggling to express individuality in a colony full of conformists.

Office Space (1999)
Comedy about the tedium of office life in a computing company.

Pushing Tin (1999) with John Cusack
Rivalry when new recruit unsettles close-knit team of New York air-traffic controllers.

Ressources Humaines (2000) with mainly non-professional cast, real workers and bosses
Management trainee scheme at a factory where father was a shop-floor worker for 30 years, used by management, labour protest over firings, 35-hour working week.

Billy Elliot (2000) with Julie Walters and Jamie Bell
Set against backdrop of 1984 miners' strike.

Bread and Roses (2000) with Pilar Padilla
Non-union immigrant Mexican women office cleaners in California take action to secure benefits and better pay.

Antitrust (2001) with Tim Robbins
Set in cut-throat world of computer software industry; lampoons Bill Gates.

Life and Debt (2003) by Stephanie Black
Account of the costs of globalisation, IMF and 'free' trade using the example of the Jamaican economy.

Books

Gaskell, E. (1855) *North and South*
An industrial novel which includes reciprocal responsibilities of employers and employees.

Sinclair, U. (1906) *The Jungle* (Penguin)
Harrowing account of Chicago meat-packing industry and the low-skilled and disadvantaged who work there.

Dreiser, T. (1912) *The Financier* (Penguin)
Set in the late nineteenth century, recounting how power and wealth were achieved.

Sinclair, U. (1919) *The Brass Check*
First use of phrase 'white-collar worker'.

Lewis, S. (1922) *Babbitt* (Harcourt Brace)
Satiric portrait of 'efficiency' and business in a medium-sized city.

Huxley, A. (1932) *Brave New World* (Penguin)
Portrayal of a brutal, standardised, emotionless society dominated by mass production.

Orwell, G. (1933) *Down and Out in Paris and London* (Gollancz)
Restaurant work as a *plongeur*.

Orwell, G. (1937) *The Road to Wigan Pier* (Gollancz)
Exploration of coal areas of Lancashire and Yorkshire at a time of mass unemployment.

Dos Passos, J. (1937) *The Big Money*
Pursuit of the American Dream, dehumanising effects on workers in age of mechanisation, efficiency, mass production and assembly lines.

Marquand, J. (1949) *Point of No Return*
Turbulent inner life of banker searching for identity in chosen profession.

Tressell, R. (1955) *The Ragged Trousered Philanthropists* (Lawrence & Wishart)
Classic novel of working conditions in the nineteenth century; important to labour movement.

Wilson, S. (1955) *The Man in the Gray Flannel Suit* (The Reprint Society)
Executives ready to bury emotions and values in the name of corporate uniformity.

Selby, H. (1957) *Last Exit to Brooklyn* (Paladin)
Highlights the often brutal nature of early postwar US labour relations.

Foot, M. (1962) *Aneurin Bevan* (Paladin)
Working conditions in mining.

Sheed, W. (1968) *Office Politics* (Simon & Schuster)
Novel about interpersonal conflicts in a publishing house.

Currell-Brown, P. (1977) *Smallcreep's Day* (Picador)
Alienation and frustration on the shop floor.

Beattie, G. (1986) *Survivors of Steel City: A Portrait of Sheffield* (Chatto & Windus)
Anthropological account of people in Sheffield after the decline of the steel industry.

Hamper, B. (1986/92) *Rivethead: Tales from the Assembly Line* (Fourth Estate)
Fascinating record of working life by an assembly worker in a GM plant.

Lodge, D. (1989) *Nice Work* (Penguin)
Compares industrial and academic worlds.

Heller, J. (1989) *Something Happened* (Dell)
Black comedy of corporate culture and executives in an office.

Kemske, F. (1996) *Human Resources: A Business Novel* (Nicholas Brealey)
HR manager and 'strange' turnaround specialist, differences in company reorganisation.

Brawer, R. (1998) *Fictions of Business: Insights on Management from Great Literature* (Wiley)
Insights on various human problems of management indicated in novels and plays.

Lively, A. (2000) *Shifts* (Cape)
Collection of stories on a range of occupations/work, geographical and historical locations.

Ehrenreich, B. (2002) *Nickel and Dimed* (Granta)
Hard-hitting look at low-wage work in the USA.

Ross, S.J. (2002) *Working Class Hollywood* (Princeton)
A trawl through films depicting labour–capital conflicts.

Schlosser. E. (2001) *Fast Food Nation* (Houghton Mifflin)
A look at the fast-food industry around the world.

Black, E. (2002) *IBM and the Holocaust* (Time/Warner)
Chilling demonstration of technology coupled with effective bureaucratic organisation and a strategic alliance with Nazis using Hollerith tabulating machines to conduct a census later used for other purposes.

Daisey, M. (2002) *Twenty-one Dog Years – Doing Time at Amazon.com* (Fourth Estate)
Organisational socialisation and culture; the author's experience of being recruited and inducted.

Toynebee, P. (2003) *Hard Work: Life in Low-Pay Britain* (Bloomsbury)
Journalist working in, and living on, low-paid work, e.g. hospital porter.

Index

graphology, candidate selection, 83–4, 89

Harvard framework, HRM, 18
human resource cycle, HRM, 19
human resource management (HRM):
    alternative approaches to, 14–16, 17, 264–5
    context of, 6, 15, 20–9
    departments, 27
    development of, 7–10, 261–3
    dynamism of, 263–4
    future of, 283–4, 285
    importance of, 10–14
    integration within organisations, 17–20, 101–2, 103, 214–16
    international comparisons, 265, 275–82
    managers, 27–8
    models of, 18–19, 28–9
    nature of, 5–6, 263–4
    and personnel management (PM), comparisons with, 16–18, 261
    study of, 11–12
    tensions in, 14–16, 17, 259–60, 261

incremental pay scales, 117, 126
individualist perspective, employee relations (ER), 201, 220–1, 225–6, 270
industrial action:
    case studies, 202–5
    international comparisons, coverage and methodology, 277, 279–82
    south-east Asia, 270–4

Switzerland, peace obligations, 233–4
see also arbitration
industrial relations (IR), definition/ development of, 198–9, 209–10, 227
see also employee relations (ER)
internal labour markets (ILMs), 22–4
interviews:
    candidate selection, 76–83, 88–9
    job analysis, 63
    performance appraisal, 183–4
Investors in People (IIP), 169–70
Ireland, employee relations (ER), 222–3

Japan, 266–70
    trade unions, 227–9, 270
    training, 137–8, 171, 267
job analysis, recruitment and selection, 61–3
job bidding, internal recruitment, 66–7
job descriptions, 63–4
job evaluation, employee rewards, 111–16
job satisfaction, 104

knowledge-based economy, 13

labour markets (LMs), 21–4
    and employee rewards, 21–2, 109–10
    and flexible firm model, 24–6
Labour Party/government, 219, 221–2, 225–6

quality circles (QCs), 247–8
question types, interviews, 80–1
questionnaires:
    job analysis, 62–3
    psychometric testing, 85, 86–7, 90
    use in international comparisons,
        HRM, 278

ranking:
    job evaluation, 112
    performance appraisal, 177, 186
rating scales, performance appraisal,
    178, 179–83, 186
recruitment and selection, 42, 58–9,
    90–1
    advertising, 73
    application forms/references, 75,
        77–8
    employment tests, 84–7
    external recruitment, methods/
        sources, 68–74
    graphology, 83–4, 89
    internal recruitment, methods/
        sources, 66–8, 73–4
    interviews, 76–83, 88–9
    job analysis, 61–3
    job description/person specification,
        63–5
    practical examples, 87–90
    recruitment, methods/sources,
        65–74
    selection, methods, 74–90
    stages of, 59–60
references (recruitment and selection),
    75

rehires, 67
relativities (employee rewards),
    110–11
resourcing, employee, 29–30, 37–9
    see also planning, HR; recruitment
        and selection
results-based rewards, 119–20, 126,
    129
retirees, as recruitment source, 70–1
rewards, employee, 30–1, 97–101,
    131–2, 248–9
    determinants of, 107–16
    equity of, 108–9, 111, 128
    and individual characteristics, 109
    and integration/business strategy,
        101–2, 103
    international variations, 130–1, 267
    and job characteristics, 110–11
    and job evaluation, 111–16
    and labour markets (LMs), 21–2,
        109–10
    packages, 104–7
    performance-related, 100–1,
        118–26, 129–30, 271
    practical examples, 126–31
    strategic, 127–8
    time-based, 117–18, 126
    types of, 102–7

selection – see recruitment and
    selection
self-appraisal, 183, 187
self-development, 146, 147–8
share options, 122–3, 124
Singapore, industrial action, 272, 274

skills-based rewards, 120–1, 129
social democratic individualism,
    225–6
software, 46–7
south-east Asia, industrial action,
    270–4
South Korea, industrial action, 273,
    274
stability index (HR planning), 50–1
statistics:
    HR planning, 48–52
    international comparisons, 277,
        279–83
stock options, 122–3, 124
strategic choice model, employee
    relations (ER), 214–16
subordinate ratings, performance
    appraisal, 183, 187
suggestion schemes, 244–5
surveys, employee attitudes, 243–4
Sweden, training, 172
Switzerland, employee relations (ER),
    233–4

Taiwan (ROC), industrial action, 273,
    274
task/work groups, 245–8
team briefings, 241
Thailand, industrial action, 272, 274
360-degree appraisal, 183, 187
time-based rewards systems, 117–18,
    126
trade unions, 215, 221–2, 225–7, 236
    Australia, 223–4, 230–2
    Ireland, 222–3
    Japan, 227–9, 270

see also employee relations (ER);
    industrial action
train operating companies, HR
    problems, 57–8
training, 136–7, 143, 190–1
    case study, 139–42
    compulsory/voluntary, implications
        of, 174
    cycle, 152, 154
    design/delivery of, 155–7
    evaluation of, 160–2, 163–6
    future requirements, determining,
        150
    government initiatives, 162–3,
        166–70
    implementation/methods, 157–9
    international comparisons, 137–8,
        170–4, 265
    lack of, UK, 137, 162–3, 170
    management development, 145–50,
        151, 168–9
    needs analysis, 152, 154–5
    system, 152, 153
    tensions in, 144–5
    trainers, 159–60
    uses of, 143–4
turnover, labour, 48–51

unitarist perspective, employee
    relations (ER), 200–1, 218,
        219–20
universities, as recruitment source,
    69–70
USA:
    compulsory arbitration, essential
        services, 234–5